PELICAN BOOKS

EXISTENTIALISM

John Macquarrie was born in Scotland in
1919. The recipient of many honorary degrees, he holds two doctorates, one in philosophy and the other in letters, from Glasgow
University. His distinguished teaching career,
begun in 1953, has included posts at the University of Glasgow and at Union Theological
Seminary in New York. He is currently Lady
Margaret Professor of Divinity at Oxford.
Among his many important interpretations of
contemporary thought are *An Existentialist
Theology*, *The Scope of Demythologizing*,
Principles of Christian Theology, *God-Talk*,
and *Three Issues in Ethics*. Professor Macquarrie is also co-translator, with Edward
Robinson, of one of the century's key philosophical works, Heidegger's *Sein und Zeit*.

JOHN MACQUARRIE

EXISTENTIALISM

Penguin Books

Penguin Books Ltd, Harmondsworth, Middlesex, England
Penguin Books Inc, 7110 Ambassador Road, Baltimore, Maryland 21207, U.S.A.
Penguin Books Australia Ltd, Ringwood, Victoria, Australia

First published by World Publishing Co., New York, 1972 in
the Theological Resources Series

Published in Pelican Books 1973

Printed in the United States of America

TO
CHARLES ARTHUR CAMPBELL
PROFESSOR EMERITUS OF LOGIC
UNIVERSITY OF GLASGOW

Contents

Preface

There are already many excellent books on existentialism. Some of them deal with particular problems or particular existentialist writers. Most of those that deal with existentialism as a whole divide their subject-matter according to authors, presenting chapters on Kierkegaard, Heidegger, Sartre, and the rest. Thus I think that there is room for the present book, which attempts a comprehensive examination and evaluation of existentialism, but does so by a thematic treatment. That is to say, each chapter deals with a major theme of existentialist philosophy, and these themes are arranged in the order of the existential dialetic. Of course, each chapter is illustrated with material from the writings of existentialists, from Kierkegaard to Camus.

In Chapters Ten and Eleven I have echoed some passages from my essay 'Will and Existence,' published in *The Concept of Willing,* ed. James N. Lapsley (Nashville, 1967); and in Chapter Fourteen some passages are reproduced from my 'Existentialism and Christian Thought,' published in *Philosophical Resources for Christian Thought,* ed. Perry LeFevre (Nashville, 1968).

I wish to thank the Reverend John P. Whalen and Professor Jaroslav Pelikan for their encouragement in the writing of this book.

JOHN MACQUARRIE

CHAPTER ONE

The Existentialist Style of Philosophizing

WHAT IS EXISTENTIALISM?

When we try to say what existentialism is, we are confronted with a certain elusiveness. Partly, the difficulty arises from the fact that what was intended as a serious type of philosophy has frequently been vulgarized to the level of a fad, so that the existentialist label gets applied to all sorts of people and activities that are only remotely, if at all, connected with existentialist philosophy. As Jean-Paul Sartre has written, 'the word is now so loosely applied to so many things that it no longer means anything at all.'[1] Partly, however, the difficulty is that a kind of elusiveness is built into existentialism itself. The advocates of this philosophy deny that reality can be neatly packaged in concepts or presented as an interlocking system. The father of modern existentialism, Søren Kierkegaard, significantly named two of his most important books *Philosophical Fragments* and *Concluding Unscientific Postscript* and engaged in polemic against the all-inclusive system of Hegelian philosophy. In the existentialist view there are always loose ends. Our experience and our knowledge are always incomplete and fragmentary; only a divine Mind, if there is one, could know the world as a whole—and perhaps even for such a Mind there would be gaps and discontinuities.

But the point that existentialists have generally been critical of metaphysical systems should not be exaggerated. It does not mean that they themselves are totally unsystematic or even that some of them do not produce some kind of metaphysic of their own.

1

According to Hermann Diem, 'Had Kierkegaard lived a hundred years later, that is, in our day, when a "system" is conceived in rather more modest terms than then . . . he would at once have been able to offer the Hegelian system competition in the form of a system of existential dialectic.'[2] Paul Sponheim has written a study to show that there is 'a systematic interrelatedness of Kierkegaard's fundamental concerns,' though this is of the particular sort 'suggested by the affirmations which form the living tissue of those concerns.'[3] Martin Heidegger certainly thought that the existential analyses carried out in *Being and Time* were scientific (*wissenschaftlich*) in character.[4] Thomas Langan is correct in his judgment that Heidegger preserves the concrete and personal approach of the existentialists 'without sacrificing the coherence and methodicalness associated with traditional systematic philosophical analyses.'[5] Furthermore, most of the existentialist philosophers, though they have repudiated the traditional metaphysical systems, have ventured some assertions of an ontological or metaphysical kind.

It does remain true, however, that there is no common body of doctrine to which all existentialists subscribe, comparable, let us say, to those central tenets that held together idealists or Thomists in their respective schools. For this reason, existentialism has been described in the title of this chapter not as a 'philosophy' but rather as a 'style of philosophizing.' It is a style that may lead those who adopt it to very different convictions about the world and man's life in it. The three great existentialists whom we have already mentioned, Kierkegaard, Sartre, and Heidegger, evidence this diversity. Yet however different their outlooks may be, we see a family resemblance among them in the way that they 'do philosophy.' It is this shared style of philosophizing that permits us to call them 'existentialists.'

What then are the basic characteristics belonging to this style of philosophizing? The first and most obvious one is that this style of philosophizing begins from man rather than from nature. It is a philosophy of the subject rather than of the object. But one might say that idealism too took its starting point in the subject. Thus one must further qualify the existentialist position by saying that for the existentialist the subject is the existent in the whole range of his existing. He is not only a thinking subject but an initiator of action and a center of feeling. It is this whole spectrum of existence, known directly and concretely in the very act of existing, that existentialism tries to express. Sometimes, therefore, this style of philosophizing appears anti-intellectualist. The existentialist thinks passionately, as one who is involved in the actualities of existence. Miguel de

Unamuno declares: 'Philosophy is a product of the humanity of each philosopher, and each philosopher is a man of flesh and bone who addresses himself to other men of flesh and bone like himself. And, let him do what he will, he philosophizes not with the reason only, but with the will, with the feelings, with the flesh and with the bones, with the whole soul and with the whole body. It is the man that philosophizes.'[6] Even though some other existentialists pay more respect to reason than Unamuno did, it is still true that they all claim to found their philosophy on a broad existential basis and eschew any narrow rationalism or intellectualism.

The concept of 'existence' will demand a more detailed treatment later, but even at this stage something must be said about it if we are to grasp the distinctive character of existentialism as a style of philosophizing. We have said that this kind of philosophy begins from man, but from man as an existent rather than man as a thinking subject. In stressing existence, it is also implied that one cannot posit a 'nature' or an 'essence' of man, and then go on to make deductions about him. It is perhaps this approach to the problem that above all gives to existentialism its somewhat elusive character. In Sartre's way of putting it, man's existence precedes his essence. He goes on to explain: 'We mean that man first of all exists, encounters himself, surges up in the world—and defines himself afterwards. If man, as the existentialist sees him, is not definable, it is because to begin with he is nothing. He will not be anything until later, and then he will be what he makes of himself.'[7]

These remarks may be sufficient to afford us a provisional notion of the existentialist style of philosophizing. A fuller understanding can be reached only as we follow in detail the working out of this philosophy in its various developed forms.

SOME RECURRING THEMES IN EXISTENTIALISM

Although we have asserted that existentialism is a style of philosophizing rather than a body of philosophical doctrines, it is nevertheless true that this particular approach to philosophy tends to concentrate attention on some themes rather than others, so that we find these themes recurring in most of the existentialist thinkers. These themes are often different from those that have traditionally occupied the philosopher. Whereas, for instance, the problems of logic and epistemology loomed large in the older schools of thought, the existentialist is inclined to pass over these rather lightly. It could be argued that some existentialists pass over these problems much too lightly and are somewhat cavalier in dismissing them as merely 'academic.' But even existentialists against whom this complaint could not be made concentrate their attention on problems that seem to be directly related to concrete human existence rather than on those that are abstract or speculative. As we shall see, some of the matters that are of great interest to the existentialists have hitherto scarcely been regarded as appropriate themes for philosophy at all.

Such themes as freedom, decision, and responsibility are prominent in all the existentialist philosophers. These matters constitute the core of personal being. It is the exercise of freedom and the ability to shape the future that distinguishes man from all the other beings that we know on earth. It is through free and responsible decisions that man becomes authentically himself. In John Macmurray's language, the 'self as agent' provides the central themes for existentialism, whereas traditional Western philosophy, especially since the time of Descartes, has concentrated attention on the 'self as subject'—and by 'subject' is understood 'thinking subject.'[8]

It should perhaps be added that one limitation of the existentialist discussion of personal being is that for the most part this discussion has centered on the individual. It is true that some existentialists or near-existentialists—Martin Buber and Gabriel Marcel are outstanding examples—have in recent times been pioneers in the investigation of interpersonal relations. Probably all the leading existentialists pay at least lip-service to the truth that man exists as a person only in a community of persons. But in the main they are concerned with the individual whose quest for authentic selfhood focuses on the meaning of personal being.

Another group of recurring existentialist themes includes such topics as finitude, guilt, alienation, despair, death. Discussion of these has not been prominent in traditional philosophy, yet we find them treated at length among the existentialists. One cannot speak in any facile way of pessimism or optimism. Some existentialists do acknowledge themselves to be pessimists, while others speak of optimism or at least of hope. Yet all of them seem aware of the tragic elements in human existence. Man's freedom and his quest for authentic personal being meet with resistance and sometimes with frustration. In any case, as far as the individual is concerned, existence ends in death. Perhaps the tragic side of existentialism is already implied in its starting point where human existence is set over against the being of the inanimate world. The contrast between these two modes of being may be conceived so sharply that existentialism comes near to assuming the shape of a dualism. Even where the contrast is not so sharply drawn, there is still the recognition of conflict and of the experiences of guilt and alienation. For the existentialist, man is never just part of the cosmos but always stands to it in a relationship of tension with possibilities for tragic conflict.

Perhaps future generations will judge that one of the most brilliant and lasting contributions of existentialist philosophy is to be found in its treatment of still another theme that recurs in the writings of its practitioners—the emotional life of man. This again is something that has been in the main neglected by philosophers of the past, or else turned over to psychology. Where philosophy has been dominated by the narrower kinds of rationalism, the changing feelings, moods, or affects that appear in the human mind have been considered irrelevant to philosophy's tasks, or even a hindrance in the way of the ideal of objective knowledge. But the existentialists claim that it is precisely through these that we are involved in our world and can learn some things about it that are inaccessible to a merely objective beholding. From Kierkegaard to Heidegger and Sartre, the existentialists have provided brilliant analyses of such feeling states as anxiety, boredom, nausea, and have sought to show that these are not without their significance for philosophy.

We have indicated some of the themes that appear most frequently in the pages of existentialist writers. Perhaps it is in the exploration and development of these themes, drawn mostly from the conative and affective elements in personal life, that the existentialist philosophers have made their most important and characteristic contributions. But of course they write on many other themes besides. The problems of language, of history, of society, even the problem of being, are taken up by one existentialist philosopher or another, and a vast field opens up. Yet wherever his inquiries may lead him, we shall find that the existentialist remains in close touch with the fundamental personal concerns mentioned above.

DIVERSITY AMONG THE EXISTENTIALISTS

While we have drawn attention to what we have called a 'family resemblance' among existentialists, to be seen in their philosophical style and in the themes they customarily treat, the divergences among them are just as striking. Indeed, it would be difficult to find many philosophers prepared to acknowledge themselves existentialists at all, and those whom we might regard as existentialists in spite of their protests could certainly not be counted as forming a 'school' in the usual sense. We have already noted how Sartre complains that the word *existentialism* has been virtually emptied of meaning. Heidegger, Jaspers, and Marcel, though they would certainly need to be included in any discussion of existentialism, have all rejected the label. Roger L. Shinn observes: 'Almost any self-respecting existentialist refuses to call himself an existentialist. To say, "I am an existentialist," is to say, "I am one of that classification of people known as existentialists"; whereas the existentialist wants to say, "I am myself—and I don't like your effort to fit me into your classification." '⁹

Writers on existentialism often point to the division between Christian and atheistic existentialists as evidence of the diversity that is possible in this style of philosophizing. While it is in fact true that the ranks of the existentialists do include convinced Christians and equally convinced atheists, this way of dividing them is not very helpful. It is oversimplified, for there are some existentialist philosophers (or philosophers of existentialist tendency) who just do not fit the scheme. For instance, Buber is a Jew, and Heidegger claims to be neither theist nor atheist. But more than this, the division of existentialists into Christians and atheists fails to take account of the fact that frequently the relation of the existentialist to his Christianity or his atheism is a highly paradoxical one, a kind of love-hate relationship in which elements of belief and disbelief are intertwined.

Let us consider for a moment Kierkegaard and Nietzsche. Kierkegaard is commonly regarded as the great Christian existentialist, and there can be no doubt about his passionate attachment to the Christian faith. Yet this was accompanied by an equally passionate hostility to the conventional and, as he believed, degenerate forms of Christianity current in 19th-century Denmark; and this hostility culminated in an all-out attack on the Church as he knew it. 'All Christianity is rooted in the paradoxical, whether one accepts it as a believer, or rejects it precisely because it is paradoxical. . . . A once fiery and spirited steed may come to lose its mettle and pride of carriage when it is held for hire and ridden by every bungler.'¹⁰ If Kierkegaard, the Christian existentialist, reveals an attitude that is paradoxical and ambiguous, we can also trace something of a love-hate relation in Nietzsche. His atheism and his rejection of Christian faith were just as sincere and passionate as Kierkegaard's striving for faith. Yet Christianity continued to exercise a fascination over him. As Karl Jaspers has pointed out, despite Nietzsche's savage attacks on Christianity there are strange ambivalences in his attitude. 'His *opposition* to Christianity as a reality is inseparable from his *tie* to Christianity as a postulate. And he himself regarded this tie as positive—not merely as something to be severed.'[11]

One might say that among many of the existentialists, elements from their religion or cultural heritages coalesced with their existentialism or even supplied the impulse toward it in the first place. In spite of Kierkegaard's increasingly severe criticisms of Luther, his existentialism is in fact inseparable from his Protestantism. Martin Buber's philosophy is intertwined with the Hassidic tradition of Judaism. The existentialism of Dostoevsky and Berdyaev is deeply rooted in the spirit of Russian Orthodoxy. Unamuno's attachment to Don Quixote and the quixotic generally is as Spanish as it is existentialist. The rich diversity among these men reflects the diversity of backgrounds out of which they responded to their philosophical vocations.

The Roman Catholic tradition has always had its Augustinian strand as well as its Thomist strand, and this may help to account for the appearance of such Catholic existentialists as Marcel. The word *existentialism* has not been popular in some Catholic circles, especially after the adverse comments contained in the encyclical *Humani generis* of Pius XII, issued in 1950. Often, however, when Roman Catholic writers mention 'personalism,' they have in mind a type of philosophy not far removed from existentialism.

Karl Jaspers and Martin Heidegger stand somewhat apart from the others. They are not Christians in the conventional sense, but they are decidedly not atheists. Jaspers has affinities with a very free-wheeling kind of liberal Protestantism, but his position is best described in his own phrase as 'philosophical faith.' There are elements of both mysticism and estheticism in Heidegger's attitude to being.[12] For a time also Heidegger associated himself with the Nazis; while this may have been due in part to political ineptitude, it could hardly be denied that there are elements in his thought that could be developed in directions compatible with German nationalism.[13]

When we come to the avowedly atheistic existentialists, such as Sartre and Camus, we might seem to be reaching existentialism in its purest form, for in rejecting any religious claim, these men seem to be asserting the complete autonomy and responsibility of the individual. Yet even here we find paradoxes. What is to be said, for instance, of Sartre's relation to Marxism? It is both positive and critical, and though apparently less passionate, it is no less paradoxical than Kierkegaard's relation to Christianity.

A final interesting question may be asked. Would the existentialist say that it is a matter of individual preference whether one achieves authentic selfhood in the choice of Christianity or of Marxism or of atheism or even of Nazism? One choice may be the right one for you in your situation, while another may be right for me in mine. Certainly some existentialists might come near to such an answer, and all of them would acknowledge the relativities of the situation. Yet I doubt if any responsible existentialist philosopher would go so far as to say it is just a matter of personal preference and personal authenticity—and I doubt further if anyone who took such a position would be entitled to call himself a philosopher. Philosophy does imply reflection. Sartre, after all, gives reasons for his atheism; Jaspers' 'philosophical faith' is backed by impressive analysis, even if it is said to be unprovable. To allow the reasons of the heart to have their say is not to abandon all rational judgment or to acknowledge that one point of view is as good as another. The fact that so many different points of view are found among those commonly called existentialists simply shows that existentialism offers no shortcuts toward the solution of metaphysical or ontological problems. Responsible existentialists are aware of this, and their philosophical efforts do not stop short at the needs and preferences of the individual.

EXISTENTIALISM AND PHENOMENOLOGY

Most existentialists are phenomenologists, though there are many phenomenologists who are not existentialists. A close tie has developed between these two types of philosophy because phenomenology seems to offer to the existentialist the kind of methodology that he needs if he is to pursue his investigation into human existence.

The word *phenomenology* has had quite a long history in philosophy. It was occasionally used by Kant to stand for the study of phenomena or appearances, as opposed to the 'things in themselves' that he supposed to lie behind the appearances. In his famous *Phenomenology of Mind* Hegel used the word for his lengthy exposition of the many manifestations of mind or spirit as this unfolds itself dialectically from naive sense-awareness at the simplest level through perception, understanding, and the many forms of consciousness up to the highest intellectual and spiritual activities. In more recent times 'phenomenology' has usually been understood as referring to the philosophy developed by Edmund Husserl in various writings, of which the best known is probably *Ideas: General Introduction to*

Pure Phenomenology. Husserl set aside or 'bracketed' questions concerning the reality or the genesis of the objects of consciousness and tried to devise a method for the detailed and accurate description of the various kinds of objects in their pure essences. It is not our business to attempt any detailed exposition of Husserl's phenomenology here; we must note, however, that the core of this phenomenology is *description*. We are offered a detailed description of the essence of the phenomenon as it is given to consciousness. To ensure the accuracy of the description, it is necessary first of all to clear the mind of presuppositions and prejudices. It is likewise necessary to stay within the bounds of description and to resist the tendency to go on from description to inference. As soon as such remarks are made, it becomes obvious that a pure phenomenology is a very difficult undertaking indeed and demands a very strict mental discipline. How can one ever be sure that one has screened out all one's presuppositions on any subject? Or how can one be quite certain where description ends and inference or interpretation begins? Husserl does in fact develop a highly complex and arduous methodology for overcoming the difficulties and concealments that stand in the way of attaining a pure eidetic knowledge.

Husserl's work has directly influenced several of the existentialist philosophers. Heidegger was one of his students at Freiburg and dedicated his major work, *Being and Time*, to his old teacher. But neither Heidegger nor the other existentialists have simply taken over Husserl's phenomenology in the form in which he taught it. The existentialists have developed phenomenology to suit their own purposes, and in fact Husserl was critical of the use to which Heidegger was putting his ideas. Furthermore, there is a general style of methodical description that might be called 'phenomenological,' although the person using it may never have read Husserl. It would, I think, be quite proper to use the word *phenomenological* for many of Kierkegaard's penetrating descriptions, though these are, of course, pre-Husserlian.

One rather sharp difference between Husserl and the existentialist phenomenologists arises from the fact that whereas Husserl lays the stress on essence and thinks of phenomenology as an eidetic science, the existentialist lays the stress on existence. We have already taken note of Sartre's famous assertion that existence precedes essence. Clearly, if the human existent generates his essence or even, as it has sometimes been expressed, if his essence is to exist, than it makes no sense at all to suspend the question of existence. On the other hand, the existentialists agree with Husserl that one cannot infer to some 'thing in itself' behind the phenomenon. They reject the Kantian dualism that supposed some hidden 'noumenon' of which the phenomenon is merely the appearance. Similarly, they are not interested in the Hegelian attempt to show a dialectical unfolding of the phenomenon (and, still less, of an underlying spirit). They agree with Husserl in contenting themselves with the description of the phenomenon as it shows itself. However, the existentialists have shown themselves equally unwilling to follow certain idealist tendencies that manifest themselves in Husserl. It is true that Husserl insisted that consciousness is always intentional, in the sense of being directed to an object beyond itself. But he did tend to absorb everything into consciousness. As we shall see more clearly later, the existentialists reject idealism. The objects of consciousness may not be confused with the consciousness of objects. Such confusion arises from falsely locating the starting point of philosophy in the thinking consciousness rather than in the total range of existence.

Let us try to understand more fully the kind of description that existentialist phenomenology offers. Although we have emphasized that phenomenology is primarily descriptive, this cannot mean that it simply describes in a naive way what is presented to consciousness. The point about phenomenology is that it offers a description in depth, so to speak, causing us to notice features that we ordinarily fail to notice, removing hindrances that stand in the way of our seeing, exhibiting the essential rather than the accidental, showing interrelations that may lead to a quite different view from the one that we get when a phenomenon is considered in isolation. These characteristics of phenomenology may be illustrated from a brief consideration of the remarks on the subject made by Heidegger and Sartre.

Heidegger goes about his explication of phenomenology in a manner that is common in his writings—he considers the etymology of the word. *Phenomenology* is derived from the two Greek words, φαινόμενον and λόγος. The word φαινόμενον, in turn, comes from φαίνεσθαι, to appear, to come into the light, a verb that may be traced back to the Indo-European root *pha*, connected with the ideas of light and clarity. The phenomenon (φαινόμενον) is that which shows itself, that which appears in the light. Admittedly, there are many variations of usage. Sometimes we talk of 'mere appearance,' implying that what shows itself is somehow unreal, and that the reality remains hidden. Heidegger does not deny, of course, that there is more to things than, so to speak, 'meets the eye.' There are all kinds of possibilities for concealment and distortion, and the truth has to be 'wrested' from the phenomena. But he is quite clear in rejecting the idea that behind the phenomena there could be an utterly inaccessible 'thing in itself.' We can know only the phenomena as they show themselves in themselves.

When we turn to the second constituent of the word *phenomenology*, to λόγος, Heidegger makes the point that this too is a showing: λέγειν, to say, is ἀποφαίνεσθαι, to show. (Incidentally, the Greek verb φάναι, to say, shows the same root *pha* as φαίνεσθαι, to appear. Speech brings to light.) When we bring the λόγος to the φαινόμενον, then, as it were, a second level of showing takes place. Speech articulates the phenomenon, so that phenomenology is letting be seen that which shows itself. It lets us see the phenomenon in such a way that obstructions are removed, and we are made to notice structures and interconnections that had hitherto been concealed or not brought into the light.[14]

Like Heidegger, Sartre also rejects the dualism in which a phenomenon is contrasted with a mysterious 'thing in itself.' Yet the phenomenon is not simply the particular manifestation that is presented to me in any given moment. The phenomenon is rather a coordinated series of manifestations. There is what Sartre calls a 'transphenomenal' reference in every particular manifestation. Whereas the Kantian philosophy sought to link the phenomenon as appearance to a reality that never appears, the task of phenomenology is to show the structural interrelatedness of the single moments or aspects that constitute the phenomenon. The 'being' of the phenomenon is more than any particular appearance of it, and it is the business of 'phenomenological ontology' to reveal to us what this being is.[15]

It is clear from the foregoing that phenomenology is not a method of proof. It describes what is seen. Furthermore, it may be the case that in making such a description, different people will see things differently. Of course, the techniques of phenomenology and its concentration on essences and universal structures are designed to reduce the effect of personal preferences and idiosyncrasies. Yet it could hardly be denied that, especially in so personal a matter as attempting a phenomenology of the human existent, a personal equation will enter into the description, and the personal attitudes of the investigator will announce themselves. No doubt, this accounts in part for the divergences among the existentialists. Yet we are not given over to the subjective preferences of the philosopher. Within limits, phenomenology does provide a scholarly and reliable method for the investigation of this elusive subject-matter, existence. The more strictly its canons are applied, the less are the possibilities for distortion and one-sidedness. And although phenomenology does not offer proof or demonstration, its truth-claim is nevertheless open to testing. The test is to compare the description offered with our own first-hand understanding of existence, i.e., to confront the phenomenological account with the phenomena themselves as we have access to them.

EXISTENTIALISM DISTINGUISHED FROM SOME RELATED TYPES OF PHILOSOPHY

Admittedly, the boundaries that separate existentialism from other types of philosophy are not always clearcut, and probably there is no philosopher so narrowly existentialist that at one point or another he does not straddle the boundary between existentialism and, let us say, pragmatism or empiricism. But in principle, distinctions can be made, and they have the effect of clarifying what is most characteristic in the existentialist stance.

The philosophies that at one point or another seem to abut most closely upon existentialism are empiricism, humanism, idealism, pragmatism, and nihilism.

1. We begin by considering the relation of existentialism to empiricism. These are probably the two dominant philosophies of our time, though for reasons that we shall consider later existentialism has flourished mainly on the continent of Europe, whereas empiricism has prevailed in the English-speaking countries. Existentialists and empiricists make common cause against the speculative rationalism of earlier times. They distrust all attempts to construct philosophy *a priori*, and they are less interested in the attempt to build comprehensive systems than in seeking such limited knowledge as can be securely based on accessible data.

However, at this point the resemblances end. The existentialist tends to turn inward for his data, and although the moderate empiricist will allow some weight to 'inner experience,' the radical empiricist tends to equate experience with sense-experience, so that his philosophical inquiry is turned outward on the world. Even man himself is to be known by empirical observation rather than from subjective experience. The difference between existentialism and empiricism at this point reveals itself as a difference between two modes of knowing. The existentialist stresses knowledge by participation, the empiricist knowledge by observation. The empiricist claims that the kind of knowledge that he seeks has an objectivity and universality about it such as confer on it a validity lacking in the more subjective assertions of the existentialist. But the latter will reply that in the case of the knowledge of man at least, the objectification and abstraction of empiricism distort the living concrete reality. Nikolai Berdyaev is specially critical of the objectifying tendency of the empirical approach, and claims that it brings these consequences: 'the estrangement of the object from the subject; the absorption of the unrepeatably individual and personal in what is common and impersonally universal; the rule of necessity, of determination from without, the crushing of freedom and the concealment of it; adjustment to the grandiose mien of the world and of history, to the average man, and the socialization of man and his opinions, which destroys distinctive character.'[16]

Of course, it is very easy to exaggerate, and undoubtedly the polemic against objectification is exaggerated and does not take sufficient account of the fact that, within limits, the empirical and objectifying approach even to man brings its own virtues. But Berdyaev is certainly correct in insisting that we need more than an empirical approach. He believes that the existentialist understanding of man can safeguard many things that a pure empiricism loses from sight: 'communion in sympathy and love, and the overcoming of estrangement; personalism and the expression of the individual and personal character of each existence; a transition to the realm of freedom and determination from within, with victory over enslaving necessity; and the predominance of quality over quantity, of creativeness over adaptation.'[17]

Our discussion helps us to see what is the difference between the various existential analyses of man and the findings of such empirical sciences as psychology and sociology. The latter are based on observable data, whereas the existentialist proceeds along the lines of a phenomenological analysis of the existence in which he participates. The existentialist is not even concerned with man as an empirical instance of existence but rather with existence as such in its basic structures. This non-empirical stance of the existentialist is reflected in the fact that he will often avoid speaking of 'man' at all, and will designate the existent by some ontological term, such as *Dasein* (Heidegger) or *pour-soi* (Sartre).

2. Humanism is hardly a philosophy in the strict sense, but it is one of the pervasive attitudes of our time. How does existentialism stand to humanism? The question is prompted in the main by Sartre's famous lecture, 'Existentialism Is a Humanism.'

The question cannot be answered simply. The term *humanism* has more than one meaning, and although existentialism is a humanism in one sense, I do not think that it is a humanism in another sense. Existentialism is a humanism in the sense that it is very much concerned with human and personal values, and with the realization of an authentic human existence. This comes out very clearly in Sartre's lecture, though one could argue that it is not clear how he makes the transition from the aspirations of the individual existent to a sense of communal responsibility. But be this as it may, one can readily agree—indeed, one must assert—that existentialism is a humanism in the broad sense described. This would obviously hold true also of the existentialism of Berdyaev, summarized a few paragraphs above.

However, there is another sense of the term *humanism*. Roger Shinn has made a useful distinction between 'open humanism' and 'closed humanism.'[18] Open humanism refers simply to the pursuit of human values in the world and would apply, for instance, to the humanism of Berdyaev. The second type of humanism carries a further implication, namely, that man is the sole creator of meaning and value in the world. Clearly this is the kind of atheism that Sartre embraces, and it is for this reason that he asserts that existentialism is an atheism. For him, existentialism is an atheism because man is abandoned to himself, to create and realize in his world such values as he can.

But must all existentialism be regarded as a humanism in this second, restricted sense? Sartre's lecture drew a reply from Heidegger, his 'Letter on Humanism.' No less than Sartre does Heidegger stress the responsibility of man in the face of an open future of possibility. But it is an open rather than a closed humanism that Heidegger advocates. Human life is set in the wider context of being. Man does not create being, but rather receives his existence from being, and becomes responsible for being and to being. Before he speaks, he must let himself be addressed by being.[19] We need not at this stage take sides in the dispute. But we can take note that although existentialism is a humanism in the broad sense, it is not always or necessarily a closed humanism.

3. Next we ask about existentialism and idealism. First of all, we must guard against a very superficial error. Because the existentialist restricts the usage of the word *existence* so that it is applied only to the kind of being that we know in human existence, this does not mean for a moment that only human or existent subjects are real. A few sentences of Heidegger make the point clear: 'The being

whose manner of being is existence is man. Man alone exists. A rock is, but it does not exist. A tree is, but it does not exist. A horse is, but it does not exist. An angel is, but he does not exist. God is, but he does not exist. The sentence, "Man alone exists," in no way means that only man really is and that all other beings are unreal or illusions or ideas of man.'[20] The word *exist* is used by the existentialist in a special way which differs from the traditional usage, and thus to say that man alone exists is far from any kind of subjective idealism.

More importantly, however, existentialism and idealism differ in a way to which we have already briefly alluded. It is true that both existentialism and idealism are philosophies of the subject rather than of the object, but whereas the idealist begins from man as thinking subject, the existentialist begins from man's total being-in-the-world. The idealist (if it is permitted for a moment to generalize) begins from ideas, whereas the existentialist claims that we already begin with the things themselves. In a critique of Berkeley's idealism, Sartre writes: 'A table is not *in* consciousness—not even in the capacity of a representation. A table is *in* space .... The first procedure of a philosophy ought to be to expel things from consciousness and to reestablish its true connection with the world, to know that consciousness is a positional consciousness of the world.'[21] In other words, all consciousness is intentional and directed upon an object outside of itself. An appearance is not something that belongs to consciousness but something that belongs to an objective phenomenon.

Thus despite its stress on subjectivity, existentialism does not follow the same path as idealism. To exist is to be in encounter with a real world.

4. Anyone who has read William James' famous essay 'The Will to Believe' could hardly doubt that there are close ties between existentialism and pragmatism. Both are in protest against abstract intellectualism, both stress the relation of belief to action, both acknowledge the risk of faith as an attitude about which we are compelled to decide by the demands of concrete existence before we can arrive at theoretical grounds for our decision, and both look for the confirmation or falsification of faith in terms of its fulfillment or diminution of our humanity.

But in spite of the resemblances, there are profound differences between pragmatists and existentialists. The pragmatist's criteria for truth are biological and utilitarian, and there is little sense of that inwardness that is a mark of existentialism. Furthermore, the pragmatist is usually an optimist, concerned with success in some limited undertaking and very little aware of that tragic and frustrating side of life as expressed in most existentialist writings. Berdyaev clearly indicates the difference between the two philosophies. After acknowledging that the pragmatist is correct in holding that truth is a function of life and that this criterion is acceptable when we are dealing with technical and scientific problems, Berdyaev goes on to say: 'Truth is nevertheless in direct opposition to pragmatism. A vitally flourishing state of affairs, success, profit, interest, all these things are marks rather of falsity than of truth. Truth is certainly not a useful and serviceable thing in this world; it renders no services, it may even be destructive and ruinous to the ordering of the things of this world; it demands sacrifices and has even led to martyrdom.'[22]

There are indeed existentialists who come close to a kind of pragmatism. Some passages in Unamuno seem like pragmatism, but these have to be set alongside the passionately subjective elements in his philosophy and his sense of the tragic. His compatriot José Ortega y Gasset came closer to pragmatism because of the powerfully vitalistic bias in his thinking, which enabled him to describe science and culture alike as 'tools of life.'[23] Yet Ortega's sense of crisis and of revolutionary challenge puts him among the existentialists. However close the existentialists may be at some points to pragmatists and vitalists, they are distinguished from them by the fact that their interest is in the intensity of life, even its tragic intensity, rather than in its outward expansion and success.

5. Existentialists are usually rebels against the establishment. In many fields—theology, politics, morals, literature—they struggle against the accepted authorities and the traditional canons. Even the Christian existentialists have seldom been orthodox. Kierkegaard's career culminated in his bitter attack upon the ecclesiastical establishment in Denmark, and most scholars believe that this last phase of his work was not an aberration but a consequence of his earlier thinking. The atheistic existentialists carry the revolt much further. Nietzsche, Heidegger, Sartre, Camus have all at one time or another been called nihilists. Is existentialism then a kind of nihilism, or does it lead to nihilism when one follows out its consequences to the end?

Presumably very few people have ever actually claimed to be nihilists. Presumably, too, nihilism is always relative to some affirmative position that is being explicitly rejected. Perhaps the very idea of a thoroughgoing nihilism is self-contradictory. Nevertheless, we can visualize a state of alienation against the existing order so extreme as to approach to nihilism. Ivan Turgenev's *Fathers and Sons*, the novel that first popularized the term *nihilism* and that was known to Nietzsche, depicts the student Bazarov as the almost complete nihilist. Bazarov claims to deny *everything*. In art and politics as well as in religion he denies all value to whatever has been traditionally valued. Furthermore, he claims that he is only required to deny and has no obligation to offer anything constructive in place of what has been denied. Yet even Bazarov seems to have thought of nihilism as a temporary or transitional attitude, necessary in order to clear the ground but not the final word: 'At present, the course most useful is denial. Therefore, we deny.'

It seems to me that those existentialists who do come close to nihilism recognize its temporary character and try to move through it. Nietzsche believed that the West had come into a nihilistic period; and although he deplored this fact, he has usually been regarded as caught in this nihilism. Yet he was certainly looking for a way beyond nihilism. 'He knew that he was himself the nihilist he accused, but he believed that he differed by carrying nihilism to its final consequences and thereby initiating its conquest.'[24] Sartre has looked toward the other side of despair, and Camus has acknowledged the need to search for reasons that lead beyond absurdity. Yet perhaps all of these men would say that it is only after the total denial of conventional beliefs and standards that new possibilities can arise and a transvaluation of values take place. In similar fashion, the Christian existentialists are sometimes in total revolt against the traditional forms of faith; they claim that only through the rejection and denial of these forms and through the consequent painful experience of having nothing left can new faith arise. For the Christian too, there can be a radical transvaluation of values, not far removed from the experience of the nihilist.

No doubt there is a pseudo-existentialism that likes to dwell in extravagant ways on a so-called 'confrontation with nothingness,' and no doubt there has been much unintelligent revolt against tradition. But radical questioning and readiness to doubt are built into the existentialist position, and where faith does finally emerge, it will be the stronger for having looked into the abyss of nihilism.

CHAPTER TWO

Existentialism and the History of Philosophy

THE HERMENEUTICS OF MYTH AND THE DAWN OF SELF-UNDERSTANDING

Although existentialism, in its developed forms, is a phenomenon of recent times, its roots can be traced far back in the history of philosophy and even into man's pre-philosophical attempts to attain to some self-understanding. Existentialist philosophy has brought to explicit awareness an attitude of mind and a way of thinking that are as old as human existence itself and that have manifested themselves in varying degrees throughout the history of human thought. Sometimes the existentialist attitude and preoccupation with those themes that we have taken to be typical of existentialism have been rather prominent in certain phases of culture. Sometimes men seem to have been relatively unconcerned with these issues. But existentialism does have a definite lineage.

The story can be traced back to the mythological stage of thought. For a long time now, the question of mythology and of its interpretation has exercised a fascination for many scholars. From Schelling and Strauss to Cassirer, Jung, Bultmann, Eliade, and a host of others, there has been intensive work on the hermeneutics of myth.

In the 18th and early 19th centuries attempts were made to rationalize myths by eliminating their fanciful elements and trying to penetrate to some supposed straightforwardly intelligible happenings that had given rise to the stories in the first place and had subsequently become embroidered with fanciful details. It is now generally agreed that such an approach to the hermeneutic of myth is a mistaken one and fails to distinguish genuine myth from legend and saga. More promising have been the attempts to treat myth allegorically, as the bearer of metaphysical truths for which no precise literal language would be adequate. Although this approach to mythology goes back to Plato, it can be criticized on the ground that it reads into the myths ideas much later and more sophisticated than those they were trying to express. One of the most persistent theories about mythology has taken the myths to be etiological, that is to say, almost as a kind of primitive science which accounted for the causal origins of natural events or human institutions. That there is something of an etiological strand in mythology cannot be denied, but this is not an exhaustive account of the matter either. The most recent theories about mythology have seen it rather as expressing in a symbolic manner truths about man's own life and thought. Psychological accounts have drawn attention to the parallels between myths and dreams, and have seen in them projections or objectifications of man's inner desires and strivings. Existentialist accounts see in mythology man's first gropings toward an identity; to tell a story of human origins, for example, is to confess a self-understanding.

I do not suggest that any one of these ways of interpreting mythology is entirely adequate by itself. A myth is a complex phenomenon, and just because it belongs to a period of human culture when specialized or differentiated forms of language had not yet arisen, every myth can yield several interpretations. It is legitimate to employ more than one hermeneutic approach in attempts to decipher the meaning of myths. Yet, among possible approaches, the existential interpretation of myth would seem to be of quite basic importance, for the question of finding an identity for himself or of gaining a self-understanding would seem to be inherent in man's very mode of existence and to be more fundamental than questions about how things began. Of course, it can readily be admitted that a certain intellectual curiosity is also native to human existence. Aristotle was surely correct when at the beginning of the *Metaphysics* he wrote his famous sentence, 'All men by nature desire to know.' Yet it is not wrong either to claim that human curiosity has an existential component, and that the further back we go in human history, the stronger the existential motivation would be. Disinterested curiosity, culminating in the detached thinking of the scientist or philosopher, would seem to be a very late development in the history of mankind.

So it may be claimed that the fundamental self-questioning that is characteristic of the existentialist style of philosophizing was already struggling for expression in the period when human thought was still mythological in character. This is specially obvious in the anthropogonic myths found in almost every culture. We ourselves are best acquainted with the Hebrew account of human origins, telling how God formed man of the earth and then breathed life or spirit into him (Gen 2:7). Before anyone thought of this story as an account of a datable event in the past, and certainly long before anyone thought of it as the embodiment of a primitive dualistic metaphysic of body and spirit, it already fulfilled the function of bringing to expression man's most primordial self-understanding, his existential awareness of the tensions and paradoxes that are constitutive of his being as one who knows in himself freedom, finitude, guilt, and the possibility of death. In the early myths man is already wrestling with the mystery of his own being and trying to find answers to its apparent contradictions. This is a pre-philosophical and pre-phenomenological attempt to express in mythological images the awareness of existence that is already given with the existence of man. Alongside subsequent philosophical investigations into the being of man, the concrete, imaginative thinking of the myths has been succeeded by the work of poets, dramatists, and novelists, so that even today we are as likely to discover the basic existential insights in the stories of Dostoevsky, Kafka, and Camus as in the philosophical analyses of Heidegger and Sartre. In any case, the last two named are themselves well aware of the power of myth, narrative and poetry to express the paradox of the human existent as one who, according to Alexander Pope's *Essay on Man*, is 'in doubt to deem himself a god, or beast.'

The eschatological myths also have a special existential interest. Death-awareness is seen by modern anthropology as a fundamental constituent of man's being, and as one of the traits that mark him off from the animal. To be aware of death is to be aware of living in the face of the end. Eschatological myths are not primarily speculations about the end of the world but rather attempts to find some framework of meaning within which to set the transience and mortality of human existence. Eschatology expresses the understanding that man already has of his existence as a 'being-toward-the-end,' to use a phrase of Heidegger.

The application of the methods of existential interpretation to mythology has unlocked great areas of meaning and revealed the complexity of archaic man's self-understanding, even if this understanding had not reached the level of an explicit awareness and was still veiled in symbols. Rudolf Bultmann's interpretations of the New Testament, Hans Jonas' work on the myths of Gnosticism, and Paul Ricoeur's study of the myths of a fall and the symbolism of evil are outstanding examples of existential interpretation. They make it clear that even at a pre-philosophical and pre-critical stage of his mental development, man was already preoccupied with those problems that have come to constitute the major themes of existentialist philosophy—the mystery of existence, finitude and guilt, death and hope, freedom and meaning. Yet this fact need not surprise us, since these problems arise out of the very structure of human existence itself.

ANCIENT PHILOSOPHY

We turn now from mythology to the first stirrings of reflective thought. There came a time when men began to wake up, so to speak, from the dreamlike world of myth, when consciousness was sharpened, and when the possibility of critical thought and radical questioning became actual. In this period we find that the existential themes, already present in a latent way in the myths, became increasingly explicit.

A valuable contribution toward understanding the emergence of reflective thought is made by Karl Jaspers' conception of the 'axial age.' As he sees it, there was a turning point in human history that has been 'the point most overwhelmingly fruitful in fashioning humanity.' This point may be dated around 500 B.C., though it is not so much a point as a period extending two or three centuries both before and after the date mentioned. In that period there took place an extraordinary and worldwide stirring of the human spirit. It was the time of the great Hebrew prophets, from Amos, Hosea, Isaiah, and Jeremiah down to the time of the prophets of the Exile. Meanwhile, the tremendous flowering of Greek culture was taking place: the world's first efforts in philosophizing ran their course from Thales, Heraclitus, and Parmenides through Socrates to Plato and Aristotle; the Greek dramatists and poets speculated on human destiny and commented on society and its laws; political institutions were developed; the first steps were taken in both the natural and historical sciences; while alongside all this the skepticism and radical questioning of the sophists made its appearance. The Western mind directs its attention primarily to the achievements of Greece and Israel when it thinks of this so-called axial period of history. But Jaspers goes out of his way to remind us that this is only a part of the story. The remarkable spiritual upsurge of those times can be traced in many cultures. This was the time of Confucius and Lao-Tse in China; the time of Zarathustra in Iran; the time of the Upanishads and later of the Buddha in India.

What then was happening in the axial period? Obviously, a great many things indeed were happening, and it would be foolish and one-sided to attempt to offer any simple formula. Rationalism has its roots here as well as existentialism, atheism as well as the higher religions, the study of nature as well as man's study of himself. It was the end of the age of myth; and the many insights, some of them conflicting, that had hitherto found expression obliquely in the undifferentiated and uncritical discourse of myth were now reaching the level of explicit awareness and were also, in some instances, coming into collision with one another.

The significance of the period for our own story of the antecedents of existentialism is well expressed in the following sentences from Jaspers: 'What is new about this age . . . is that man becomes conscious of being as a whole, of himself and his limitations. He experiences the terror of the world, and his own powerlessness. He asks radical questions. Face to face with the void, he strives for liberation and redemption. By consciously recognizing his limits, he sets himself the highest goals. He experiences absoluteness in the depths of selfhood and in the lucidity of transcendence.'[1]

Of course, the characteristics mentioned by Jaspers were not always and everywhere present with anything like the same intensity. 'Terror of the world,' for instance, appears among some peoples and in some historical circumstances, but by no means in all. Even in the mythological age, there had been differences. Henri Frankfort mentions the difference in temperament between the people of Egypt and Mesopotamia: 'The feeling of insecurity, of human frailty, which pervades every manifestation of Mesopotamian culture, is absent in Egypt.'[2] Likewise in the axial age there are very great differences from one culture to another—from the outward direction of early Greek natural philosophy to the inwardness of Indian thought, from the ethical and prophetic character of Hebrew religion to the experiences of Eastern mystics, and so on—the contrasts can be multiplied indefinitely. Yet in all of these cultures and in all of the different modes of experience which they exhibit, we do indeed see, as Jaspers claims, man confronting himself in a new way and wrestling with the problem of understanding himself.

A glance at each of three major areas of culture in the axial age will show us how existential questionings, the precursors of the philosophy of existence, were taking shape in this early period. The three areas are Hebrew religious thought in the time of the prophets, classical Greek culture, and Eastern religious philosophy.

The strongly existential character of the teaching of the Hebrew prophets is obvious, and has been expounded in such books as Martin Buber's *The Prophetic Faith*. A key notion in this teaching is *teshuvah*, which, according to Buber, is better understood concretely as a 'turning of the whole person' than as 'repentance.' In any case, it certainly does imply a *revolution* in human existence, a quest for a genuinely human existence. In particular, the prophetic summons was to 'turn' from idolatry, from cults that were routine and frequently dehumanizing to a responsible relationship toward God and society. It implied an acknowledgment of guilt, an acceptance of responsibility, a quest for individual integrity and for social justice.

Not only was the prophetic message a summons out of an empty cultus. It could also be interpreted as a summons out of the mythological mentality, insofar as this was a timeless mentality in which the sequence of events repeats itself in a never-ending series of cycles. Natural religion, based on the seasons of the year, on seedtime and harvest, visualizes a time in which nothing radically new ever happens. The myths of the pagan cults against which the Hebrew prophets fought were 'myths of the eternal return.'[3] But the turning demanded by the prophets was not merely a turning away from these myths but, in Buber's language, a 'turning to the future.'[4] In other words, the prophets called on men to face the radically temporal and historical character of human existence and to come out from the timeless womb of mythology.

Guilt, turning, responsibility, the quest for a fully human existence, the acknowledgment of the reality of time and history—these are all themes that take a prominent place in the teaching of the prophets, and they are all themes recognized as of importance for the existentialist philosophers. We should notice that there is another more questionable aspect of the prophetic teaching that also foreshadows a theme not uncommon in the existentialists. Bultmann points out that in protesting against the dehumanizing elements in pagan culture the prophets tended to romanticize the simple life of the desert before the establishment of the state. They 'combined their preaching of social righteousness with a protest against all political and economic progress as such.'[5] Modern existentialists have sometimes been criticized because they too have, in some instances, seemed to disclaim responsibility for the technological age and to show a nostalgic longing for the supposedly more human and personal conditions of life before the coming of the Industrial Revolution. This is a question which we shall have to consider in due course.

It might seem that when we turn to Greek culture, we are confronted with a totally different phenomenon, and one in which the strong existential tendencies of Hebrew religious thought are lacking. Does Greece not present us with the example *par excellence* of the rationalistic and intellectualistic attitude toward life and the world?

Unquestionably the intellectual achievements of Greece in philosophy and science were unequalled in the ancient world. But the conventional contrast between Greek and Hebrew ways of thinking has frequently been exaggerated. Rationalism and intellectualism are by no means the whole story about the Greek mentality. In a notable study, E. R. Dodds acknowledges on the one hand that even as early as Homer we find among the Greeks 'an intellectualist approach to the explanation of behavior,' and that this 'set a lasting stamp on the Greek mind' and already foreshadowed the doctrine that virtue is knowledge; yet after bringing forward an impressive array of evidence, he comes to the conclusion that 'the men who created the first European rationalism were never—until the Hellenistic Age— "mere" rationalists: that is to say, they were deeply and imaginatively aware of the power, the wonder and the peril of the irrational.'[6]

It is true that Greek philosophy begins with the so-called 'physicists,' Thales and his successors, and that it seems therefore to have been directed outward upon the world rather than on the specific being of man. Yet it is among the pre-Socratic philosophers that Heidegger has found the authentic beginnings of Western philosophizing, and especially the insight into the relation between being and knowing, or between being and thinking, which he attributes especially to Parmenides and also to Heraclitus.[7] According to Heidegger's view of the matter, this early insight was almost immediately lost, and the subsequent history of philosophy in the West has been the 'forgetting of being' and the rise of a thinking that is calculative rather than existential. However, the connection of being and thinking was a Greek insight, and it is precisely this connection that the modern existentialists are seeking to reestablish.

Socrates is of special significance in the genesis of a philosophy of existence, for with him a revolution took place in Greek philosophy. Attention was shifted from nature to man himself as the center of philosophical inquiry. Self-questioning became the method and self-knowledge the goal of philosophy. Conventional beliefs about piety, courage, justice, and the like were shown to be inadequate, and men were asked to probe more deeply into the understanding of life which as men they already shared. It is easy to understand Kierkegaard's admiration for Socrates: 'With what wonderful consistency Socrates remained true to himself. . . . He entered into the role of midwife and sustained it throughout; not because his thought "had no positive content," but because he perceived that this relation is the highest that one human being can sustain to another.'[8]

We may notice that two contrasting aspects are brought together in Socrates. On the one hand, he is the great champion of rationality, almost the patron saint of reason. Yet as a martyr for truth he is also the most existential of rationalists, and at the furthest remove from what is called a 'mere rationalist.' Existentialism has sometimes been tempted to irrationalism, in the bad sense of a despising of reason. Socrates remains as the great witness to the truth that rationality is an essential element in any truly human and personal existence, and from Socrates to Jaspers there has been a healthy tradition of a philosophy of existence that profoundly respects reason.

Beyond philosophy, we may take brief note of important aspects of Greek culture that yield further evidence of existential stirrings. Such were the mystery religions with their quest for salvation and the great tragic dramas that set forth and explored the collision between the being of man and the being of the cosmos. Enough has been said to show that even in Greece, the first great home of rationalism, the existentialist themes were being opened up in the axial age.

The third cultural area (or, rather, series of areas) that demands notice is the East. Of all contemporary existentialist philosophers Jaspers has undoubtedly been the one most open to the ideas of Asian philosophy and religion and most aware of the parallels which may be traced between these Eastern ideas and the existentialism of the West. On the Eastern side, perhaps the possibilities for dialogue have been most clearly perceived by Japanese Buddhist scholars. One can scarcely read the books of D. T. Suzuki, for instance, without becoming impressed with the many similarities between his version of Zen Buddhism and the teachings of existentialism.[9]

Some of these similarities are made explicit in any essay by Yoshenori Takeuchi, entitled 'Buddhism and Existentialism: The Dialogue between Oriental and Occidental Thought.'[10] He claims that with the rise of existentialism in the West, 'our several ways of philosophical thinking appear to be converging more than they have for many centuries.' Some of the themes of existentialism are, it is said, those with which Eastern philosophy, especially Buddhism, has been concerned for two and a half millennia. Takeuchi mentions as particularly significant the notions of 'being' and 'nothingness,' and the phenomenon of anxiety to which the encounter with nothingness gives rise. He sees in the common preoccupation with these matters the possibility for increased mutual understanding between East and West.

There are, of course, many facets of Eastern philosophy and religion other than those prominent in Japanese Buddhism. Also, there is much in Western philosophy besides existentialism, and there are perhaps other possibilities of contact between East and West. It may be worth recalling that fifty years ago European idealists and Indian philosophers were finding common ground. However, our aim here is simply to show that already in the axial age, in that first conscious reflective thinking that has influenced all the thinking that has taken place since, the great themes of existentialist philosophy were already finding expression, and that they appeared in such diverse cultures as the Hebrew, the Greek, and the Buddhist.

FROM THE RISE OF CHRISTIANITY TO THE MIDDLE AGES

The teaching of Jesus continued and intensified the motifs that had first appeared among the Hebrew prophets. Like them, he protested against the mechanical and legalistic features of the established cult and called for responsible and inward obedience. But the prophetic message was now set in the context of an all-pervading eschatological expectation. Life was understood as existence in the face of the end, and this lent to the prophetic message an existential urgency and intensity beyond that of the classical prophets, though to be sure the note of urgency and the prediction of judgment to come had not been absent in their teaching either.

Bultmann has pointed out that Jesus' teaching avoids the more fanciful speculations of Jewish apocalyptic. The existential character of the teaching is evident in the stress laid on the end-time as a *time of decision*. It is a time to turn or repent, to move away from formalism to radical obedience in readiness for the approaching end. Although Jesus talked of rewards and punishments, he saw the chief motive for obedience in the desire to gain one's authentic being: 'Whoever seeks to gain his life will lose it, but whoever loses his life will preserve it' (Lk 17:33).[11]

Apart from the teaching of Jesus, there is much else in the New Testament that is perhaps best interpreted as a way of understanding human existence and the path to its fulfillment. The teaching of St. Paul affords an outstanding illustration of such an existential type of theology. Bultmann sees St. Paul's conversion primarily as his attaining of a new self-understanding, and believes in turn that Paul's theology reflects the conversion experience, since it can be interpreted as a new understanding of man in the light of the Christian proclamation.[12]

Needless to say, the expressions *understanding* and *self-understanding* as used in this context do not have a narrowly intellectualist sense but refer to an understanding that rests on participation in a way of life and finds expression in taking up a concrete existential attitude—the attitude of faith. St. Paul's understanding of existence differs from that of Jesus and is expressed in very different language. The total Pauline theology can be well expressed in terms of two contrasted understandings of man, one representing the state of man prior to faith, and the other the state subsequent to faith. The apostle had an extraordinarily rich vocabulary of terms for setting forth his existential theology: sin, flesh, spirit, soul, body (almost in the sense of person), life, reason, conscience, heart, freedom, faith, hope, love—these represent only a selection from his more important terms. Perhaps the modern psychologist or existentialist would think that St. Paul's vocabulary was scarcely a precise one and that some of the terms employed still savor of animism. Yet when we compare this language of St. Paul with the older language of the myths, we see what a tremendous stride forward had been taken. By the apostle's time a vocabulary was available that could be used to describe in a manner phenomenological rather than mythological the basic structures of human existence and the nature of the transition that must be made in the quest for authentic selfhood.

At least part of the vocabulary in which the Christian doctrine of man found expression in the New Testament was probably derived from the widespread and diverse sects of the Hellenistic world loosely known as the Gnostics. Bultmann remarks that 'Gnosticism and its myth offered a stock of terms that were intelligible to great numbers of people.'[13] Gnosticism was such a dangerous rival to Christianity in the early centuries of our era because of the resemblances between them. Both offered ways of understanding man and his destiny and promised redemption from the powers that diminish and distort the true life of man.

However, Gnosticism stands much closer to modern existentialism than does New Testament Christianity. If Gnosticism and Christianity had their resemblances, they also had their differences. In particular, Gnosticism taught an ultimate dualism that was irreconcilable with the Biblical doctrine of creation. The New Testament also knows a dualism, but this is not ultimate. To the Gnostic, the world was utterly alien and demonic, and the contrast between man's being and that of the world was represented with an intensity that foreshadows the similar contrast to be found in some existentialist writers of modern times. Again, although the notion of attaining a true self-understanding is one that is found in the New Testament, it does not have there the overwhelming importance accorded to it in Gnosticism. For the Gnostic, redemption depended on attaining the true gnosis, awakening to the knowledge of one's identity and destiny.

A penetrating interpretation of that mixture of philosophy and mythology which constitutes Gnostic lore is offered by Hans Jonas in his book *The Gnostic Religion*. To the second edition of this book he added an essay with the title 'Gnosticism, Existentialism and Nihilism.' He tells us in this essay that when he first turned to the study of Gnosticism, he found that the hermeneutic key to an understanding of its strange teaching was provided by the concepts of existentialism. But in turn he discovered that contemporary existentialism gets a reciprocal illumination from Gnosticism. And this, he argues, can only be the case because of a deep affinity between the two. The basis for this affinity he sees in a kind of 'cosmic nihilism' which affected man in the early centuries of the Christian era and affects him again today. In both periods men have felt themselves lost and alone in a vast, alien world. Gnosticism and existentialism embody, in different but related ways, a possible response to the sense of not being at home in the world. Jonas quotes some lines of Nietzsche that could almost pass for a Gnostic fragment:

> The world's a gate
> To deserts stretching mute and chill.
> Who once has lost
> What thou hast lost stands nowhere still.[14]

Of course, one must avoid the dangers of oversimplification, but there is surely a strong case for seeing in Gnosticism an historical antecedent of existentialism, and particularly of some of its bleaker forms.

Returning to the mainstream of Christian theology in its early stages of development, we find that its existential character tends to recede as dogmatic and metaphysical interests become dominant. It is perhaps an oversimplification to see this change as a result of Greek philosophical influences on the content of the original Christian proclamation. Everyone knows Harnack's famous pronouncement that 'dogma, in its conception and development, is a work of the Greek spirit on the soil of the Gospel.'[15] Although Harnack seems to have thought of this 'work of the Greek spirit' as to some extent a deterioration, he acknowledged its necessity: 'Christianity without dogma, that is, without a clear expression of its content, is inconceivable.'[16] But what remains unexplained, even when this has been said, is the reason why dogma assumed a metaphysical, objectified form. It is certainly not enough to say this was 'Greek' as against 'Hebrew,' for we have already taken note that Greek thought did not lack its existential motifs and that the conventional Greek versus Hebrew dichotomy is usually exaggerated.

Although the dogmatic, propositional, metaphysical type of theology was in the ascendant in the patristic period, an existential interpretation of faith was never quite absent and may be seen, for instance, in such different writers as St. Ignatius and St. Athanasius. But it is with St. Augustine (354–430) that we come to the most powerfully existential presentation of Christianity since St. Paul, and one that has been of such enduring significance that even today existentialists, Christian and non-Christian alike, acknowledge an affinity with the great North African scholar.

Augustine finds man himself to be an inexhaustible mystery: 'If by "abyss" we understand a great depth, is not man's heart an abyss? For what is there more profound than that abyss? Men may speak, may be seen by the operation of their members, may be heard speaking; but whose thought is penetrated, whose heart is seen into? . . . Do not you believe that there is in man a deep so profound as to be hidden even from him in whom it is?'[17] Truth and understanding, therefore, are to be found not so much in propositions as by exploring the depth of one's own existence, by direct experience of life: 'What is understanding except by the light of the mind itself to live a more enlightened and perfect life?[18] However, this is not a call to rest in the subjective recesses of the self. What comes through clearly in Augustine's understanding of the self is precisely the modern existentialist insistence on the restlessness of the self, as always going out from itself. So Augustine can write: 'Remain not in thyself; transcend thyself also. Put thyself in him who made thee.'[19] As this quotation indicates, Augustine understood man's self-transcendence as directed toward God. One recalls the famous words, 'Thou hast created us for thyself, and our heart knows no rest until it may repose in thee,'[20] or, in similar vein, 'With a hidden goad thou didst urge me, that I might be restless until such time as the sight of my mind might discern thee for certain.'[21] These two quotations come from the *Confessions*, and it is toward the end of that book that Augustine sets forth his philosophical theory of the self in temporal terms, as it relates itself to past, present, and future. This theory again anticipates modern views of the self in a remarkable way. One could mention many other things in Augustine's thought, such as his view of love, or his understanding of what he calls 'chaste fear,' not far removed from the 'dread' (*Angst*) of Kierkegaard. But perhaps enough has been said to indicate Augustine's outstanding position in that tradition of thought that lies behind existentialism.

As Christian theology moved on into the Middle Ages, it became again rationalistic, propositional, and metaphysical. It may be true, as recent Thomistic scholarship has claimed, that the writings of St. Thomas Aquinas (1225–74) have in the past been interpreted in a fashion that was too exclusively essentialist, and that insufficient attention has been paid to the existential aspect of his philosophy. Yet even if we concede this, we should be careful not to be misled by the very different way in which existence is understood by Thomism and by modern existentialism.

The medieval antecedents of existentialism are to be sought not in St. Thomas but rather in some of the intellectual currents that began to flow in opposition to the prevailing rationalism. I refer especially to the rise of a new style of mysticism that turned again to the depths of human life. There were many representatives of this mysticism, but Meister Eckhart (1260–1327) is perhaps its most typical figure and is one who has exerted an influence on German philosophy right down to Heidegger. The notions of 'being' and 'nothing' are prominent in Meister Eckhart's thought, together with that of man as one who experiences the solitude of a wilderness. 'It is God's nature to be without a nature,' he declares.[22] Man, being made in the divine image, affords a clue to the mystery of God: 'To get at the core of God at his greatest, one must first get into the core of himself at the least, for no one can know God who had not first known himself.'[23] It should be added that Eckhart strongly insisted that the kind of mysticism which he advocated should not rest in contemplation for its own sake, but should be fruitful in bringing human life to fulfillment.

Can we assign any reason for the renewal of existential themes in the later Middle Ages? Historians of the period have pointed to the plagues, wars, political and ecclesiastical ferments as shaking confidence in rationalism and in philosophies that may seem to tie things up into too neat a package. Life has too many 'loose ends' for that. The struggle between rival philosophies was to be intensified in the subsequent periods of Western thought.

REFORMATION, RENAISSANCE, AND ENLIGHTENMENT

Of the great Reformers, Martin Luther (1483–1546) is the one in whose teaching the typically existential themes emerge most clearly. He was, of course, seeking to restore Christianity to what he supposed to be a purer form, and it seems to have been the existential elements in the Christian tradition that made a special appeal to him, especially the writings of St. Paul and St. Augustine.

Luther's own early writings revive in a new situation the prophetic protests that form an important part of the texture of both the Old and the New Testaments. Against sacerdotalism, legalism, ecclesiastical rigidity, and the corruption of religion, Luther pleaded for the freedom of the Christian man and for responsible individual existence within the Christian community.

Central to his new understanding of Christianity was his idea of faith, and this remains the most intensely existential item in his teaching. Faith, as Luther saw it, had become too much a matter of giving assent to dogmas and too little a personal or existential relation between man and God. Here the expressions *for me* or *for us* give the clue to Luther's understanding of faith. True faith understands the acts of God as *for us* and does not simply acknowledge them as realities of an external history. The same understanding of faith can be seen from a different angle in the stress that Luther laid on the word *your* in the divine declaration, 'I am the Lord your God' (Ex 20:2). In declaring himself 'your God,' God has promised or committed himself to his people, and thus he is no merely metaphysical or speculative God but God impinging on human existence.

Perhaps this existential understanding of faith and of theology comes through most clearly in Luther's handling of Christology. He is impatient with the scholastic distinctions and the metaphysical wrestlings with the problem of the God-man. Again, it is Christ 'for us' that affords the clue. The starting-point for Christology is the lordship of Christ in the life of the believer. Luther's younger colleague Philipp Melanchthon (1497–1560) gave expression to this existential type of Christology in his famous claim that 'to know Christ is to know his benefits.' It is true that both Luther and

Melanchthon retreated from their bolder sallies into existential theology, but they did begin a way of thinking about the person of Christ that has persisted in Lutheranism and may be seen in new forms in Ritschl in the 19th century and in Bultmann in the 20th.

The more somber elements of existentialist thought were also represented in Luther. A sense of human impotence and guilt, together with the desire for salvation, were prominent in Luther. Alongside this went a distrust of reason, a distrust that sometimes issued in violent denunciations of reason.

This darker side of Luther's thought provides a contrast with the rising humanism of the Renaissance. In a famous controversy, Desiderius Erasmus (1467–1536) took issue with Luther precisely on the question of man's freedom and responsibility, which, as it seemed to Erasmus, the Reformation had too severely discredited. Yet Erasmus and the great humanists of the time were also in revolt against scholasticism, and elements of their teaching can be seen in retrospect as sympathetic to some aspects of modern existentialism, especially the type represented by Karl Jaspers, which stresses the freedom, dignity, and rationality of man.

This may be illustrated by a remarkable passage from an *Oration on the Dignity of Man* by the Italian Renaissance scholar Giovanni Pico della Mirandola (1463–94). This writer attacks the scholastic or essentialist idea that man has a fixed and inalterable nature, and in effect anticipates Sartre's claim that man must define himself. Yet this is seen in connection with man's dignity and rationality. God is represented as saying to man: 'A limited nature in other creatures is confined within the laws written down by Us. In conformity with thy free judgment, in whose hands I have placed thee, thou art confined by no bounds and thou wilt fix limits of nature for thyself. . . . Thou, like a judge appointed for being honorable, art the molder and maker of thyself; thou mayest sculpt thyself into whatsoever shape thou dost prefer.'[24]

However, Renaissance science had introduced a new factor that was bound to affect man's understanding of himself. We allude to the new cosmology, constructed on the basis of the work of Copernicus, Galileo, Kepler, and Newton. It took time before the full implications of earth's displacement from the center of the universe were understood, but more and more man was becoming aware of his apparent insignificance in the immeasurably vast expanse of space and time. Blaise Pascal (1623–62) was one of the first to give expression, in his *Pensées*, to the new feeling of man's pilgrim status in the universe, and it has often been noted how his thought anticipates existentialism at various points. The confidence that man experienced when he thought of himself at the center of things has given way to a terror before the silence of the infinite spaces. Proofs of God's existence and of man's eternal destiny seemed no longer to carry conviction. Yet even if they did, would the God established by such proofs be the God whom man really needs? Or is this God to be known only by faith—'God of Abraham, God of Isaac, God of Jacob, not of philosophers and scientists.' Whatever one may think of Pascal's wager argument for belief in God (approximately, that we should bet our lives on the existence of God, for if we are wrong, we shall lose nothing by our bet, whilst if we are right, we shall gain an infinite reward), one must at least acknowledge that he faced up to the essentially ambiguous character of the universe and to the fact that man must make his most fundamental decisions in risk, without certain knowledge. As Pascal also said, we do not see the faces of the cards.

From Descartes onward, the mainstream of Western philosophy was rationalist and intellectualist. Sometimes this was a confident rationalism, as in the case of Christian Wolff, the leader of the German Enlightenment, who believed that even the truths of religion could be mathematically formulated. Sometimes, as with Hume and Kant, reason took a more skeptical turn. But in either case, the reign of reason was unquestioned.

Nevertheless, even in this period some voices were raised in behalf of a position that we would nowadays recognize as existentialist. Notable among them was Johann Georg Hamann (1730–88). He was a critic of Kant and of the rationalism of his time and was later to influence Kierkegaard, whose ideas he anticipated at many points.

Like Kierkegaard, Hamann had to wrestle with Christianity and the problem of faith in an age of reason. He rejected the idea that reason can support faith or construct a system of belief which will include matters of faith. 'I have no aptitude for truths, principles, systems; but for crumbs, fragments, fancies, sudden inspirations.'[25] Or again: 'If it is fools who say in their heart, "There is no God," those who try to prove his existence seem to be even more foolish. If that is what reason and philosophy are, then it is scarcely a sin to blaspheme it.'[26] Faith involves a leap beyond reason. More relevant to faith than reason of the mathematical sort is self-knowledge; and self-knowledge is a passionate kind of knowledge—Hamann can even talk of 'the hell of self-knowledge.'[27] The Bible itself yields self-knowledge: 'All biblical history is a prophecy which is fulfilled in every century and in the soul of man ... I read the course of my own life.'[28] Hamann seems strangely out of place in the neat rational world of the 18th century, but we can recognize in him the continuation of the existentialist protest, soon to receive still more forceful expression from Kierkegaard.

MODERN EXISTENTIALISM—THE 19TH AND 20TH CENTURIES

So far we have been dealing only with scattered hints and tendencies, with philosophies or religious movements having affinities with what we nowadays call existentialism but scarcely to be described directly by that name, save at the risk of anachronism. Yet we have been trying to show that the modern phenomenon has a long pedigree; and when it finally bursts upon the scene in recent times, we recognize it as having been long in gestation, and we even see how its varieties reflect earlier differences.

The end of the 18th century had already brought the conflict between the rationalism of the Enlightenment and the rising spirit of Romanticism. One cannot, however, link existentialism to Romanticism, except in the sense that they were both opposed to what they took to be a narrow intellectualism. The existentialists have been just as much opposed to estheticism and sentimentalism as to rationalism.

Søren Kierkegaard (1813–55) is commonly regarded as the father of modern existentialism, and is the first European philosopher who bears the existentialist label. We have already briefly mentioned him in discussing the varieties of existentialism (see above, p. 6). No extensive summary of his views will be given at this point; his work is too diffuse and voluminous to admit of summary, and, in any case, we shall be continually alluding to him throughout this book. Nevertheless, Kierkegaard remains in many respects the typical existentialist, and something must be said about his place in the historical development of existentialism.

We may notice first of all the connection between life and thought, which has undoubtedly been an important factor among many existentialist philosophers. Kierkegaard had a stern religious upbringing and seems to have been haunted by a sense of family guilt. Then there was his unhappy love affair, his engagement to the young Regina Olsen and his subsequent breaking of the engagement. Along with this went an introspective and melancholy disposition—at the age of twenty-three he was already writing of himself in his journal as 'inwardly torn asunder' and 'without any expectation of leading a happy earthly life.'[29] It is perhaps hardly surprising that in such a person the notion of the individual or the exceptional man would come to be a major category, or that subjectivity and intensity should be prized as the criteria of truth and genuineness.

In this view we touch reality in the intense moments of existence, especially moments of painful decision. 'In making a choice, it is not so much a question of choosing the right as of the energy, the earnestness, the pathos with which one chooses. Thereby the personality announces its inner infinity, and thereby, in turn, the personality is consolidated.'[30] These moments are also characterized by a deep anxiety, 'the dizziness of freedom, which occurs when freedom looks down into its own possibility.'[31] Life as known in such moments cannot be reduced to a system of ideas, for it has fundamental discontinuities that cannot be smoothed out without distortion of the reality. Hence arose Kierkegaard's bitter attack on Hegel's 'system,' as he understood it.

Like Hamann, Kierkegaard was preoccupied with the religious problem and with how to become a Christian. The progress of the human self is from the esthetic through the ethical to the religious stage, but again this cannot be rationalized or presented in a logical way. Christianity itself is the paradox and demands the leap of faith. What commonly passes for Christianity, the doctrines and ceremonies of the conventional Church, is a perversion. Toward the end of his life Kierkegaard became increasingly violent in his attacks on Christian institutions. In his last journals he sees Christianity more and more in world-renouncing terms and as the inward decision of the individual. 'Christianity in the New Testament has to do with man's will, everything turns upon changing the will, every expression (forsake the world, deny yourself, die to the world, and so on, to hate oneself, to love God, and so on)—everything is related to this basic idea in Christianity which makes it what it is—a change of will. In Christendom, on the other hand, the whole of Christianity has been transferred to intellectuality; so it becomes a doctrine, and our whole concern is with the intellectual.'[32]

Kierkegaard had no immediate successors. Indeed, his work was not highly esteemed in the 19th century, and only in the present century has he come into his own. Yet the tendencies which he represented were soon appearing in different forms. Friedrich Nietzsche (1844–1900) must be reckoned as important as Kierkegaard in the genesis of contemporary existentialism. Both Heidegger and Jaspers have written at length about Nietzsche and regard him as a key figure in the rise of existentialism—and, indeed, in the history of philosophy generally, for Nietzsche ends the classical age of Western philosophy and ushers in the strange new world of the present.

Like Kierkegaard, Nietzsche was of religious background, the product of a clerical family. His sensitivity of mind ended in madness. Yet, as we briefly noted above (see p. 6), in spite of his similarities to Kierkegaard, Nietzsche's 'existential syndrome' (if we may call it such) issued in a very different form. Whereas Kierkegaard's preoccupation was with becoming a Christian, Nietzsche's was with getting away from Christianity—or, better expressed, getting beyond it. Christian faith Nietzsche considered to be 'a continuous suicide of reason.'[33] Perhaps Kierkegaard could accept such a *sacrificium intellectus*, but not Nietzsche; for he understood Christianity as involving the sacrifice and even mutilation of the human spirit and its freedom. Christianity is to be overcome by putting in its place the doctrine of the superman: man surpassing himself. This is a doctrine of the affirmation of the world and of life, and so reverses the world-renunciation of Christianity.

Much has been written about the 'death of God' in Nietzsche's thought: 'God is dead! God remains dead! And we have killed him!'[34] In one sense, the death of God liberates man. But there is another, melancholy side to Nietzsche's philosophy. The death of God brings us into the age of nihilism. Man's self-affirmation takes place therefore against the background of a godless and absurd world, whose law is the law of eternal recurrence. As with Kierkegaard, Nietzsche's philosophy ends in paradox—a paradox in which, one may speculate, the philosopher himself was destroyed. One of Nietzsche's commentators, M. M. Bozmann, has written: 'The will to glorify will, the will to achievement and victory, the will to say "Yea and Amen" to life, combined with belief in the dogma of eternal recurrence and his own many failures and sufferings seems at times to have caused Nietzsche terrible mental anguish.'[35] In a sense, we might say that this anguish was the anguish of the age, concentrated in the philosopher; it was also the basic anguish of existentialism.

Perhaps the anguish of Nietzsche was impossible to sustain. At any rate, subsequent German existentialism (or 'philosophy of existence,' as its practitioners prefer to call it) has sought to break out of the impasse in which Nietzsche found himself. Karl Jaspers (1883–   ) began his career as a psychiatrist and soon became interested in what he calls the 'limit situations' of life, those situations where we come against a wall, as it were: the human resources are exhausted and a 'shattering' or 'foundering' takes place. However, the conclusion is not nihilism, for it is in precisely such situations, according to Jaspers, that there opens to us the reality of Transcendence. His voluminous and somewhat repetitious writings explore the relations between the human existent and the world, on the one side, and between the existent and Transcendence on the other. While all our knowing is of the subject-object pattern, we have some disclosure too of the 'encompassing' or 'comprehensive,' that which embraces both subject and object.

Jaspers' thought leads him in the direction of a 'philosophical faith' that cannot be proved and is not objective knowledge. Yet it is not just a subjective attitude; and although Transcendence is not known, it nevertheless speaks through a language of 'ciphers.' Many of these ideas will have to be discussed in subsequent chapters of this book.

Martin Heidegger (1889–   ) likewise avoids the nihilist impasse, though there are moments in his philosophy when he seems headed toward it. Among the formative influences in his thinking are the phenomenology of Husserl, an interest in the question of 'being' derived from Brentano, and a preoccupation with language, which he attributes to the days spent in a Jesuit seminary. Noteworthy too is his interest in the pre-Socratics. With this breadth of interest, it is not surprising that Heidegger rejects the title of existentialist. In particular, he dissociates himself from the humanistic existentialism of Sartre.

Nevertheless, Heidegger's major work, *Being and Time*, dating from 1927, is by common consent the most impressive analysis of human existence to have come out of this whole movement in philosophy. The prominence of such themes as care, anxiety, guilt, finitude, and above all death, in Heidegger's account might be taken as indications of a trend toward a kind of nihilism. This impression might be further strengthened by his famous inaugural lecture given at Freiburg in 1929 on the theme, 'What Is Metaphysics?'; for in this lecture we learn that metaphysics has to do with nothing.

But no more than Jaspers does Heidegger end up in nihilism. By a *tour de force* he argues that the 'nothing' of which he writes, though a 'non-entity,' is precisely being. 'This wholly other to all entities is the non-entity. But this nothing essentiates as being.'[36] The way opens into the philosophy of the later Heidegger, a quasi-mystical, quasi-poetical, yet none the less philosophical meditation upon being, thought, and language.

Alongside the German *Existenzphilosophie* just considered, there has been a related movement which, though it could hardly be called existentialism, has certainly close affinities. Its lineage is traced not to Nietzsche but to such philosophers of life and action as Hermann Lotze (1817–81) and Rudolf Eucken (1846–1926). This philosophy is related to existentialism chiefly in the sense that it has become increasingly interested in the problem of interpersonal relations, and because of the tendency toward individualism among many existentialists, this other type of approach provides a needed corrective.

This interpersonal approach has had many representatives, such as Eberhard Grisebach and Ferdinand Ebner, but best-known of all is the Jewish philosopher Martin Buber (1878–1965). Whereas existentialists have tended to concentrate on the problem of man's relation to the world or sometimes on his relation to God or Being, Buber has been more interested in men's relations with each other and rightly holds that there cannot be an existent apart from his relation to other existents.

French existentialism has become probably the best-known of all existentialisms. The non-Christian type has its philosophical roots in German existentialism, especially that of Heidegger, but it has strong roots also in the French (and European) experience of the 20th century. F. Temple Kingston, one of the most penetrating analysts of French existentialism, has written: 'All of the existentialists admit that human beings in this century are threatened to an unusual degree in their very existence by abstract philosophies, by all-powerful totalitarian states, and by the misuse of scientific inventions. This awareness has been made especially vivid to the French philosophers by France's defeat in the war and by the present tension between Communism and American democracy.'[37]

This French existentialism, as we see it in Jean-Paul Sartre (1905–   ), remains, in some respects, close to Nietzsche. In a godless world man himself has to take the place of God. 'Man being condemned to be free carries the weight of the whole world on his shoulders; he is responsible for the world and for himself as a way of being.'[38] But, as with Nietzsche, there is also the dark side to this situation of freedom, for man's desire to be God is essentially self-contradictory and self-frustrating.

Alongside Sartre may be mentioned Albert Camus (1913–60). He developed a kind of existentialism of the absurd and has been described as an 'anti-theist' rather than an atheist. For him, Sisyphus is the symbol of mankind—the ancient hero who was condemned to spend his days rolling a boulder to the top of a hill, always to see it escape him and crash back down to the bottom.

However, there is another type of French existentialism, a more personalistic type that is not directly derived from German sources but that draws on a native French tradition. Maurice Blondel (1861–1949) is not usually classed as an existentialist, but his philosophy certainly prepared the way for a personalistic kind of existentialism. In his famous book *L'Action* Blondel argued that the starting-point of philosophy should be sought not in the abstract 'I think' but in the concrete 'I act,' and from this point of departure he constructed a dialectical philosophy of action. One of his most recent commentators has remarked: 'Although the term is greatly abused, we must agree that Blondel was an "existentialist." '[39]

Gabriel Marcel (1889–) is the best-known representative of this other kind of French existentialism. As against the pessimistic elements in Sartre and Camus, he offers a 'metaphysic of hope' (the subtitle of his book *Homo Viator*), based on a theistic conception of the universe, and the individualistic tendencies in Sartre are confronted in Marcel with a sense of human community that is not inferior to Buber's.

While Germany and France have been the countries where existentialism has attained its greatest development, the existentialist type of thinking has appeared in many other countries besides. The Spaniard Miguel de Unamuno (1864–1936) and the Russian Nikolai Alexandrovich Berdyaev (1874–1948) deserve to be counted among the most brilliant representatives of existentialism. We have confined ourselves to the mention of men who were first and foremost philosophers; the list could be greatly widened if we were to mention literary men whose novels, plays, and poems expound something like an existentialist point of view—Dostoevsky, Kafka, Eliot, Beckett, and a host of others. At this point, however, one has to be careful not to broaden the term *existentialism* to the point where it becomes a jejune expression.

Thus, from its first hardly articulate stirrings in the earliest periods of human reflection, existentialism has gradually taken shape until in the 20th century it has become one of the major forms of philosophy. Why should it have blossomed forth in our own time, and why should it have found such congenial soil on the continent of Europe?

The answer to these questions has surely become clear in the course of our historical survey. The existentialist style of thought seems to emerge whenever man finds his securities threatened, when he becomes aware of the ambiguities of the world and knows his pilgrim status in it. This also helps to explain why existentialism has flourished in those lands where the social structures have been turned upside down and all values transvalued, whereas relatively stable countries (including the Anglo-Saxon lands) have not experienced this poignancy and so have not developed the philosophizing that flows from it.

CHAPTER THREE

The Idea of Existence

ESSENCE AND EXISTENCE

The distinction between existence and essence is one of the oldest in philosophy and has very wide applicability and usefulness. To say that anything 'exists' is simply to point to the fact 'that it is.' Existence is characterized by concreteness and particularity and also by a sheer givenness. The silver dollar lying on the table exists as a particular item in the world, and its existence is presented to me as a fact to be accepted. I can neither wish it into existence nor wish it out of existence, though indeed I can change the form in which it exists. But as soon as we talk of 'the form in which it exists,' we are already beginning to move away from existence to essence. If the existence of anything has to do with the fact 'that it is,' its essence consists in 'what it is.' The essence of an object is constituted by those basic characteristics that make it one kind of object rather than another. The essence of the silver dollar would be described in terms of its color, metallic luster, composition, weight, specific gravity, shape, inscription, and so on. One would have to mention all the characteristics that are necessary to define this as a dollar rather than anything else. It follows then that essence is characterized by abstractness and universality. Furthermore, essences lend themselves to the operations of rational thought, to analysis, comparison, and synthesis, in ways which the sheer contingency and 'thatness' of existence resist.

Throughout the history of philosophy, sometimes essences and sometimes existences have dominated thought. The whole tradition that stemmed from Plato has exalted essence at the expense of existence. This tradition has seen existence as belonging to the realm of the contingent and changeable. Reason turns away from this realm and looks for unchanging and universal essences, for a realm of forms and ideas. One may even be pushed to the paradoxical conclusion that existence is unreal (it does not really exist, so to speak!) and that reality belongs to essences. But always philosophical common sense comes to rebel against such conclusions, and then we have periods in the history of philosophy when the existent, the concrete, the particular is asserted over against the essential, the abstract, and the universal. Modern existentialism begins with Kierkegaard's championing of the concreteness of existence over against what he took to be the essentialism of Hegel.

But while the broad distinction between essence and existence is clear enough, we soon find that the relation of essence and exist-ence is a very complex one, and that the very notion of *existence* is far from being as simple as it seems at first sight and has in fact been understood in many different ways. Apart from the fact that the contemporary existentialist uses the word *existence* in a more restricted sense than it bore in the philosophical tradition, it does not require much thought to see that even in that tradition *existence* was by no means a univocal expression.

We may begin with etymology. To 'exist' or 'ex-sist' (Latin: *ex-sistere*) meant originally to 'stand out' or 'emerge.' Thus the verb probably had a more active *feel* about it than it has now. To exist was to emerge or stand out from the background as some-thing really there. Putting it more philosophically, to exist is to stand out from nothing. Nowadays, however, the notion of existence has become altogether more passive. To 'exist' is more likely to be understood as 'lying around somewhere' than as 'standing out somewhere.'

Indeed, the commonest meaning of *existence* is not very far from just 'lying around.' To say that anything exists means that you will come across it somewhere in the world. If someone makes the assertion, 'Unicorns exist,' he means that somewhere in the world you will come across a unicorn if you search long enough and hard enough. The expression *somewhere in the world*, which we have used twice already in this paragraph, does not seem to be accidental. To 'exist' is to have a place (and time) in the real world.

However, there have been philosophers who, for one reason or another, have sometimes found it necessary to claim that the world itself exists, that it is not an illusion or a mere appearance but is the real world. What is meant when it is said that 'the world exists'?

Obviously, in this case 'exists' cannot be construed in terms of 'coming across in the real world,' for the world itself is not something in the world. It is not my business at the moment to discuss the meaning of the word *existence* when we say 'the world exists.' (The reader who is interested in pursuing this particular meaning will find an excellent discussion in Milton K. Munitz, *The Mystery of Existence*.)[1] I believe that it makes sense to claim that the world exists, but I only want to establish the point here that this kind of existence must be very different from the existence of particular things or animals or persons, since this latter kind of existence is understood to imply that the existent in question occurs in the world.

The existence of God raises still another problem. What does it mean to say, 'God exists'? Whatever or whoever God is, he is not an object within the world. Even if he is in some measure immanent in the world, he is certainly not an item within it. To say that he exists cannot mean that there is the possibility that we might come across God in the world, as we might come across a unicorn. Some theologians think that we should give up talking about the 'existence' of God, because such talk is almost bound to convey the impression that he is a particular item to be discovered in the world. However, the logic of the word *God* is in some respects similar to the logic of the word *world*, so if it makes sense to say that the world exists, perhaps it also makes sense to say that God exists, though in each case one is using the word *exists* in a different (though presumably related) sense to the one it bears when we assert the existence of anything within the world. I suppose too that 'exists' has a different sense when used with respect to God from what it has when used with respect to the world. Except perhaps for a pantheist, God and the world 'exist' in different ways. But it might seem that they have this in common, namely, that in some sense their existence enables or empowers the existence of particular existents in the world. Especially in the case of God, 'existence' would have to be understood in a supremely active sense, placing this kind of existence at the opposite pole from an existence that can be understood as a mere 'lying around.'

We are still far from having exhausted the meanings of 'existence.' What, for instance, is meant by asserting the existence of the soul? In the Western world, our ways of thinking have been so dominated by the notion of thinghood as the paradigmatic mode of existence that to assert the existence of the soul might be taken to mean that there exists a subtle and possibly indestructible soul-substance. But if we escape from this way of thinking and still want to assert that the soul exists, then we have to visualize still another mode of existence appropriate to souls or selves, conceived in a formal rather than a substantial way.

One could continue this exploration into the traditional usages of the word *existence*. Do numbers exist? Certainly the mathematician makes a distinction between 'real' and 'imaginary' numbers. But what kind of existence would one ascribe to a number? Was Bertrand Russell's suggestion that, with respect to numbers, relations, and the like, one should speak of 'subsistence' rather than of 'existence' any more than a verbal convention?

It is important to recognize that while the existentialists use the word *existence* in a special sense, which they are at pains to distinguish from the traditional ways in which the word is used, nevertheless some of the traditional meanings still cling to the word even among contemporary existentialists. Thus, while it may be true to say (see above, p. 30) that the efforts of some recent writers, such as Étienne Gilson, to show that Thomism is existential rather than essentialist employ the traditional rather than the contemporary existentialist concept of existence, this is not sufficient to dispose of such efforts or to show that they are mistaken. There is sufficient affinity between the traditional and the contemporary notions of existence to establish a measure of validity for Gilson's interpretation, though certainly it would fall far short of establishing a fully 'existentialist' version of Thomism, in the modern sense of 'existentialist.' Similarly, it seems to me that Heidegger's complaint that Sartre uses the notions of existence and essence in their traditional metaphysical sense when he declares that existence precedes essence[2] does not dispose of Sartre's contention, which indeed takes up the traditional distinction of essence and existence but goes on to incorporate it into the development of a new conception of existence.

Of course, what is distinctive in the way the existentialists use the word *existence* is that they confine it to the kind of being that belongs to man. But it has been worth our while to spend a little time in clarifying the traditional meanings of the word, for we shall find that these are still influential in determining, affirmatively or negatively, the existentialist understanding of 'existence'; and we shall find further that leading existentialists are by no means agreed among themselves about the precise meaning of this key term in their philosophy.

HOW SOME EXISTENTIALISTS UNDERSTAND THE WORD 'EXISTENCE'

We have noted that in existentialist philosophy the word *existence* is restricted to the kind of being exemplified in man. It should hardly be necessary to remind ourselves that although only man (and any other beings who may have the same ontological constitution as man) 'exists,' this does not for a moment imply some kind of subjective idealism. Trees and mountains, factories and highways, perhaps God and angels, all *are*; they have reality and being. But in existentialist terminology, they do not exist. What then is existence, the peculiar mode of being that we ourselves, as human beings, know at first hand?

In order to answer this question, it may be helpful first of all to pass in review what some leading existentialists have said about existence.

Kierkegaard, the first of the modern existentialists, is a writer for whom 'existence' does mean primarily the unique concrete being of the individual human person. The existent then is the contingent, the particular, that which refuses to fit into some system constructed by rational thought. Essentialism, as Kierkegaard knew it in Hegelianism, tried to bring men and all things into an organic structure within which contradictions would be overcome. But to be aware of existence is to be aware of precisely that which is discontinuous with a system and which remains paradoxical. The real (the existent) refuses to conform itself to the pattern laid down by rational thought. 'The difficulty that inheres in existence with which the existing individual is confronted is one that never really comes to expression in the language of abstract thought, much less receives an explanation. Because abstract thought is *sub specie aeterni* (i.e., from the standpoint of an absolute spectator) it ignores the concrete and the temporal, the existential process, the predicament of the existing individual arising from his being a synthesis of the temporal and the eternal situated in existence.'[3] The last few words of this quotation perhaps point to the heart of the matter in Kierkegaard's understanding of existence. Man paradoxically joins in himself the temporal and the eternal, the finite and the infinite; and thought will never 'make sense' of this or combine two sides of man's being in a unitary whole. Existence is not an idea or an essence that can be intellectually manipulated. Indeed, man becomes something less than human if he allows himself and his being to be absorbed into some organic scheme of being or some rational system of thought.

Man fulfills his being precisely by existing, by standing out as the
unique individual that he is and stubbornly refusing to be absorbed
into a system.

Heidegger employs a threefold terminology in an attempt to
avoid confusion over the word *existence* (or its German equivalents).
The German word *Dasein* has been traditionally used for existence
of various kinds; it was often used, for instance, of the existence
of God. But Heidegger restricts *Dasein* to the being exemplified
in man. Strictly speaking, *Dasein* is not equivalent to 'man.' *Dasein* is
an ontological term. It designates man *in respect of his being*: and
if this kind of being is found elsewhere than in humanity, then the
term *Dasein* could be appropriately applied. For the traditional
term *existentia*, Heidegger proposes the German expression *Vor-
handenheit*, which may be translated 'presence-at-hand.' This expression points to that rather passive kind of existing that we have
called a mere 'lying around'; it is something that one may come
across in the world. The third of Heidegger's terms is *Existenz*,
'existence.' Heidegger declares that in his writing 'the term "existence"
(*Existenz*), as a designation of being, will be allotted solely to
Dasein.'[4] Heidegger goes on to say that 'the "essence" (*Wesen*) of
Dasein lies in its existence,' and he explains this to mean that *Dasein's*
'essence' is constituted not by properties but by possible ways of
being. Elsewhere he offers this interpretation of the sentence: 'Man
has an essence such that he is the "there," that is to say, the clearing
of being. This "being" of the there, and only this, has the basic
characteristic of ex-sistence, that is to say, the ecstatic standing-in
in the truth of being.'[5] This interpretation obviously stands in need of
further interpretation, and we hope to offer this as we develop the
notion of existence. For the present, we may note that Heidegger is
seeking here to avoid a purely subjectivist or 'man is the measure
of all things' reading of his assertion that 'the "essence" of *Dasein*
lies in its existence.'

It was just this subjectivist interpretation that Sartre placed upon
Heidegger's sentence, which, in his philosophy, takes the form:
'Existence precedes essence.'[6] I am not concerned with the question
whether, as Heidegger has maintained, Sartre misunderstood him.
Sartre builds up his own conception of existence, and it has to be
considered in its own right. It may be true that 'existence' in Sartre
retains more of its traditional sense than it does in Heidegger. 'Concrete individual being here and now' is the definition of Sartre's
'existence' offered by Hazel Barnes.[7] But Sartre, like Heidegger,
introduces terms of his own to clarify distinctions that get blurred in

the traditional terminology. It is the *pour-soi* ('for-itself') of Sartre that corresponds to the *Dasein* of Heidegger, and to *Existenz*. But Sartre's *pour-soi* gets defined in terms of negation and freedom. The *pour-soi* comes into being (exists, emerges) by separating itself from the *en-soi* ('in-itself'). The *en-soi* has its being in itself, and this is essential being. The *pour-soi* is free to choose its essence. Its being is its freedom. Yet, paradoxically, its freedom is also its lack of being. For Sartre as for Kierkegaard there is an inner contradiction in existence. For Sartre this might be expressed by saying that freedom and being stand in inverse ratio to each other.

In Jaspers we find still another way of talking about 'existence.'[8] He can use the expression *Dasein* or *existence* simply to refer to the fact that we find ourselves in the world. In this sense 'we find existence as the unreflecting experience of our life in the world. It is immediate and unquestioning, the reality which everything must enter so as to be real for us . . . we never get over the awe of this "I exist." ' However, this kind of existence must not be confused with another kind, designated by the German *Existenz*, a term often left untranslated in English versions of Jaspers, just as *Dasein* is left untranslated in English versions of Heidegger. Concerning *Existenz*, Jaspers makes three points: 1) '*Existenz* is not a kind of being; it is potential being. That is to say, I am not *Existenz* but possible *Existenz*. I do not have myself, but come to myself.' Here Jaspers regards *Existenz* as the fulfillment of mere existence (*Dasein*), just as we have seen that in Kierkegaard 'existence' can mean the fulfillment of man's being. 2) '*Existenz* is freedom . . . a freedom not of its own making, which may fail to appear. *Existenz* is freedom only as the gift of Transcendence, knowing its donor . . . . There is no *Existenz* without Transcendence.' The reference to the gift of freedom and the relation to Transcendence at this point differentiate Jaspers' conception of existence rather sharply from that of Sartre. 3) Finally, we are told that '*Existenz* is the ever-individual self, irreplaceable and never interchangeable.'

I shall not pursue this question of the peculiarities of different existentialists in their use of the expression *existence*. Even allowing for confusions of translation, we can see that there is considerable diversity. In the next section, I shall try to construct a coherent concept of existence. This will be neither an amalgam of the views of the philosophers just considered nor an attempt to harmonize them, but an exposition of the most typical characteristics of existence. This exposition will also make clear to us how some of the differences have arisen.

BASIC STRUCTURES OF EXISTENCE

If we restrict the word *existence* to the kind of being exemplified in man, and if we ask what are the basic characteristics distinguishing this kind of being from the being of plants, mountains, animals, and whatever else, then it seems to me that at least three such characteristics call for mention.

1. We have seen that 'ex-sistence' is taken by existentialists in its root sense of 'standing out.' If we take seriously this notion of standing out, then a little reflection shows that it is much more apposite to the kind of being that belongs to man than to other modes of being which traditionally have been called existence. It is true that all beings 'exist' in the sense of 'standing out' from nothing. But man exists in the further sense that among all the beings that may be observed on earth he 'stands out' as the only one that not only *is* but takes over its being in awareness of who or what it is and of who or what it may become. And this points to still another and more important sense of the 'standing out.' Man keeps on standing out or emerging from where he is at any given moment. Perhaps one should speak of a 'going out' rather than of a 'standing out,' for what we have in mind is something fundamentally dynamic—man's constant movement beyond where he is at any given time. He is always on the way to somewhere else. Other language which may be used and which has been used includes the terms *ecstasy* and *transcendence*. To say man exists 'ecstatically' is, strictly speaking, to utter a tautology, for *ecstasis* is nothing but the Greek cognate of 'existence.' Yet the introduction of the word *ecstatic* does help to stress the dynamic quality of human existence. When a man is 'ecstatic' or 'in ecstasy,' he goes beyond himself. The claim of the existentialist is that we should not think of man as 'ecstatic' only in those rare experiences of vision or trance for which we normally reserve the word; man is 'ecstatic' in respect of his very being. We can also say that man is 'transcendent' in his being. We should notice that the word here has none of its theological connotations. It is a word that even Sartre can use about man. To talk of the 'transcendence' of the human existent is simply to point again to the fact that man is at any moment transcending or going beyond what he is in that moment.

So the first basic characteristic of existence is its emergent, ecstatic, transcendent elusiveness. Most objects within the world can be described in terms of a few fixed characteristics—a metal, for example. But man is not just constituted by some given properties.

He thrusts himself into possibilities of existence.

Would not the same be true of animals and plants? Admittedly the ontological status of living things would seem to be intermediate between that of the human existent and that of, let us say, a rock or a mountain. Yet even at the biological level it would seem that man stands in a kind of openness and possibility of transcendence that are uniquely his. Theodosius Dobzhansky writes: 'The ancestors of man had begun to transcend their animality perhaps as long as 1,700,000 years ago.' He goes on to describe this transcendence in words borrowed from a fellow biologist, but they could equally well have been written by an existentialist philosopher: 'Man is a self-reflecting animal in that he alone has the ability to objectify himself, to stand apart from himself, as it were, and to consider the kind of being he is, and what it is that he wants to do and to become.'[9]

We could put the matter in another way by saying that 'hominization'—to use Teilhard de Chardin's expression for the appearance of man on earth—is not just a biological phenomenon presented for empirical observation. It can be understood only through an introspective phenomenology that penetrates to its inner meaning. What distinguishes man's 'existing' from biological evolution is that man does not transcend his given situation in terms of 'laws of nature' operating from outside, but in terms of images of himself which he seeks consciously to realize—he considers 'the kind of being he is, and what it is that he wants to do and to become.'

Does man have a nature? It seems clear from what we have just been saying that man does not have a *fixed* nature. However, if 'nature' is defined in a sufficiently flexible way, there is presumably no harm in allowing that there is a 'human nature.' Some Catholic philosophers and theologians do in fact talk of the 'nature' of man, while at the same time insisting that this is an 'open' nature, which is in process of self-transcendence. The question whether man has a nature cannot be answered by pointing to the 'nature' he shares with other mammals. Even man's animality is transformed in the relation to his humanity. But, in any case, man would have to be defined in terms of what is distinctive to his humanity rather than in terms of what he shares with the animals. In general we may say that the question about a 'nature' in man must be answered negatively if nature is conceived in either static or subhuman terms, but it may be answered affirmatively if one has developed a sufficiently dynamic conception of nature, appropriate to the human existent.

Another traditional word may be briefly considered at this point.

Is not man 'spirit,' and is this not what is distinctive in him? To be sure, one can have no quarrel with such a point of view. But what is meant by 'spirit'? We must certainly purge our minds of the animistic view of spirit as itself some kind of subtle essence. What is most characteristic of spirit is 'procession,' a going forth. 'Spirit' too is a dynamic notion, not to be seized in terms of a static nature. The spiritual man is so far from static that he is precisely 'ec-static,' that is to say, he exists. 'Spirituality' is the disciplined path along which 'existence' is enhanced.

It is in the context of the foregoing remarks concerning man's dynamic self-transcending that we must come back to the problem of existence and essence. We have noted some disagreement among existentialists over this problem. Heidegger declares that man's 'essence' lies in his existence, Sartre that existence precedes essence.

I take it that Heidegger and Sartre, together with other philosophers of existence, are agreed that man has no fixed essence, given in advance. As Sartre says, he is not like a manufactured thing. Kierkegaard's insistence that existence cannot be reduced to rationally manipulable ideas and Nietzsche's thought of man moving toward superman are on similar lines. For all of them man is unfinished and incomplete.

Yet the difference (and I think it is a deep difference) would seem to be this. For some of these philosophers, there are clues or guidelines given, perhaps in existence itself, that point toward human fulfillment. Heidegger seems to belong here, with his statement that the essence of man lies in existence, and still more with the later development of his philosophy in which existence comes to maturity as it responds to the call of being. Jaspers also belongs here. We may recall his statement, quoted above, that 'there is no *Existenz* apart from Transcendence.' The theistic existentialists would belong here, for they think of human existence as transcending toward God. On the other hand, Nietzsche, Sartre, and Camus see human existence transcending into the nothing. There is no God. So man is entirely abandoned to fixing his own norms and determining his values and what he will become. And Sartre might well complain that if it is otherwise and God somehow imposes an 'essence' on man, then after all, man does not truly exist but is just another manufactured object, though in this case the manufacturer is a transcendent Creator. To this I think it might be replied that there is no question of 'imposing' an essence, and that Heidegger is probably correct when he holds that Sartre is here using the ideas of existence and essence in a very traditionalist manner.

But a fuller discussion of this difficult problem must wait until we look at the idea of authenticity and, at a still later stage of our discussion (see below, p. 213), examine the structure and the viability of an existentialist ethic.

2. The second basic characteristic of existence is the uniqueness of the individual existent. An existent is not just an 'it'; the existent says 'I,' and in uttering the personal pronoun lays claim not just to a unique place and perspective in the world but to a unique being. 'Mineness' is a term that has sometimes been used to express the awareness that my existence is unique and distinct from the existence of everyone else. I am not just a specimen of a class. I am I. And this last statement is not merely a tautology. It is an assertion of my unique individual being as an existent who stands out as this existent and no other.

Of course, these remarks need both clarification and qualification. On the one hand, it may be said that every particular thing in the world is unique. Two newspapers, fresh from the presses, are very much alike, but a close examination would show minor differences. However, the point is that these differences do not matter. It is a matter of *indifference* what paper I pick up and read; and having read one, I have no interest in the hundreds of thousands of others, nearly identical with it, that have rolled off the presses. If we think of animals rather than of newspapers, no doubt individual differences are more important and more marked than in the case of manufactured items. Animal life is a mode of being somewhere between existence and mere presence-at-hand. Yet even in the case of the animal it will generally be a matter of indifference to the biologist which particular specimen he uses for his experiment or dissection. Now sometimes human beings can be treated as merely specimens. The very useful sciences of psychology and sociology proceed in this way. But when human beings are represented merely statistically, let us say, an abstraction has taken place that screens out what is most distinctively *human*—namely, the precise individuality of each. Jaspers hit on the important words when, in the sentence quoted earlier, he said of the human existent that he is 'irreplaceable' and 'never interchangeable.' One might add that there is an inexhaustible interest in individual human beings. These qualities of irreplaceability, non-interchangeability, and inexhaustible interest go to constitute that uniqueness or 'mineness' of personal being, marking it off from all other modes of being.

On the other hand, it may be argued that the uniqueness of each individual existent is simply a physical uniqueness and is at bottom no different from the tiny differences that distinguish one butterfly from another of the same species, or even one silver dollar from another. Everyone knows, of course, that there are physical differences between one human being and another. Each one has his own unique face or appearance. Of recent years we have learned much more about the physical basis of uniqueness. The science of genetics has taught us that each individual person has in his genes a unique 'recipe,' as it were, and that the possible combinations and permutations of molecular structure on which the profusion of individuals depends is almost infinite. However, the discovery of this physical basis of individual uniqueness certainly does not 'reduce' the existential phenomenon of such uniqueness to a merely physical phenomenon, to be regarded as comparable to the physical differences that make every animal, every crystal, and even every manufactured object unique. Whatever its biological or physico-chemical basis, the uniqueness of the human existent has emerged as a uniqueness of a distinct order. No animal, no crystal, no manufactured thing says 'I.' The uniqueness of the human existent lies in the felt 'mineness' of that existence which knows itself as 'I,' almost a microcosm or a 'monad,' as Leibniz called it, a unique center different from every other, at once lonely and cut off, yet also in a sense embracing the world and embraced by it.

That I am this 'I' and no other is a basic datum and characteristic of human existence. Why this should be so is a mystery. Perhaps it does not make sense to talk about a 'why' or perhaps that word in this context only expresses a kind of wonder. On the other hand, people have speculated about the why—stories of creation or, again, about metempsychosis or the transmigration of souls have, in some measure, been motivated by the sheer givenness of I-hood. We shall return to the theme when we consider the phenomenon called by existentialists 'facticity.'

3. A third basic characteristic of existence is self-relatedness. This follows from the points already considered. We have seen that the existent is on his way as the unique person that he is. Either he is himself, he is existing as this unique existent, standing out from the world of objects and going out from any given state of himself; or he is not himself, he is being absorbed into the world of objects as just another object, he decides nothing for himself but everything is decided for him by external factors. The extraordinary complexity of existence and selfhood is implicit in sentences such as these. To exist as a self (or better expressed, on the way to selfhood) is to stand in the possibility of becoming at one with oneself, of fulfilling oneself

(though this might be by giving up oneself) or of being divided in oneself, separated from what everyone knows how to call his 'true self.' In the language of some existentialists, these two possibilities are to exist 'authentically' or 'inauthentically.' But this terminology does little more than translate into Greek, for in that language an αὐθέντης is one who does things for himself (αὐτός), the actual perpetrator of a deed. In our usage, an authentic Rembrandt is a picture that Rembrandt himself painted. The German equivalent, *eigentlich*, would be literally rendered in English as 'own-ly,' that with which one identifies oneself.

The problem of the existent's self-relatedness and his predicament as one who may either lay hold of his existence or let it slip raises again in a new way the question of existence and essence. How do we distinguish authentic and inauthentic existence? What is the criterion? Or are there any criteria?

Does authentic existence depend solely on the intensity and 'own-liness' of the choice? And does this mean, on the other hand, that conformity to rules is *ipso facto* inauthentic? Would one go on to draw the conclusion that perhaps a thief or a pervert or a tyrant is an authentic man, because he has really chosen to be thief, pervert, or tyrant; and that the law-abiding citizen must be adjudged inauthentic, especially if his law-abiding character is the result of unthinking habit?

On the whole, the atheistic existentialists find themselves impelled toward the first of the two alternatives, though they seek to ward off its most anarchical and antisocial consequences. Sartre, for instance, holds that values are created *by our choices*. We do not choose an antecedent good but make something good by choosing it. However, he also maintains that we cannot choose anything as better 'unless it is better for all.'[10] It is admittedly not easy to see how this apparently Kantian principle coheres with his general philosophy. But in any case, I think we must say that the principle is only *apparently* Kantian. Kant's distinction between autonomy and heteronomy might seem at first sight to be similar to the existentialist distinction between authenticity and inauthenticity, but it is not really so. Both are protests against the unthinking acceptance of an externally imposed code of morals, but Sartre's view is infected with a subjectivism quite absent in Kant because of the Sartrean rejection of an objectively valid 'practical reason.'

As against these subjectivist tendencies, the Christian existentialists and the German philosophers of existence seek to bridge the gap between the freedom and autonomy of the individual existent

and the demands of God or of being. But to bridge this gap is by
no means easy if one is to avoid the error of invoking a ready-made
'essence of humanity' as the criterion of authenticity. A good apple
or a good tennis racket earns its appellation because it conforms to a
standard laid down and exhibits the properties demanded by this
standard. But the existentialist, whether Christian or atheist, precisely denies that man can be measured like an apple or a tennis
racket.

A detailed discussion of these difficult matters must be deferred
for the present (see Chapters Eight and Twelve below). Meanwhile,
to the basic characteristics of existence earlier noted we add this
third one—that to 'exist' is not simply to 'be,' but is rather to be
faced with the choice to 'be or not to be,' to gain existence in the
full sense or to let it slip away.

THE POSSIBILITY OF EXISTENTIAL ANALYSIS

This chapter has been devoted mainly to exploring and clarifying
the notion of 'existence,' with special reference to the way (or ways)
in which this notion is understood among existentialists. At this
point the first assessment of existentialism becomes feasible. We
are ourselves human existents and have firsthand acquaintance with
what it means to exist. When we reflect on our existence, do we agree
with the basic description offered by the existentialists—the in-
completeness and fluidity of existence, its uniqueness in every case,
and its possibility for realizing itself or getting lost? If we do not
agree, then perhaps we should not pursue existentialism any
further.

On the other hand, if we do find this basic description of the
human condition accurate and even (compared with essentialist
views) exciting, the question arises, 'Where do we go from here?'
Has not this very description of existence in its basic structures
made impossible anything like a *philosophy* of existence? We can see
how the individual existent is, in virtue of the fact that he has to
decide about his own existence, compelled to reflect on that existence
and to reach such understanding of it as he can. In the terminology
employed by some existentialist writers, *existential* philosophy has
an *existentiell* root, where the adjective *existential* is understood as
referring to the universal structures of existence while *existentiell*
refers to the concrete situation of the individual existent. Other
writers reject this terminological distinction. But perhaps they all
agree that the basic motivation of a philosophy of existence arises

from the individual existent's need to come to terms with his own existence.

But how can one possibly move from the concrete individual existence known at first hand into a philosophical account that, in virtue of the fact that it calls itself 'philosophical,' would seem to be making some claim to universal validity? More especially, if human existence is always incomplete and elusive, how can anyone claim to give an adequate account of it? Again, if each individual existent is unique and cannot be regarded as a specimen of a class, how can one generalize about human existence, as a philosophy of existence seems compelled to do? Finally, if there are no objective criteria that determine an authentic existence and allow us to distinguish it from an inauthentic one, then are we not purely at the mercy of individual whims and arbitrary preferences, so that freedom in Sartre or heroic absurdity in Camus or the superman in Nietzsche or Christianity in Kierkegaard or death in Heidegger or whatever it may be, gets exalted to the level of an ultimate? However, this tells us nothing about philosophy but only about the psychological idiosyncrasies of these writers.

These objections are certainly formidable, and to anyone who embraces either a narrow empiricism or a narrow rationalism and who wants to treat man and human action precisely as one might treat any natural phenomenon, they may seem fatal. But it may be that they simply urge us to develop, for the study of man, more flexible and more complex methods of inquiry than are demanded when minerals or plants form the object of our investigation. The three critical questions raised in the last paragraph can be met. The fact than man is unfinished and on his way does not mean that a description is impossible, but that such a description must be directed to possibilities rather than properties. The fact that each individual is unique does not mean that we are confronted with a formless and indescribable multiplicity, for there are limits or horizons within which all these unique existents fall, and there are structures that can be discerned in all of them. And while existence fulfills itself in many ways, we may well discover that there are some norms, internal rather than external, that determine the direction of an authentic fulfillment.

So we must now pursue our inquiry further. It will take the form of a phenomenological analysis of that mode of being called *existence*, of which the basic characteristics were set out in the preceding section.

CHAPTER FOUR

Existence and World

EXISTENCE AND ENVIRONMENT

Although we talk often enough about the 'world,' a moment's reflection is enough to convince us that the expression has many meanings, and some of them are far from clear. What is the world? Perhaps we are tempted to answer the question by saying that the world is everything that there is. But such an answer immediately shows the difficulties we are in. No one knows the extent of all that is or the content of all that is, so how is it possible to make any meaningful pronouncement about it? It would seem that when anyone talks about the 'world,' he could mean at most everything of which he is aware or of which he can form some idea, but he could never claim to be talking of everything that is.

The expression *world* then would seem always to include the point of view of the person who is talking about the world. It does not stand for something altogether independent of those who talk about it, but rather for their total environment as they are aware of it. It is senseless to pronounce about 'everything that is,' without qualification. But the world is not just everything that is but everything that forms the human environment and provides the setting in which human life has to be lived. The very word *world* is derived from the Old English compound, *weor-old*, in which *weor* means 'man' and *old* means 'age' or 'era,' so that, taken etymologically, 'world' is the era of man.

Strictly speaking, then, there is no world apart from man. This is not to be taken for a moment in the sense of some kind of subjective idealism, as if the material universe depended for its existence on the minds that perceive it (*esse est percipi*). If there were no human beings, there might still be galaxies, trees, rocks, and so on—and doubtless there were, in those long stretches of time before the evolution of *Homo sapiens* or any other human species that may have existed on earth. But the total sum of these things would not constitute a world, for we have seen that the world is not just 'everything that is.' When I say that there is no world apart from man, I am not making a metaphysical pronouncement on the mind-dependent character of material things, but am simply making a linguistic point: whenever we talk of world, we talk at the same time of man, for the expression *world* implies a human standpoint from which everything is seen as environment.

Man organizes his world. Even to speak of 'world' is to imply some kind of unity. A world is not a chaos. The Greeks called the world *kosmos*, 'order.' Man orders phenomena into a world. Perhaps he does not succeed in wholly unifying his world. There will always be loose ends. This raises in turn the question whether such unity as there is gets imposed by the human mind, or whether the mind can impose order and unity only because these are already in some sense present in and given with the phenomena. This question can hardly fail to remind us of a somewhat parallel question raised in the last chapter—whether values and the idea of an authentic existence are created by the human mind, or whether man is responding to some moral order or moral demand from beyond himself (see above, p. 51). On both questions, existentialist philosophers differ among themselves, and the line of division on this second question would follow a similar direction to that which it took on the first, with the atheistic existentialists stressing man's part in bringing order and meaning into a meaningless manifold, while those existentialists oriented toward theism or some religious view would argue that man can project meaning on the phenomena only because this possibility is given with the phenomena themselves. But all existentialists would agree that there is an important human factor in the concept of the 'world,' and that we see the world from a definitely human point of view.

This becomes more obvious when we remember that there are many 'worlds,' each organized in relation to some special point of view. The 'world in general' is an extremely vague notion. If we read in the newspapers that the 'world' is torn by tensions we understand that the writer has in mind the world of international relations. But if we turn on to the sports section, it is quite possible that we may read there something about the 'world' of baseball. The woman's page may have something on the 'world' of fashion. There are innumerable worlds, varying in importance and extent. All of them, however, are 'environmental,' that is to say, they are all settings for human activities and are organized from the standpoints of such activities. All human activity requires a world in which it may take place. In this sense, the notion of world would seem to be *a priori*—not any particular world and not the content of any world, but the formal notion of world.

Up till now, I have been stressing the human or existential factor in the meaning of 'world,' even to the point of asserting that there is no world apart from the human mind that helps to constitute it. I also said, however, that this does not imply a doctrine of subjective idealism. Perhaps it is now time to redress the balance with the compensating assertion that there is no human existent apart from the world in which he exists. The human existent is not a self-sufficient point of consciousness to which a world gets added on, so to speak. To exist is already to be in a world. And if it is true that the human existent organizes his world, it is also true that the world has an independence over against him, that there are elements in it which stubbornly resist man's efforts to comprehend things in a unified order, that the world reacts on man as surely as man acts on the world. Sartre, who stresses the obstinate and opaque *en-soi* character of the things that make up the world, neatly summarizes the reciprocity between self and world in these words: 'Without the world there is no selfhood, no person; without selfhood, without the person, there is no world.'[1]

To put the matter in another way, man is nothing apart from his environment. Although it is true that Kierkegaard has much to say about subjectivity, existentialism is not a subjectivism, still less a solipsism. To exist is already to be in confrontation with that which is other than oneself. If indeed by definition 'ex-sistence' is a standing out, then the environment from which he stands out is just as primordial as the existent himself. One might say, with Sartre, that the existent constitutes himself by an act of separation. The problem (perhaps one should say, pseudo-problem) of the reality of the 'external world' is not a matter that exercises the existentialist as it has done those philosophers who begin with a subject on one side and a world on the other and try to bring them together. The existentialist begins with concrete being-in-the-world, and out of this initial unity self and world arise as equiprimordial realities.

However, although there is no self without a world, and to exist is to be in a world as well as to stand out from the world, the existent, as being-in-the-world, is never just part of the world. Here we take note of still another shade of meaning that attaches to the expression *world*. Especially in the language of religion, the world has sometimes been regarded as a threat to a genuine humanity and the so-called 'worldly' man is taken to be one who has 'fallen' from the normative human condition. To be sure, such expressions have often been associated with a false religiosity and other-worldliness, which in extreme cases has been little short of a Manichaean dualism. But even in the context of a genuinely Biblical faith, the assertion of the goodness of the world as God's creation is accompanied by the warning that man can be lost in the world if it gains the mastery over him. The ambiguity of the world finds expression in many forms of existentialism. If there is on the one hand the assertion that the world is a necessary constituent of existence, so that if there is no world, there is no self, there is on the other hand the awareness that the self can be absorbed into the world. If this should happen (and presumably it never happens completely) then man would cease to 'ex-sist' and become just another item among the objects that surround him. In this connection, Heidegger makes a useful distinction between 'being-in-the-world' (*In-der-Welt-sein*) and 'innerworldly being' (*das innerweltliche Seiende*). The human existent is 'being-in-the-world,' which implies a certain transcendence of the world in virtue of his 'standing out'; but he is constantly threatened by a kind of drag into 'innerworldly being,' to the loss of his distinctive existence and his absorption on to the level of subhuman, subexistent, unreflective, irresponsible being. There is a fundamental paradox in human existence, in that the existent can exist only in virtue of a world to which he is constantly related by the closest ties, yet the same world that enables him to exist also threatens to diminish his existence or even to take it from him.

THE EVERYDAY WORLD

We have noted that there are many worlds, each constituted by a particular interest and perspective of the human existent. We begin by considering the 'everyday' world. The classic existentialist analysis of the everyday world has been given by Heidegger,[2] and in the main Sartre follows him in this. The expression *everyday* is meant to designate the mode of existence in which we spend most of our lives, that is to say, the daily round of tasks and duties, most of them performed in routine and habitual ways or according to a schedule. Everyday existence is practically oriented and concerned with the satisfaction of ordinary human needs. It is probably not only the commonest but also the most fundamental mode of existence, other modes being derived from it. Hence the everyday world, the world that is organized in correlation with everyday existence, has also a fundamental role.

Our everyday existing is often designated by such words as *living* or *dwelling*. What does it mean to live or dwell in the world? Obviously such expressions mean much more than just being physically located in the world. Such 'location in' is certainly a part of the meaning, and later we shall give consideration to the spatiality of existence in the world (see below, p. 70). However, to live in the world is to be related to it in innumerable ways besides the spatial relation. This holds even for the way an animal lives in its world (if the expression *world* is permissible here). A whole complex branch of biology, namely, ecology, studies the nature of dwelling, the relation of the organism to that environment which forms its οἶκος or home.

The term *concern* has been used by existentialists to refer to the complex relation designated by the 'in' of being-*in*-the-world. 'Concern' is understood in a very general sense as covering the almost endless ways in which man's interests impinge on the beings around him. Handling and using, eating and drinking, building and manufacturing, finding the way, telling the time, transporting himself, sowing and reaping—these are a mere fraction of the modes of concern whereby man relates himself to his environment and harnesses it to his needs. Other activities like destroying, pushing aside, removing obstructions are also instances of concern, though these constitute its negative modes. To be in the world is to be concerned with the world, to be engaged in ceaseless interaction with the things we find within the world.

From the point of view of practical concern, therefore, a 'thing' is viewed primarily in a pragmatic way. This means in turn that the world of everyday existing is an instrumental world. A child's first question about anything is very often: 'What is it for?' The notion of a bare thing-in-itself, inert, indifferent, would seem to be a very sophisticated idea and certainly one that is remote from everyday existing. In concern, we are constantly looking around, and whatever presents itself is viewed from the perspective of practical concern and will almost certainly be pressed into service in one way or another.

In an earlier discussion it was said that the expression *existence* has sometimes been used in the history of philosophy in a sense not far removed from 'just lying around', (see above, p. 42). But man, as being-in-the-world and concerned with the world, is not content to leave things lying around. He finds them at hand, so to speak, as potentially serviceable to his needs. He is constantly expanding his world and making it more complex by incorporating new things into the range of his concern. New tools and new substances are discovered in their serviceability. However, it is not only man-made instruments that are to hand in the world. Natural objects, even those over which man has little or no control, become instruments also. The river becomes an instrument as it is used for irrigation or transportation, and long ago man learned the serviceability of the heavenly bodies themselves as a natural clock or as guides to navigation.

There is a sense in which one might say that the progress of man has consisted in the bringing of more and more items into his instrumental world. I do not mean, however, that man is at first confronted with inert, independent things to which he subsequently assigns (or in which he subsequently discovers) an instrumentality. Concern is there from the beginning. Sartre remarks: 'The thing is not first a thing in order to be subsequently an instrument; neither is it first an instrument in order to be revealed subsequently as a thing. It is an instrumental thing.'[3]

Instruments are interlocking. They imply one another, in systems and subsystems. A pen implies paper; the paper implies a postal system; the postal system implies methods of transportation; and so on. Today, as we often hear, we live in the context of a world of immense complexity where everything seems to affect everything else. What articulates this world and gives significance to each single item within it is human concern. The everyday world is correlated with the range of human concern. This is what gives unity and system to the multifarious items embraced within the world. We see how large a part the human factor plays in constituting the everyday world, and we see also how the notion of worldhood is in a sense *a priori*, for the concept of world is already presupposed in every single instrument.

As the *a priori* condition of all concernful dealing with things, the notion of world is not even noticed for most of the time. The world, after all, is not another thing, besides the things in the world. We already live in the world, just as we breathe in the air, and the medium is so close to us and we are so accustomed to it that we remain unaware of it. Perhaps we become conscious of the air we breathe only when there is a danger of its being cut off. In a similar way Heidegger suggests that the world gets 'lit up' for us when something goes wrong and, so to speak, shocks us into an awareness of the instrumental complex that all the time we take for granted. The instrument that is nearest to hand we pay no attention to—our mind is fixed on the end we are achieving through it. When I talk into the telephone, I am not interested in the telephone itself but in the person at the other end of the line. But when the instrument ceases to be serviceable—for instance, if the telephone goes dead—I suddenly become aware of it. In the midst of our busy modern civilization we are sometimes made aware, suddenly and unpleasantly, of the vast interlocking international apparatus on which life has come to depend, for instance, when a heavy snowstorm or a dock strike paralyzes a city.[4]

The idea of the world as an instrumental system that derives its unity and meaning from the organizing concern of man is one that might seem to have considerable relevance to the age of technology. At an ever increasing rate, the whole planet—and now the moon as well—is becoming transformed into a man-made and man-centered world. More and more, cities, industrial installations, airports, and so on roll back not only 'wild nature' but even cultivated land. Technology stands ready to exploit even the ocean floor. The few sizeable areas of land left in more or less natural condition are likewise incorporated into the instrumental system as parks or recreation areas. Thus the world (in the sense of the everyday world) becomes more and more humanized. If when we first talked of the idea that if there is no self, there is no world, this seemed a subjective notion, we now see more clearly that the human factor in constituting the world constantly increases, though the world retains its measure of independence. Perhaps it would not be going too far to say that the everyday world is an extension of man. At the beginning of the century Bergson was pointing out that tools are simply extensions of man's body, and similar ideas have been taken up more recently by Marshall McLuhan. But the total instrumental system within which these tools have their place and significance, namely, the world, is also an extension of man.

At this point, however, the ambiguity of the world begins to emerge. I have just mentioned that although to a considerable extent man constitutes his world, it retains a measure of independence and will continue to do so, no matter how far the triumphs of technology may reach. The world reacts on man. At the most, man can never be more than co-creator of the world. The material is given him, though he imposes the form. Later we shall have occasion to attend to the 'facticity' of existence, the givenness in the human condition. For the present we simply note that there is a reciprocity in the man-world relation; if man shapes the world, the world also shapes man. It is for this reason that the world, though the necessary condition of existence, can also constitute a threat to existence. Man can become subjugated to his own creations. I need hardly enlarge on the dilemma that confronts us today. The technological process continually accelerates, and we find ourselves being hurried along before we can rightly decide where we want to go or before we understand all the consequences of what we are doing. Even more threatening is the ambiguity of every advance and above all the frightening possibilities for destruction that have come about with the harnessing of atomic power.

However, the existentialist philosophers point to dangers more subtle than those of pollution or nuclear warfare. As man extends his instrumental world, he tends to be drawn into it himself, to become a part of it and even a slave of it, and so to cease to 'exist' in the full sense, that is to say, as fully personal and fully human. Gabriel Marcel is the philosopher who has most carefully analyzed the relation of 'having' to 'being,' especially in his book *Being and Having*. To have something is not just to stand in an external relationship to it. The very having of something affects the person who has it. He becomes anxious about it and instead of having it, it begins, so to speak, to have him. There is real danger to our humanity as the world becomes increasingly industrialized, computerized, automated. To be sure, being and having are not to be taken as simply opposed. Deprivation dehumanizes just as surely as a surfeit of possessions. A minimal level of 'having' seems to be necessary before there can be a truly human life with any dignity and independence, and it is possible for technology to bring this minimal level to more people than ever before. But rising affluence brings new dangers. It leads to the acquisitive society, the rat race, the infinite desire to possess. In its relation to the world, as in so many other aspects, human existence finds itself at the center of a tension and must survive in the face of opposing pressures.

THE WORLDS OF SCIENCE, ART, AND RELIGION

The everyday world described in the preceding section is not the only world. It is indeed the world in which we live for the most part, in our everyday practical concerns. But existentialist philosophers do not usually believe that 'existence' fulfills itself most adequately in such everyday patterns of living. These tend to become routine, unthinking, and humdrum, so that in them the distinctive characteristics of existence tend to become obscured. The existent 'stands out' more clearly in those moments or activities of his life in which he breaks out of the routine and transcends his immediate concerns. These are the creative moments of existing. In them, the world is perceived in new ways, though presumably the worlds built up in scientific discovery or artistic imagination or religious vision are modifications of the fundamental everyday world that lies nearest to us. Certainly they are not dream worlds.

At first sight the world as described by the sciences seems to have an objectivity that is lacking in the everyday world. Is not the world of science precisely the world from which human concerns, all subjective likes and dislikes, preferences and evaluations, have been screened out, so that we are allowed to see things as they are in themselves? And is not this the fundamental world, from which the everyday world is itself derived as things get related to human needs?

Although there is a measure of plausibility in this account, the existentialist philosopher turns it around and maintains his claim that the world of science is derived from the more fundamental everyday world. We are not first of all observers and spectators who subsequently develop an interest in what we observe. Rather, from the beginning we are beings-in-the-world, deeply involved in our concerns with it. It calls for a great deal of sophistication to be able to reduce the level of concern to the point (or near to the point) when we become simply observers. But even this would seem to be a matter of degree. It is doubtful if there is any 'value-free' science. Even the sciences are modes of concern and, of course, they require their own techniques. But it may be readily conceded that the concern of the scientist differs from that practical concern that is directed toward use, enjoyment, and the like. Hence the world revealed by the sciences has an objective and impersonal character as compared with the world of practical concern. Yet, as has been clear enough since the time of Immanuel Kant, the world of science too has its human factor since it is in part constituted by those conceptual and imaginative structures by which we organize the intuitions of sense and build out of them an ordered world.

Let it be frankly said that many existentialist philosophers have done less than justice to science. They seem to feel that the abstract and theoretical point of view characteristic of scientific research is somehow a threat to a full human experience of the world. Of course, there are exceptions to this attitude. One must mention particularly Karl Jaspers, who will have no part in the anti-rational tendencies that sometimes show themselves in the existentialists.

I would suggest at this point that existentialist philosophy must recognize more clearly than it has done the intellectual drive in man. We have a fundamental desire to know and to understand, and this may be just as primordial as our practical concern. The two, of course, are never entirely separable. But the extent to which one or the other can come to dominance is illustrated by the great distance between the everyday world of concern and the world of the scientist. We may recall Sir Arthur Eddington's famous description of his two tables.[5] 'One of them has been familiar to me from earliest years. It is a commonplace object of the environment which I call the "world." ' This is the everyday table, the one we use in a commonsense way. The other table is 'my scientific table. It is a more recent acquaintance and I do not feel so familiar with it. It does not belong to the world previously mentioned—the world which spontaneously appears around me when I open my eyes, though how much of it is objective and how much subjective I do not here consider. It is part of a world which in more devious ways has forced itself on my attention.' He then goes on to describe the very different 'scientific table' as understood in this 'other world' of science—a table that is mostly empty space with innumerable electric charges scattered through it.

We turn next to the world of the artist—whether the world as seen by the painter or as depicted by the poet or through some other art medium. It might seem that the world as perceived by the artist is at the opposite extreme from the world of the scientist. Whereas the latter aims at rationality and objectivity, the artist employs imagination, and it might seem that every artist has his own private world. However, I have said that none of the worlds we are talking about are just dream worlds. The artist employs imagination, but he may do so in the hope of evoking reality.

There are many styles of art and many ways in which artists and poets understand what they are doing. I do not suppose there is any one way of describing the multifarious ways in which the arts are pursued. But I think it may be claimed that if the scientist builds a second world with a second table and all the rest, the artist builds still a third world. Both for himself and for those who understand his work, he breaks out of the routine everyday world. So far is he from the attitudes of manipulation and exploitation that are characteristic of everydayness that he rather lets the world and whatever is within it come to us. To do this, he may by his art cause us to notice features of the world or of things that had hitherto been concealed from us because our attention had been directed elsewhere. The artist opens up new depths and dimensions of worldhood beyond those that we know in either the everyday world or the world of science.

Can one speak also of the world of religion, that is to say, of a distinct way of perceiving the world constructed from the perspective of religion? I think there is such a way. The foundation this time lies in one's existential attitude to the world as a whole. Of course, in line with our earlier discussion, we have to remember that no one ever knows the world as a whole in the sense of knowing everything that is. But we do speak in religion of faith rather than of knowledge. Faith involves a leap beyond that which is known with reasonable certitude. Essentially, faith is an attitude of trust and commitment. The man of faith, therefore, is the man who takes up such an attitude in the face of the world. The world as a whole is, finally, a mystery that cannot be grasped except in partial and fragmentary ways. But faith thrusts beyond the partial and the fragmentary in order to place trust and commitment in the mystery itself.

Although faith goes beyond what is known, it is not merely arbitrary nor is its way of taking the world totally unfounded. Faith takes its rise from some partial insight, and on the basis of this adopts its attitude of trust and commitment toward the whole. Many religions talk of revelation, and a revelatory event is simply some particularly impressive experience that stands out from the common run of experience and is made interpretative for the whole. In the Christian religion, for instance, the 'event' of Jesus Christ is believed to be revealing of the meaning of all history. It becomes a kind of paradigm for the interpretation of all experience. It founds a 'world,' for it provides a basic perspective (or 'blik,' as it has sometimes been called) from which one looks out on experience and in the light of which events are evaluated and one's own conduct is regulated.

Of course, faith has taken many forms, and there have been many 'worlds' constructed by the religious consciousness in the course of human history. The world itself has sometimes been deified and made the direct object of faith and commitment, as in pantheism. In the Jewish and Christian traditions the world has been understood as creation, and the attitude of trust and commitment has been directed toward God, understood as transcending the world, yet at work in it. Also possible is the attitude of unfaith, where the world is perceived as indifferent or hostile. Since the nonbeliever, no more than the believer, is able to comprehend the final mystery of the world, his attitude too must arise from a leap beyond the fragmentary knowledge of the world that is available to us. Here again some limited but impressive event has been taken as paradigmatic, or some series of events or range of data.

To the everyday world, then, we must add the worlds described in this section; the abstract world constructed by the intellectual procedures of the sciences; the world in its esthetic dimensions revealed by artists and poets; the world in its mystery, before which men have to decide about their ultimate concerns and take up attitudes of faith or unfaith. Perhaps there are other worlds that may be constructed in different ways. Whatever we do or think, we are always 'in a world' by which we orient ourselves, yet which we ourselves have helped to constitute.

When I say that we must 'add' these other worlds to the everyday world, I do not mean, of course, that these worlds are somehow separate and unconnected. Rather, they are all different ways of interpreting one world. Perhaps the language of 'dimensions' would be appropriate. The world has many dimensions, and these get opened up to us in different ways, so that the world appears under different aspects. Presumably the 'everyday' world is the basic world, our nearest experience of the world. But human life would be sadly impoverished if it remained on the level of the everyday and if the world were known simply in an unending series of tasks, calculations, manipulations, momentary enjoyments, and the like. In such a case we come near to falling below the level of 'ex-sistence,' that is to say, of standing out from the world and transcending it. In such a case, the world threatens to tyrannize man and absorb him. Man truly exists as new dimensions of the world and new ways of constructing the world open up for him.

THE BODY

To be in the world is to have a body or to be a body, or, as Marcel expresses it, to be incarnate. There is a tiny part of the world that is, so to speak, my own territory. This part of the world, my body, I occupy and indeed constitute. It is only through existing in bodily form that I can be in the world. Through the body I perceive the things and persons that make up the world. Through the body I am able to act upon them and, conversely, they are able to act on me.

The existentialist acknowledges that existence is being-in-the-world, and there is no existence without environment. He must therefore acknowledge the body as constitutive for existence, for one cannot be in a world or interact with an environment except through the body. In actual fact, not all existentialists have been clear about the bodily character of existence. We have taken note that existentialism has some affinities with Gnosticism (see above, p. 27), and distrust or neglect of the body is not uncommon among existentialist philosophers. Kierkegaard, especially in his latest writings, moved increasingly in the direction of asceticism. Heidegger, while offering a full-scale analysis of human existence and while certainly conceiving this as an existence in the world, has hardly anything to say about the body by which we have the possibility of being in a world. But if the body has been neglected by some existentialists, we find that there are others who have devoted attention to this problem. Among them, one may mention especially Marcel, Sartre, and Merleau-Ponty.

The reason for the neglect of the body in philosophy lies deep in the tradition of Western thought. Although existentialism has revolted against that tradition (or many elements in it), the transition to new ways of thinking takes time. From Plato to Descartes and modern idealism, the belief has been that the true self or the real man is somehow within, and that the body is an appendage or a framework of some sort. This is the understanding of man that Gilbert Ryle castigated as the 'ghost-in-the-machine' theory in his book *The Concept of Mind*. This is also the understanding of man that led into all the insoluble metaphysical problems about how two such disparate entities as a soul (*res cogitans*) and a body (*res extensa*) could stand to one another in the intimate relation which they obviously enjoy in a person. If we begin with two separate and incommensurable 'things,' we shall never be able to make a unity out of them. We must begin with the unity of being-in-the-world, and this means man as a psychosomatic unity.

I can see my body, or at least part of it, but it is not just a thing in the world. It is a part of *me*. I do not say 'My body is thirsty,' but 'I am thirsty.' Merleau-Ponty remarks: 'When my right hand touches my left, I am aware of it as a "physical thing." But at the same moment, if I wish, an extraordinary event takes place: here is my left hand as well starting to perceive my right.'[6] This kind of reciprocity illustrates very well the point that the body is not just a thing or a machine, which somehow 'I' animate or control. Yet on the other hand, 'I' am not just a body, understood as a physical organism. If contemporary philosophy is moving away from the ghost-in-the-machine conception of the soul, it is equally holding off from the reductionist view that man is nothing but a complicated machine. 'There is nothing behind the body. But the body is wholly "psychic." '[7]

It is because the body is at once part of me and yet I am more than my body that, at the beginning of this section, I said that to be in the world is to have a body or to be a body. Which expression is more correct? Should I say, 'I have a body' or 'I am a body'? Both expressions have just claims. I can rightly say, 'I have a body,' because I can transcend my body, I can within limits objectify it, I can make it my instrument (and so treat it as part of the instrumental world). But I must also say, 'I am my body,' for I am nothing apart from it, when I touch myself I am thereby touched; when my body experiences pain or pleasure, it is I who experience them.

There are two quite different ways in which we can think of the body. We can think of it in anatomical and physiological terms, as a highly complex organism made up of muscles, bones, nerves, and all kinds of organs. But this we have learned from dissection (or from books describing the dissection) of *other people's bodies*, that is to say, from bodies that have been made *for us*, not for the people themselves, things within the world, available for objective investigation. For the most part, I think of my own body quite differently and experience it quite differently. Most of the time, I am hardly aware of it at all, for, as mentioned earlier, I transcend my body and am much more occupied with the environment to which the body relates me than with the body itself. But when I do experience my body, it is in quite a different manner from the perceptions that are foundational to anatomy and physics. Hunger or indigestion may make me aware of my stomach, but this immediate awareness is of a different order from reading a description of what happens in hunger or indigestion as observed by the physiologist.

The interest of existentialist philosophy in the body is oriented to the immediate awareness of the body as a constituent of my being-in-the-world. It differs therefore from all physiological research into the body and even from psychological investigations into those sensations which arise from the body. It is concerned with the meaning of 'body' for the philosophical concept of existence. Existentially, the body might not even be a material thing, if it is possible to imagine a non-material world; for then my body would be my mode of presence in that world. Actually, St. Paul does talk about a 'spiritual body,' which he contrasts with the 'natural body' (1 Cor 15: 44). Of course, this is a difficult conception, as is the whole related imagery of a 'resurrection of the body.' But one thing that is quite clear is that for St. Paul all existence is somatic, in the body, whether this body be the familiar body by which we are present in the world of space and time or whether it is some speculative 'spiritual body' by which we might be present in a world to come.[8]

Existentially, then, the body is our mode of participation in a world. It is both the focus from which we look out on the world and organize it according to our concerns and interests, and it is also the center on which the world reflects back, so to speak, so that each one of us is a kind of microcosm, a world in miniature. Existentialism, however, is not a monadology in the manner of Leibniz; for the existentialist does not begin with a multitude of separate self-contained entities that have subsequently to be coordinated. He begins with the unity of being-in-the-world, so that the existent is already outside of himself.

A consequence of the foregoing remarks on the body is the finitude of existence. To have a body is to occupy a place in the spatio-temporal series. Existence as *Da-sein* is being-there. Insofar as the existent *is* his body, he is there. This point will be developed later when we consider more fully the finitude of existence.

Finally, we may notice that the same kind of ambiguity that showed itself in the discussion of the world arises also in the case of the body. We saw that a world is necessary to existence and enables existence; yet it could also be detrimental to existence when the latter is absorbed into its world and is deprived, in some degree at least, of that 'standing out' that is its essence. Similarly, the body is an integral factor in existence, but the body too can distort existence, becoming a tyrant or a burden. Gabriel Marcel explains the ambiguity in terms of our double relation to the body—we both *have* bodies and *are* bodies. It is possible to become alienated from the body, to 'have' the body almost as an exterior possession that we may use in various ways. But this alienated body may in turn react against us to destroy us, as happens, for instance, in drug addiction. No doubt this possibility of alienation has been a driving motive in the long history of men's distrust of the body, and something of this is found even among some existentialists. But existentialist teaching about the body as an essential factor in existence directs men rather toward seeking to be at home in the body.

SPACE AND TIME

The world is in space and time. We too are in space and time.

As we might expect, the account of space and time is given by philosophies of existence in terms of the spatiality and temporality of the existent. This, however, does not imply a subjectivizing of space or of time. Kant reckoned space to be a 'form' of perception; we do not see things as they are 'in themselves,' but under the form of space. Heidegger seems to be explicitly differentiating his own position from Kant's when he writes: 'Space is not to be found in the subject, nor does the subject observe the world "as if" that world were in a space; but the "subject" (*Dasein*), if well understood ontologically, is spatial.'[9] On the other hand, Heidegger prefers to say that space is in the world, rather than that the world is in space.[10] Presumably if there were no world, there could be no space. Space itself does not objectively exist, as a spatial object exists. However, the language of 'subjective' and 'objective' is not really applicable in the context of an existential analysis of spatiality. Like the world itself, space is neither subjective nor objective. If we begin with the unity of being-in-the-world, then we are beginning with the existent as already spatial.

In the foregoing paragraph, I have talked mainly of space and left time aside. Time does in fact have a very special role in existentialist philosophy, and it is not regarded as simply a fourth dimension in addition to the dimensions of space. Unlike the process philosophers, existentialists do not speak of 'space-time'; thus we shall discuss space and time separately.

Our basic understanding of space arises from the fact that we exist spatially and already are oriented to space. This is in virtue of the fact that we are bodies, occupying space and located at particular points in space. Space is from the beginning organized in terms of our bodily participation in space. The fundamental directions of left and right are based on the body. They are therefore notoriously difficult to define—we learn them by existing ourselves as bodies having spatial orientation. *The Random House Dictionary* defines *left* as: 'of, or pertaining to, the side of a person or thing that is turned toward the west when the subject is facing north.' Though cumbrous, this definition is correct and, for that matter, objective, since it relates left and right to west and east. However, there is little doubt that the existential directionality of left and right is more fundamental than the points of the compass. It is interesting to note that in some languages the points of the compass are defined in terms of right and left. South Arabia, for instance, is known as the Yemen, that is to say, the country on the right hand (*yamin*) as one faces toward the rising sun. There can be little doubt that the points of the compass were defined in terms of the spatiality of the body long before the process was turned around so as to provide 'objective' ways of defining existential directionality. Right, left, above, below, in front, behind—these are the fundamental ways of organizing space, and they arise from the existent's own spatiality.

Furthermore, the existent proceeds to organize his space in a system of 'places.' Just as the world is built up by incorporating things into the instrumental system based on concern, so space is organized in terms of places related to concern. A place is not a mere location. It is a 'place *for* . . .' In the workshop or study, everything is assigned its place. We know where to find it, and the several places are organized among themselves in the way that is most effective for carrying out our tasks. Just as in the case of the world, this 'space of concern,' as we may call it, lies unnoticed for most of the time. Our attention is drawn to it when something is not in its place or when we move into new quarters and have to construct a new system of places.

The space of geometry or the space which gets accurately measured is subsequent to the existential space of daily concern. It is reached when practical concern is 'bracketed,' so to speak, and we approach the point at which we consider space in a detached, objective manner. This is a specialized way of understanding space. For most of the time, it is with the space of concern that we have to do. In the contemporary United States, if one asks the distance between two cities, the answer is more likely to be given in hours and minutes than in miles; for it is understood that the question is related to the concern of getting from one city to the other, and therefore to such matters as the state of the highways and the like, rather than to the objective fact of the precise linear distance between the two points.

When we turn from space to time, we notice that time too gets organized in terms of our concerns. There is a time to go to work, a time to have a break, a time to go to bed, and so on. Man is aware of time through the fundamental rhythms of his life in the world before these get correlated with a 'clock-time' that is the same for all and by which our several activities are coordinated.

Existentialists were not, of course, the first to point to the difference between time as the existent knows it in experience and time as measured by the clock. Men have long been aware that for the conscious existent time may pass more quickly or more slowly, even if the clock ticks steadily away. Bergson drew attention to the

continuous, unbroken character of time as it is known in consciousness, as against the broken up series of 'instants' that constitute
clock-time.[11]

But these remarks on time must be broken off at this point,
for the further development of the understanding of time in existentialist philosophy does not parallel the discussion of space. We
shall see later the fundamental role assigned to time and temporality
in the analysis of existence.

NATURE

In this chapter we have discussed, in the context of existentialist
philosophy, the concepts of 'world,' 'body,' 'space,' and (in a
provisional way) 'time.' It remains to say something about the concept of 'nature.'

On the whole, existentialist philosophers give the impression
of not being greatly interested in nature. Their philosophizing
takes its rise from man, and sometimes it tends to go no further than
man. Certainly, they eschew any romantic approach to nature.
This has already become apparent in our discussion of the everyday
world, in which man is continually bringing the 'merely natural'
into the complex instrumental system that gets built up out of his
own practical concerns. Even the scientific approach to nature fares
somewhat badly among many existentialists; for they distrust
both the intellectualism of science and the practical applications of
scientific research, believing that both of these can, in different
ways, be deleterious to the full development of human existence.
In sharp reaction against easy-going beliefs in the progress of man
through science, the existentialist is more likely to say, with Berdyaev,
'all modern history, with its rationalism, its positivism, its belief in
science, has been a period of night rather than of day.'[12] Strictly
speaking, however, it is 'scientism' rather than science which the
existentialist criticizes. He recognizes the legitimacy of the scientific
perspective on the world, but is at pains to deny that this is the only
perspective that can yield truth or even that it is the fundamental one.

Nevertheless, in spite of the general disinterest in nature, existentialism has the capacity for offering some account of nature,
and there is indeed considerable strength in its way of approaching
the problem, though I doubt if anywhere the consequences have been
fully worked out. The approach is by way of a reductive analysis of
existence itself. Man is an existent, a person; but he is also a living
organism; and finally, from one point of view, he is a material

object, made up of carbon, oxygen, calcium, and whatever other elements are to be found in the body.

Heidegger argues as follows: 'Life, in its own right, is a kind of being; but essentially it is accessible only in *Dasein*. The ontology of life is accomplished by way of a privative interpretation; it determines what must be the case if there can be anything like mere aliveness.'[13] Heidegger does not himself develop the point, but he does indicate that this kind of operation is more than just a question of manipulating plus and minus signs. We do not arrive at a notion of life just by subtracting the more obvious human characteristics, any more than we can build up the picture of man by adding a few properties to the idea of a living organism.

The British philosopher John Macmurray has many affinities with the existentialists. He points out that the self or personal being of man was, in the course of modern philosophy, first understood on the model of a material thing or substance, and then, with the rise of biology, on the model of a living organism. But Macmurray, rather like Heidegger, claims that both of these models are inadequate for understanding a person and that we must rather work the other way around, understanding organism and even substance out of our own personal experience, which subsumes both the organic and substantial modes of being.[14]

How would one expect the scientist to react to this kind of argument? No doubt different scientists would react differently. We may note, however, the remark of a biologist, John Habgood. 'We can ask physical and chemical questions (about a complete living creature). . . . But what is it to understand an animal *as a living creature*? I believe it means to recognize that it has a certain kinship with ourselves; that we belong to the same family.'[15] This remark suggests that as well as the approach 'from below up,' through physics and chemistry, an understanding of life requires also the approach 'from above down,' that is to say, from our own immediate awareness of what it means to be alive. However, if the existentialists criticize some scientists and philosophers for dwelling too exclusively on the first of these approaches to the being of natural phenomena, it may be argued that they themselves are too exclusively concerned with the second.

CHAPTER FIVE

Existence and Others

BEING-WITH-OTHERS AS FUNDAMENTALLY
CHARACTERIZING EXISTENCE

In the preceding chapter we discussed the idea of 'world' and saw that existence is impossible apart from a world—that, indeed, existence is 'being-in-the-world.' But the human environment is not just a world, if this is understood (as in general we have understood it) as a world of things. There is also the personal environment. The existent lives in constant interaction with other existents, or, to put the matter in another way, existence is 'being-with-others' or 'being-with-one-another.' In the present chapter we shall be concerned to analyze this particular aspect of existence. The discussion will be broadly parallel to that of the last chapter; just as we began then by showing that there is no existence without a world, we shall begin now by showing that other people are just as primordially implied in the notion of existence as is a world. Existence is fundamentally communal in character, and without the others I cannot exist.

At first sight, this claim might seem to contradict some of the things that have been said earlier. In the preliminary analysis of existence, much was made of the idea of the uniqueness of every existent. It was said that existence is characterized by 'mineness' (see above, p. 51). Subsequent analyses seem to have confirmed that stress on the solitary character of the existent. We have seen that to be inserted in a world by one's body is to look out upon that world from a unique point of view and, in turn, to be constituted as a unique microcosm through the reflection of the world upon oneself. We have also seen that to have a body is to be a body, in the sense that one has an intimate and immediate relation to the body that one *is*, perceiving it from within, as it were, whereas one is 'outside' of every other body and can perceive other bodies only by external observation. Is there not then an inevitable privacy from which no existent can break out? And is not this privacy of being bound to the existence that I call 'mine' far more characteristic of existence than any communal character? If indeed we relate to others, as we all do, is not this something subsequent, something that gets added on, so to speak, to the individual existent?

Although it has often been supposed that society is formed by the banding together of individuals, most contemporary anthropologists and sociologists would argue that individuals emerge from a society that is prior to them. It is true also that many existentialists do give the impression of being strongly individualistic. Kierkegaard made the individual a major category of his philosophy, and both he and his successors have stressed that untransferable responsibility laid upon the individual as he faces the decisions that existence lays upon him. Undoubtedly they have drawn attention to something that is quite fundamental to existing as a human being. Each person has to decide in his own unique situation, and he has to take on himself responsibility for his decision. There are aspects of existence that seem to be essentially lonely. The facing of death is another illustration.

Yet further existential analysis must also stress the communal character of man's being. It is impossible to say very much about existence without stumbling into its polarities and paradoxes. Whatever assertion is made must be made in the context of a dialectic that allows also for the assertion of the other pole. No polarity of human existence is more deeply pervasive of our being than the polarity between the privacy and the community of existence.

The polarity is, moreover, a subtle one. If the individualism of a Kierkegaard strikes us as exaggerated, we must equally shun a collectivism that indiscriminately assembles human beings in a uniform mass. We shall later have occasion to criticize those inauthentic modes of being-with-others, modes that are just as detrimental to a truly human existence as the most solitary individualism (see below, p. 88). Of course, such collectivism really misses the meaning of community. As the very word *collectivism* implies, it begins from the thought of separate individuals who are collected or gathered together to form a collection. Individualism and collectivism are, at bottom, different forms of the same error. We can avoid them only if we begin with the concreteness of existence as 'being-with-others.' 'With-others' is not added on to a pre-existent and self-sufficient being; rather, both this being (the self) and the others find themselves in a whole wherein they are already related.

That community belongs to the essential or primordial constitution of the existent may be established in various ways. It may, for instance, be established as a corollary of the 'being-in-the-world,' explored in the last chapter. For although each person has his own unique perspective on the world, the very notion of 'world' implies a common world. This is very clear, for instance, in the conception of an instrumental world. We have noted that no instrument can be understood in complete isolation—it implies all kinds of other instruments and materials, and the context of tasks in which these are used. But equally the instrumental world implies other existents. The typewriter I use implies not just the paper on which to type and the machinery that produced the typewriter, but also the people who designed, produced, and marketed the typewriter, and the people who are going to read what I type on the paper. The everyday world, then, is already a world that implies an indefinite number of people engaged in interlocking and mutually supportive tasks. We have seen that this world is an *a priori* condition of all my practical concerns (see above, p. 56 ff.). So one may also claim that the others are *a priori*—they are conditions of existence rather than 'extras' that are added on to existence.

The foregoing argument from the instrumental world could be paralleled by similar arguments based on the spatiality and the temporality of the existent. The tendency to 'objectify' space and time arises from the need of coordinating the spatiality and temporality of existence. The space that stretches out beyond my body is not a private space but a space already shared with other existents, each of whom has his own perspective upon it.

However, being-with-others can be established as a fundamental constituent of existence in more direct ways. If it is equally primordial with being-in-the-world, then we need not derive it from being-in-the-world as a corollary but can allow it to stand in its own right. In the words of Martin Buber, 'There is no "I" taken in itself, but only the "I" of the primary word "I-Thou" and the "I" of the primary word "I-It." '[1] In the terminology we have been using, Buber's sentence could be expressed: 'There is no (human) existent taken in itself, but only the existent who constitutes being-with-others or being-in-the-world.' Buber puts being-with-others before being-in-the-world; and indeed, a little reflection on what it means to exist as a human being indicates that the idea of a solitary existent is delusory. Buber's own point is that the 'I' and the 'Thou' are derivatives of the primary word 'I-Thou,' that is to say, to speak the word 'I' is already implicitly to recognize the 'Thou' from which the 'I' distinguishes itself. Prior to either 'I' or 'Thou,' taken separately, is 'I-Thou,' the social or communal reality which makes selfhood and individual personality possible.

There are many other considerations that support our contention that community is fundamental to existence and is constitutive for it. One may mention two basic characteristics of being human—sexuality and 'linguisticality.' Both of these will require more extended treatment later (see below, p. 85 and p. 109). It is immediately obvious, however, that both sex and language imply that no human individual is complete without others. Sex refers to the fact that although the human body contains several complete 'systems' (nervous, alimentary, respiratory, and so on) it has only half of a reproductive system and is thus incomplete without another person of the opposite sex. Moreover, this is not just an empirical or biological fact, which one might also observe in many other creatures besides man. In man, sex is humanized so that it becomes a definite existential phenomenon. Berdyaev notes: 'Man's sexual nature cannot be placed on the same level as other functions of his organism, such as the circulation of the blood. In man's sexuality, we perceive the metaphysical roots of his being.' Or again: 'Sexuality is not a special differentiated function of the human being. It is diffused throughout man's whole being, penetrates all his cells and determines the whole of his life.' Berdyaev goes so far as to claim that 'the categories of sex, male and female, are cosmic categories, not merely anthropological ones.'[2]

Much the same might be said about language. One essential function of language is communication, meaningful exchange between persons. There is no such thing as a private language, but there could be no existence (in the limited sense) apart from language. Thinking is scarcely conceivable (except, perhaps, under very unusual conditions) apart from language; but language is what externalizes thought and makes it accessible to the other person. Some existentialist philosophers would make for language the same claim that Berdyaev makes for sex—that it is not just a human phenomenon but has a more ultimate ontological significance. It is true that language is a fundamental human power, and without language one could not be human. But, as Heidegger asks, 'how could man ever have invented the power which pervades him, which alone enables him to *be* a man?'[3]

At this stage of our discussion, however, we need not become involved in these ontological questions concerning language or sex. It is enough for us to note that these pervasive characteristics of being human testify to the essential sociality of existence. The solitary individual is not the unit from which communities and societies are built up. When we try to isolate this solitary individual, we find that he escapes us. Even in the most fundamental ways of his being, the human existent spills over, so to speak; he transcends the bounds of an individual existence and is intelligible only within a broader social whole that we have designated 'being-with-others.'

INTERPERSONAL RELATIONS

We have seen that existence requires not only a worldly environment but also a personal environment. Within the world I meet persons, but these are not objects belonging to the world. I know them as co-existents, so to speak. They are in the world in the same way that I am in the world, that is to say, as centers of concern in terms of which the world is structured. They are not available as instruments. They are like myself agents. They shape the world.

Just as existentialist philosophers do not seek 'proofs' of the existence of an 'external' world, so they do not seek to prove that there are other existences. Solipsism cannot be a problem for a philosophy that begins neither with a pure thinking subject nor with a solitary individual but always with concrete being-in-the-world and being-with-others.

The relation between the self and the everyday world was described in terms of *concern*. The relation between one existing self and another we shall call *solicitude*. These particular terms are taken from the English translation of Heidegger's *Being and Time* and represent the German expressions *Besorgen* and *Fürsorge* respectively. The terminology used is in itself unimportant, but it is very important that we should have some words to express the distinction between the two kinds of relationship, and the words *concern* and *solicitude* are convenient for the purpose. In using these words in a quasi-technical way, we must remember that they will not always bear their usual connotations. We have already noted that concern may be expressed in the negative mode of pushing things out of the way rather than using them (see above, p. 60). Likewise solicitude does not always take the form of actively caring for the other; regrettably, it is just as likely to show itself as neglect or resentment. But we shall still include such attitudes under the broad category of solicitude, which is here a purely formal idea.

Although we have made the preliminary distinction between the two kinds of relation in language borrowed from Heidegger, our actual analysis will be based rather on Buber, who among recent thinkers has surely had preeminence in this field. There are, he tells us, two primary words, 'I-Thou' and 'I-It,' and these reflect two primary ways in which we may relate ourselves. The first distinction he makes between them is this: 'The primary word "I-Thou" can only be spoken with the whole being. The primary word "I-It" can never be spoken with the whole being.' Such primary words then are more than mere labels or logical operators. They have existential force. 'When a primary word is spoken, the speaker enters the word and takes his stand in it.'[4]

What does Buber mean by saying 'I-Thou' language is spoken with the whole being, 'I-It' language never with the whole being? We get a clue to this if we reflect again on the nature of concern, the attitude that finds expression in the 'I-It' language. Concern has to do with the satisfaction of some particular need, and that with which we are concerned is considered as an instrument. Concern is partial and that with which we are concerned remains external to us. In the 'I-Thou' relation, however, we relate totally to the other and we do so by becoming open to him. He is not just externally 'there' for us; nor is he an end to some satisfaction beyond himself.

Here we must pause to notice that the relations designated 'I-Thou' and 'I-It' or 'solicitude' and 'concern' (though these pairs of terms are not precisely synonymous) are not absolutely distinct. One form can wander over into the other, so to speak.

The tragic aspect of this mutability is that the 'I-Thou' relation frequently degenerates into the 'I-It.' We relate to another person not in wholeness and in openness but turn him into a thing, an instrument. Extreme instances of this are slavery and prostitution. But it happens continually in a thousand more subtle ways, wherever there is exploitation or discrimination or prejudice, and persons are treated as less than personal.

However, there is the other possibility that an 'I-It' relation may blossom into an 'I-Thou.' Buber suggests that this kind of relation is possible not only between man and man, but between man and nature, and between man and what he somewhat vaguely describes as 'spiritual beings.'[5] One can relate to a tree in all kinds of practical and concernful ways, in which the tree is one's object or even one's instrument. But a kind of total relation to the tree is also possible: 'It is bodied over against me and has to do with me as I with it. . . .

Relation is mutual.' Is this a kind of panpsychism? Buber will not say so. 'I encounter no soul or dryad of the tree, but the tree itself.'[6]

As well as the possibility of one type of relation 'wandering' over into the other, we must also recognize the possibility of inter-mediate cases. Harvey Cox has sensibly suggested that in many cases an 'I-You' relation is more appropriate than an 'I-Thou' relation. An 'I-You' relation is one that respects the personality and humanity of the other but does not seek to establish with him the depth and intimacy that are customarily associated with the notion of the 'I-Thou.'[7] Of course, Buber did not intend that one should go around forming intense personal relations in an indis-criminate way, but the distinction made clear in Cox's terminology is a useful one.

One might speculate also on the God-man relation and its place on the spectrum. Buber does indeed speak of God as 'the eternal Thou,' but clearly a relation to God is not quite the same as a relation to a finite 'Thou.'

However, let us return to elucidate further the nature of inter-personal relations as Buber interprets them. Perhaps this elucidation can best be done by reviewing some of the key terms he introduces. For these, we draw not only on *I and Thou* but on the writings in which Buber developed his insights further and in more systematic ways, especially the collection of essays *Between Man and Man* and the late work on philosophical anthropology, *The Knowledge of Man.*

Very characteristic of Buber's thought is his use of the word *dialogue.* To say that the interpersonal relation is dialogical is to insist on that 'mutual' character already mentioned in one of our earlier quotations from Buber. A genuine relation to another person cannot be onesided, dominating, or possessive; it must consist in openness and willingness to listen and receive as well as to speak and to give. Here again we note a fundamental difference between the relation to a person and the relation to a thing. *Relation* and *distance* are other words that Buber uses to express his thoughts on these matters. He confines the word *relation* to the relation between persons, and we have already seen that this relation is a fundamental and pri-mordial one in human existence. But there is a dialectic here. The fact of relation implies the equally primordial fact of distance. The drama of the interpersonal is played out, so to speak, in the tension of relation and distance. Sometimes the other slips into the distance, the genuine relation is lost or fails to be actualized, and the 'I-It' supervenes. But even where the relation is established, some distance must remain.

People are too ready to think of the interpersonal relation in terms of union. But a true relation preserves the other in his otherness, in his uniqueness. It leaves him room to be himself, so to speak. Unlike possessive affection on the one hand or mystical love on the other, the dialogical relation does not permit one side to be merged in the other. Buber is particularly insistent that we have respect for the other and not try to change him in accordance with our idea of what he ought to be. Still another idea is 'confirmation.' I am confirmed by the other, that is to say, I really become myself through the relation to the other. Here again is the insistence that there can be no 'I' without a 'Thou.'

Such is a sketch of the 'between,' the region of interpersonal relations, as Buber describes it. Although he is sometimes critical of Heidegger, there is nevertheless considerable similarity between Buber's descriptions and what is said about the relation to the other in *Being and Time*. We have already noted that Heidegger's distinction between 'concern' and 'solicitude' corresponds, though only in an inexact way, with Buber's distinction between 'I-Thou' and 'I-It.' But Heidegger's further remarks on the subject in *Being and Time* move in a direction similar to Buber's ideas. Thus Heidegger recognizes 'two extreme possibilities' in which solicitude manifests itself. In one case, we 'leap in' for the other. 'This kind of solicitude takes over for the other that with which he is to concern himself. The other is thus thrown out of his own position; he steps back, so that afterwards, when the matter has been attended to, he can either take it over as something finished and at his disposal, or disburden himself of it completely.' In this we recognize the dominating mode of solicitude, and Heidegger suggests that it is very prevalent, especially in our everyday existence. The contrasting mode of solicitude is that in which one 'leaps ahead' of the other, 'not in order to take away his "care" but to give it back to him authentically as such for the first time.' In this kind of solicitude, one helps to open up for the other his own possibilities of being. 'It helps the other to become transparent to himself in his care, and to become free for it.'[8]

But although there are some very suggestive ideas in Heidegger's remarks, he does not himself develop the analysis of interpersonal relations on anything like the scale of Buber. One has to turn rather to Gabriel Marcel for a detailed and appreciative study of the interpersonal. Two expressions that are very characteristic of Marcel's understanding of the relation to the other are 'availability' and 'fidelity.' The English word *availability* translates the French *disponibilité*: I must be willing to put myself at the disposal of the other. The sad truth, however, is that people are largely unavailable to one another. The unavailable person is preoccupied with himself and thus closed against the other. His existence is something that he 'has,' and his unavailability arises from his anxiety to maintain himself. But the way to genuinely human being lies through being open, through being able to expend oneself, and to do this generously or even extravagantly. There are clear echoes of New Testament teaching in these notions.

It is in virtue of this kind of availability that one person is *present* to another. 'Presence,' writes Marcel, 'denotes something rather different and more comprehensive than the fact of just being there; to be quite exact, one should not actually say that an object is present.'[9] Presence depends on a person's coming out of himself or transcending himself toward the other.

One of the most typical ways in which men do transcend themselves is by making pledges or promises or engagements. This is a basically human action. We are continually engaging ourselves: 'I shall see you after the meeting'; 'I shall write that letter tomorrow'; and so on. Community is built on the basis of fidelity, our faithfulness to the engagements we have taken upon ourselves. The idea of fidelity is not far from that of loyalty, and Marcel himself sees a resemblance between his own teaching and that of the American philosopher of an earlier generation, Josiah Royce, who saw in 'loyalty to loyalty' the foundation of morality and of human community. Person, engagement, community, reality are seen by Marcel as a continuous series. The inclusion of reality in the series indicates that for him the way of engagement and fidelity leads finally to God.

Our attention has so far been directed on those existentialist thinkers whose teaching about the relation to the other has a more or less strongly affirmative character. But there is another side to the story.

With Kierkegaard, the other can be a barrier to a relation with God. This is the substance of Buber's critique of Kierkegaard. He quotes the Danish philosopher's statement that 'everyone should be chary about having dealings with others and should essentially speak only with God and himself' and interprets this to mean that for Kierkegaard it is necessary to become a 'single one' in order to have a relation to God. Of course, behind this lies Kierkegaard's own history. He broke off his engagement to Regina Olsen because he thought it conflicted with God's claim on him as an extraordinary individual. However, this is just the point at which Buber (and per-

haps many Christian theologians also) would want to quarrel with
Kierkegaard. Do we relate to God by turning away from the other
person, or do we relate to God precisely by turning toward the other
and finding the 'eternal Thou' through the finite? I do not myself
think that this disjunction is an absolute one or that God can be
known *only* in interpersonal relations. But certainly a fruitful way
to God is through the relation to other persons and through involvement (or engagement) in the life of the human community. One
would need to be very suspicious of any point of view that consistently advocated detachment from other (finite) persons for the sake
of a supposed relation to God. But, in fairness to Kierkegaard, we
have to remember that there is much more to his teaching, and the
relation to the other is affirmatively evaluated and finely described
in such a book as *Works of Love*.

In Sartre we again meet a philosopher with whom individual
being seems to weigh more than communal being. Everyone is
familiar with the famous (or infamous) line from his play *No Exit*:
'Hell is other people.' In a sense, one might say that the reasoning
behind this is very similar to Kierkegaard's: it is for the sake of the
relation to God that the other has to be adjudged an obstacle in
the way. Of course, this is understood in a very different way from
that in which Kierkegaard understood it. For Sartre, God is not an
independent reality. 'God' is only a name that may conveniently
designate that fulfillment which every human being seeks. The
finite existent is the desire to be God. However, the fact that there is
in the world a plurality of existents frustrates the desire. We cannot
all be gods. Thus the other is seen primarily as an obstacle to the
fulfillment of existence. Of Sartre's subtle analysis of interpersonal
relations we shall have more to say when we ask about the role of
the body in these relations, and especially about the phenomenon of
sexuality (see below, p. 85). For the present, however, we must
seek to do justice to him, just as we have tried to do in the case of
Kierkegaard. It may be that the other is essentially a hindrance to
one's self-fulfillment; in any case, the desire to become God is a
senseless and absurd one. In practice, Sartre too agrees about the
necessity of engagement and having regard to the well-being of the
other.

In this section we have become aware of the deep tension to be
found among existentialist philosophers, even sometimes in one
and the same philosopher, as they are torn between the individual
and communal poles of existence. We have argued that the deeper
insight lies with those who claim that being-with-others is a more

primordial structure of human existence than any being-for-onself. But only at a later stage of our analysis (see below, p. 188 f.) shall we be able to see the justification of some existentialist tendencies toward individualism as protests against oppressive collectivism and in-authentic being-with-others.

THE BODY AND THE OTHER, WITH SPECIAL REFERENCE TO SEXUALITY

We have seen that it is in virtue of being and having a body that the existent is in a world. Likewise, his being-with-others is possible only through his being or having a body. I am aware of the other because I touch him, see him, hear him through the organs of sense. I communicate with him through the medium of language, but language is made possible by those bodily organs that are capable of producing the sounds of speech or that are receptors for such sounds. Sometimes, indeed, we hear reports of telepathy and of thought-transference, where communication apparently takes place apart from the ordinary means of speaking or writing. But even if it is granted that such phenomena do occur, it would probably still be the case that in some way or another they would be found to depend on the body. However, such phenomena are in any case exceptional in a high degree. All normal communication between persons, whether by speech, looks, gestures, physical contacts, or other ways when they are present to each other, or by writing, telephone, radio, or other methods when the communication takes place over a distance, is a function of the bodies of those involved. Being-with-others implies bodily existence.

Among existentialist philosophers, some of the best and most careful analysis of the role of the body in interpersonal relations has been done by Sartre.[10] Some other existentialists, among them Heidegger, scarcely mention the body, and this must be counted an unfortunate omission or even a kind of docetism. We shall begin our own analysis by letting Sartre be our guide. But since he finds interpersonal bodily relations to be inherently self-frustrating—this is bound to be the consequence of his view that each existent is the desire to be God, so that the other is seen initially as a hindrance—we shall try to give a more affirmative account of the matter, especially when we come to discuss sexuality, the most intimate and intense mode by which the body relates to existents.

We have already said something about the ways in which the existent relates to his own body (see above, p. 67). As far as the other is concerned, there are two possibilities: he is a body for me, the object of my vision, touch and so on; or I become a body for him, and experience myself as his object.

Sartre makes two acute observations concerning the way in which I perceive the body of the other. The first is that the other's body is perceived in terms of a total situation. For instance, a room with its chairs, illumination, and various fittings is structured with a view to bodily existence; so the body is seen in relation to world not as an item in the world but as world user. The second point is that we perceive the other's body as a whole; we do not say, 'His hand went up' but 'He raised his hand'; for we do not see the movement of the hand in isolation, but 'Pierre-who-raises-his-hand.' For these reasons, Sartre claims that 'my perception of the other's body is radically different from my perception of things.'[11]

The other's body is not a thing. It *is* the other person. 'Pierre's body is in no way to be distinguished from Pierre-for-me.' To understand this is to understand that my body is an object for the other, just as much as his body is for me. When he looks at me, I am aware of myself as object of his look. 'My body is there not only as the point of view which I am but again as a point of view on which are actually brought to bear points of view which I could never take; my body escapes me on all sides.'[12] Hence there is a sense in which I become alienated from my own body. This finds expression in such affective states as shyness, shame, embarrassment. For I become aware of my body not as it is for me but as it is for the other.

How is the relation to the other resolved, so that one escapes being his object? It is not surprising that Sartre uses the language of sexuality in reviewing the various possibilities, for this language is peculiarly appropriate. But we should be aware that for Sartre 'sexuality' bears a wide meaning, and that such sexual possibilities as masochism or sadism are interpretative of relations that are not sexual in the narrower sense.

It is in exploring these relations that Sartre brings out what he supposes to be the inescapably contradictory and frustrating character of the interpersonal and sexual relation. I try to escape being object to the other through love. In this context, love is understood as possessive love. It is the desire to assimilate the other to myself. But in order that this may happen, the other has to love me; and to make the other love me, I have to become an object to excite that love. So the relationship becomes endlessly ambiguous and frustrating, oscillating between love and hate, the desire to possess and to be possessed, even the desire to become merely flesh in its character as *en-soi*. In any case, whatever partial satisfaction may be obtained in the sexual act is dispersed by its consummation.

Without for a moment wishing to deny that there are many acute insights in Sartre's treatment of sexuality, I think it may be fairly claimed that a more affirmative account may be given. The ecstatic character of the sexual act points to the central existential role of the body in sex, for *ecstasis* is 'ex-sistence,' the going out of oneself. In the sexual relation the individual goes out from himself to the other in a unity of being-with-the-other. The sex act is not only ecstatic, it is also total. In a discussion of Henry Miller, Arthur Gibson has made the point that 'the mystery of sex is the mystery of total contact between created existents.'[13] Sex is thus an attempt at a total sharing of being. If Berdyaev is right (as I believe he is) in insisting that human sexuality is not just a biological function but has its inescapable ontological dimension (see above, p. 78), then even so-called 'casual' acts of sex cannot be regarded as merely peripheral to existence but are bound to affect the persons concerned quite deeply; for in them too something of the totality of being-with-the-other is expressed, however badly.

Here we may remember that Buber drew the distinction between 'I-Thou' and 'I-It' precisely in terms of the difference between something that flows from the whole self and something that flows from less than the whole self. No doubt there is a type of sexual exploitation in which the exploiter regards the other as an 'It,' though I have suggested that we may be so constituted that, even if we are not aware of it, the sexual act affects us totally. However, if it is characteristic of an 'I-Thou' relation that the whole person is involved, then there is a sense in which the sexual act is the paradigm of such a relation. It is total *ecstasis*, total contact, and total mutuality.

When we set the sexual act within the context of 'I-Thou' relations, we can also answer Sartre's complaint that the consummation of the act frustrates its drive toward union. Sartre's error at this point is obvious—he is regarding the sexual act in isolation, as something complete in itself. But the act (or better, a whole series of such acts) takes place in the context of a relation between two persons. This relation is much wider and richer than the sexual act itself, but the latter concentrates the relation from time to time and nurtures it. The climactic *ecstasis* of sex by which persons become, in the Biblical phrase, 'one flesh' belongs within a constant *ecstasis* of a much broader kind whereby two persons interpenetrate each other's existences in innumerable ways and are involved in a 'total contact.'

Nowadays, through the development of contraceptive methods, it has become possible to separate the sexual act from reproduction. Insofar as this frees persons for the sexual relation, which is good in itself, within the wider context of an 'I-Thou' relation (marriage), contraception should be welcomed to the extent that it can enrich human relations. However, in spite of the fundamental role of sex as the way whereby, through his body, the existent transcends himself in order to be-with-the-other, there is a danger here of an *égoisme à deux*. Like most discoveries contraception is ethically ambiguous—it can enrich interpersonal relations within a responsible context, but it can also arrest community at the stage of being-with-the-other before one comes to being-with-others. The link between sexuality and creativity cannot be severed. If sexuality is the bodily foundation of the simplest kind of community (sexual union or marriage), it is also the act that has the potentiality to found the next order of community, the family.

We have tried in this section to depict the fundamental role played by the body in the relation between persons. Although we have concentrated attention on sex as having a peculiar place among bodily relations, there are, of course, other ways of being physically related. Yet these other ways can often be interpreted on the sexual model. What does become clear from even a brief survey of these matters is the varied and ambiguous ways of relation. Sex itself, with its endless variations and deviations, indicates something of the range of possible relations. In the extreme case I may assault the other person, I may seek to destroy his body in order to be rid of him. But even to take this negative attitude to the other is proof of the inevitability of being bodily with others, in one way or another.

INAUTHENTIC AND AUTHENTIC BEING-WITH-OTHERS

Most of this chapter has been taken up with stressing the inevitability of being-with-others. No man is an island, and this becomes clear in the course of existential analysis. But we have also encountered the counterpoint, as it were, in that individualism that appears to characterize many existentialist philosophers. How do we reconcile the fact that existential analysis reveals the fundamentally communal character of existence with the equally plain fact that existentialist philosophers are in many cases individualists?

Actually, it is not too difficult to show how this seeming contradiction has arisen. Practically all existentialists, even those who lay most stress on the notions of 'I and Thou' and being-with-others, are agreed that human social relations, as we normally find them, are sadly distorted. The everyday being-with-others is inauthentic; that is to say, it does not really involve the selves of those who take part in it, it does not flow from whole selves. The way in which people are normally together does not deserve the name of community. What we find is a distorting and distorted relationship, and it is out of the experience of this that we are to understand the existentialist critique of society and the summons to the individual to come out from the crowd and take the burden of his being upon himself.

Kierkegaard, the father of modern existentialism, sets the pattern for much that was to follow. He has little use for the 'crowd' or the 'public,' and indeed he got little sympathy from them in his own career. 'A crowd in its very concept is the untruth, by reason of the fact that it renders the individual completely impenitent and irresponsible, or at least weakens his sense of responsibility by reducing it to a fraction.'[14] Although penitence and responsibility are not quantifiable or divisible, this is nevertheless how they get treated in the crowd, and this means that they are in fact eliminated. The collective mass gains power over the individual in a frightening manner. 'If once men are allowed to coalesce into what Aristotle called the "multitude," a characteristic of beasts, this abstraction (instead of being regarded as less than nothing, which in fact it is, less than the lowliest individual man) will be regarded as something, and no long time will elapse before this abstraction becomes God.'[15] Kierkegaard may have had in mind here some of the radical 19th-century philosophers who were in fact arguing that 'God' is really a mythological name for society. But apart from this, he was protesting against those absolute powers that society is not slow to assume over the individual, and his warning about the multitude turning into God found its outcome a century later in the Nazi deification of the state.

We must note, however, that in his own lifetime Kierkegaard saw the stifling effects of collectivism and institutionalism above all in the Christian Church, in the established Christendom that had, as he believed, utterly departed from the religion of the New Testament.

It must be said, and as outspokenly as possible, that the so-called Christendom (in which after a sort all men are Christians in a way, so that there are just as many, precisely as many, Christians as there are men)—it must be said that not only is it a wretched edition of Christianity, full of misprints disturbing to the sense, and of senseless omissions and editions, but that it has abusively taken Christianity's name in vain.[16]

What Kierkegaard decried as the 'crowd' is designated in Nietzsche by the still less complimentary term, the *herd*. The herd has devised the value-system that controls the life of mankind. Nietzsche too thinks of the herd as having taken over the prerogatives of God: 'Now, admitting that faith in God is dead: the question arises once more: "Who speaks?" My answer, which I take from biology and not from metaphysics, is: *the gregarious instinct speaks*. That is what desires to be master: hence its "thou shalt!"—it will allow the individual to exist only as a part of the whole, only in favor of the whole.'[17] The herd is characterized precisely by mediocrity. It can tolerate nothing great, nothing exceptional. It is egalitarian and levels everything to the familiar and harmless.

Surely there are echoes of Nietzsche in Heidegger's descriptions of the 'they' (*das Man*), the faceless anonymous power that governs us all. Heidegger's expression, the *they*,[18] is well-chosen, for the word is frequently on our lips. 'They will send a man to the moon this year.' 'They never get around to the real issues.' 'They' can be anybody or everybody or nobody. They are the 'others,' but they are not definite others. Yet our lives are dominated by them. It would be repetitious to quote Heidegger's comments on the 'they' in any detail, for he says much the same things as Kierkegaard and Nietzsche. The 'they' takes away choice, disburdens the individual of his responsibility, levels everything down to mediocrity, determines standards of taste and morals. But Heidegger does make an interesting new point about the relation of the individual in his everydayness to the 'they.' 'Everyone is the other, and no one is himself.' This is elaborated in the statement that 'the self of everyday *Dasein* is the "they-self," which we distinguish from the authentic self—that is, from the self that has been taken hold of in its own way. As "they-self," the particular *Dasein* has been *dispersed* into the "they," and must first find itself.'[19] This certainly implies an inevitable entanglement of the individual with the others; but it is a relation that deprives the individual of his true selfhood. He is completely dominated by and subject to the others, yet paradoxically he himself contributes to this dominance of the impersonal 'they.'

Karl Jaspers uses the expressions *mass-existence* or the *mass* to indicate the domination of life and standards by the unthinking multitude. He sees this danger as one that is prevalent to a peculiar degree in the close living conditions of the modern industrialized and urbanized state, especially in his book *Man in the Modern Age*.

Even Martin Buber, though he stresses what is affirmative in interpersonal relations, is well aware of the other side of the coin, even if he remains at the furthest remove from individualism. 'I-Thou' relations are in constant jeopardy of sinking into the 'I-It.' The truly interpersonal is a rare flower, and speedily withers.

What is the criterion by which one distinguishes an authentic from an inauthentic being-with-others? Authentic being-with-others is precisely that mode of relation to the other that promotes existence in the full sense; that is to say, it lets the human stand out as human, in freedom and responsibility. On the other hand, inauthentic being-with-others suppresses the genuinely human and personal. Whatever kind of relation to the others depersonalizes and dehumanizes is an inauthentic one. Thus there is a paradox involved here. A purely individual existence is not possible and could not properly be called an 'existence'; yet existence with the others is to be judged authentic to the degree that it lets individuals be free to become the unique persons that they are. True community allows for true diversity.

Inauthentic being-with-others is the kind that imposes uniformity, perhaps in the name of a mistaken egalitarianism. Any kind of excellence is suppressed. The existentialist critique of mass-existence has sometimes been considered an aristocratic bias. Undoubtedly there is such a bias in some existentialist writers. However, I think it should be noted that the crowd is just as intolerant of weakness as it is of strength, of inferiority as of superiority. This was seen plainly enough by Nietzsche: 'My teaching is this, that the herd seeks to maintain and preserve one type of man, and that it defends itself on two sides—that is to say, against those which are decadents from its ranks (criminals, etc.), and against those who rise superior to its dead level.'[20]

What the inauthentic collective kind of being-together cannot tolerate is the *different*, anything that departs from the accepted norm. Hence, it is a mistake to think that it wishes only to level down the privileged. It is the same existential attitude that underlies prejudice against the person of different color or race. He is different, he is 'not one of the crowd,' as we say in a particularly revealing colloquialism. Even handicapped persons, in spite of all the compassionate *talk* about their several conditions, are frequently the victims of discrimination. They do not fit the norm, they are not like 'them.' Since the existentialist critique of the 'crowd' is usually considered in terms of leveling down the 'exceptional' persons who rise above the average, it is worth remembering that the collective drive toward uniformity has just as little use for those unfortunate people who fall below the average.

At the everyday level of relations between persons, no doubt much so-called community is of the inauthentic kind. It is simply the crowd, the herd, the mass, the they, or whatever one may wish to call it. It is the pressure toward uniformity, which has been enormously heightened in modern times by the mass media of communication and the mass products unloaded upon a consumer society. It is against this background that the individualism of the existentialists is to be understood. Perhaps it is only by breaking out of a distorted being-with-others that the possibility of building a genuine community can arise. One might compare the 'black power' phase in the struggle of the American Negro toward full citizenship. An oppressive relationship has to be broken and a sense of independence and dignity enjoyed before an affirmative and genuine relation can be built up.

Even so, however, there would still seem to be a fundamental division of opinion between two types of existentialism on this question of being-with-others. One type holds that the individual break with inauthentic society is the first step toward being free for genuine relations with others. The second type holds that all attempts at reaching an authentic being-with-others are doomed to frustration. This second point of view would seem to have been held by Sartre, at least at the time when he wrote *Being and Nothingness*. But the ambiguity of human relations and the tendency of one role to pass into its opposite need not lead to pessimistic conclusions. Sartre's study of the sexual relation is in fact very much like a reminiscence of Hegel's subtle analysis of the master-slave relation.[21] What has to be remembered is that this particular relation was far from being the last word in the dialectic of spirit.

If the existentialists seem to show that interpersonal relations are usually at an inauthentic level and if they seem to recommend individualism as a revolt against this inauthenticity, this is by no means the last word in the analysis. It must be acknowledged, however, that in most of these philosophers, the shape of an authentic being-with-others is not adequately delineated.

CHAPTER SIX

Knowledge and Understanding

EXISTENTIALISM AND EPISTEMOLOGY

The problem of knowledge (epistemology) and the problem of being (ontology) are inextricably bound up with each other. Any claim to have knowledge would seem to imply an assertion about what is and what is not; while any assertion about the real is also a claim to knowledge. Because of this reciprocity, it is hard to know whether it makes any sense to say either that epistemology is prior to ontology or that ontology is prior to epistemology.

Nevertheless, in the history of philosophy, one or other of the two problems, the problem of knowledge or the problem of being, has usually been accorded a priority. In modern philosophy priority has usually been assigned to the epistemological problem. Descartes on the rationalist side and Locke on the empiricist side gave new impetus to philosophical inquiry into the grounds of human knowledge and understanding. Above all, Kant investigated the conditions, limits, and validity of our knowledge in a manner that has been influential for all subsequent philosophy. What can be known with certainty? This question has been made fundamental, and only when it has been answered (so it has often been maintained) is one entitled to ask about what is real.

With the advent of existentialism, however, the familiar order is reversed and the longstanding dominance of epistemology is challenged. The avowed starting place of existentialist philosophy is existence—and, let it be noted, this does not mean the *idea* of existence but concrete existing itself, immediately accessible to us as existents. Since this philosophy begins with reality (existence), the question of knowledge arises only subsequently and is subordinate to the existential question. As Heidegger puts it, 'knowing is a kind of being which belongs to being-in-the-world.'[1]

He immediately goes on to ask whether this statement does not nullify the problem of knowledge. In a sense it seems clear that it does. Existentialists have, in fact, spent little time in discussing the problem of knowledge as traditionally formulated. This is not because, as some seem to imagine, all existentialists are anti-intellectualists, creatures of feeling and impulse who care little for knowledge or strict understanding or truth. The existentialists have been not so much neglectful as impatient of the epistemological problem; and the reason for this impatience is their conviction that the customary way of going about the problem of knowledge is a mistaken one and sets up a pseudo-problem.

The mistake is to begin with two entities that are supposedly quite disparate, and then to try to put them together. If one begins with a thinking subject (*res cogitans*) and a material universe (*res extensa*), how does the subject ever get out of his subjectivity so that he can know the world? Certainly, the first step in Descartes' own reasoning has usually been regarded as one of the strongest arguments in philosophy: *cogito, ergo sum*; I think, therefore I am. My most skeptical doubt is itself a thinking which proves my existence. But the existentialist criticizes this classic argument as abstract. I am not primarily a thinking subject. I am first of all an existent; existence is something much broader than thinking, and prior to it.

The existentialist is therefore inclined to turn the argument around: I am, therefore I think. But what does it mean to say 'I am'? 'I am' is the same as 'I exist'; but 'I exist,' in turn, is equivalent to 'I-am-in-the-world,' or, again, 'I-am-with-others.' So the premise of the argument is not anything so abstract as 'I think' or even 'I am' if this is understood in some isolated sense. The premise is the immensely rich and complex reality, 'I-am-with-others-in-the-world.' This reality is not something that has to be established by means of an argument or an epistemological theory. It is the initial datum that has to be unpacked in subsequent reflection.

The attempt to move the starting-point of philosophy from the abstract thinking subject to a more concrete base in the total, multidimensional human experience of involvement in a world of affairs has been carefully explored by John Macmurray. In his terminology the 'I act' (the self as agent) replaces the 'I think' as the place where philosophy finds its beginning. It is not that the

'I act' and the 'I think' are opposed to one another. It is rather, as he puts it, that 'the concept of "action" is inclusive.'[2] Action (as opposed to mere random activity) includes thinking. The thinking subject is an abstraction from the totality of the self as agent. The relations between the self as agent and the self as subject are summed up by Macmurray in four propositions: 1) The self is agent and exists only as agent. 2) The self is subject, but cannot exist as subject; it can be subject only because it is agent. 3) The self is subject in and for the self as agent. 4) The self can be agent only by being also subject.[3]

Macmurray argues that the adoption of the 'I act' rather than the 'I think' as the starting-place would circumvent many of the problems that have proved to be most intractable in philosophy. Especially it avoids an initial dualism of mind and matter, body and soul, self and world; and this dualism has been at the root of the antinomies of modern philosophy.

Macmurray's position on these matters is very close to that of many existentialists, and we have felt free to take Macmurray as our example because of the clear and detailed discussion of the problem to be found in his writings. This does not mean that he is being annexed to the 'existentialists'—but, after all, who is willing to accept that label?

However, we must face the question whether the existentialist (or someone akin in his thinking to the existentialist) is bypassing the problem of knowledge and conveniently avoiding a discussion of what has been long accounted one of the toughest and most central problems in philosophy. Is there an attempt here to take a shortcut, to assume what ought to be demonstrated? I do not think so. If the problem of knowledge has proved to be a tough one, even an apparently insoluble one, may this not be due to its having been formulated in the wrong way? If one begins with knower and known as separate entities, then perhaps it just is impossible to put these two together or to get out convincingly from the solipsist trap. The existentialist, as we have already stressed, begins not with two things that have to be put together but with the unity of being-with-others-in-the-world. From the ground up, as far as he is concerned, there is no isolated subject on the one side that has to be related to a world or other subjects standing over against it. But this does not abolish the epistemological question, the problem of the conditions, limits, and truth of our knowing. Rather, it gives to the problem a different form. Because existence is regarded as inclusive of knowledge (or action of thinking, or the agent of the subject), knowledge is taken to be a mode of being-with-others-in-the-world, that is to say, as one strand that goes to make up this very complex and multiform relationship. The epistemological problem remains, but it is seen as the problem of sorting out and exposing to view this particular strand, and of giving a phenomenological analysis of the self-world relation in its specifically epistemological character. Such an analysis would have to cover such themes as the nature of understanding, the modes of knowing, and the problem of truth.

The foundations for this part of our inquiry have been laid in the preceding chapters. The very notion of existence as a going out of oneself already had important implications for a theory of knowledge. In choosing 'ex-sistence' as the basic description of the human condition it was already being asserted that man is characterized by a fundamental openness or, at least, the potentiality for such. To exist is already to be outside of oneself and alongside other entities. Man never was an eremite, a subject shut in on himself, a selfsufficient and self-enclosed entity who might subsequently come out to develop relations with a world or with other subjects. Primordially, he already stands out, out of himself among things and other persons. We can say that he *is* only because he stands in these relations.

What was already implicit in the notion of existence has become clearer in the discussions of the world and of other existents. We have seen that there is no existence without a world and without other existents, and already knowing the world and knowing the other are included. Not least important has been our discussion of the body. To exist is not just to *have* a body but to *be* a body; and it is through being a body that we can have the perceptions or sensations that constitute the content of knowledge. In saying that the existent *is* a body, that is to say, a psychosomatic unity, the existentialist is again refusing to begin with a dualism of body and soul; but he is not thereby excused from giving the best account that he can of how perception, understanding, and knowing are possible within the unity of being-in-the-world.

UNDERSTANDING, PROJECTING, INTERPRETING

It must be acknowledged that explicit or thematic discussions of the nature of knowing and understanding are not frequent in the writings of the existentialists. It is perhaps only to be expected that these writers, in rebelling against what they regard as the abstractness of much traditional philosophy, should devote more attention to feeling, willing, and acting than to the intellectual side of man's being; and, of course, they maintain that even our knowing is passional, and our understanding always colored by some affective mood. Yet it is a pity that in the main they have not devoted more attention to the problem of knowledge.

Like Kant, the existentialist considers human knowledge to have a double root. There is the given, the data of the senses; and then there is our own mental contribution by which we organize the given in accordance with *a priori* forms. In the words of Berdyaev: 'By its most profound nature, perception cannot be only an obedient reflection of reality, an adaptation to the data at hand; it is also an active transfiguration, giving meaning to being.'[4]

It is with this active, meaning-giving element in understanding that we shall be chiefly concerned in this discussion. The activity that we meet here has been aptly called *projecting* in the writings of Heidegger and Sartre. The existent is constantly projecting—indeed, this is part of his existing, his going out of himself. He is constantly projecting himself upon his surroundings.

In Heidegger's *Being and Time* one meets an almost bewildering variety of usages in which 'projection' gets mentioned. There is projection of the self, of existence, of understanding, of possibilities, of meaning, of a world, of nature, as well as projection *upon* possibilities, *upon* meaning, *upon* the world, to name only some of the more common occurrences.[5] Whether Heidegger has been quite consistent in his talk about projecting may be doubted. The general meaning, however, is fairly clear. To 'project' is to throw forward or to throw forth. The existent, in his self-transcendence, throws himself forward into his possibilities; he throws these possibilities forth into his environment; he understands his environment in terms of the possibilities that he throws upon it. It is thus that he projects meaning and builds an intelligible world. Here our present discussion links up with an earlier one of the constitution of the world (see above, p. 56 ff.). The world itself is a project, or a system of projects. Of course, the content or raw material of the world is given. But its strict worldlihood, its character as world, is constructed in terms of projects that are rooted *a priori* in the concerns of the existent.

The nature of everyday understanding has been anticipated in our earlier discussion of the everyday world. We understand something when we have projected our concern upon it and grasped its serviceability. A child understands something when he learns 'what it is for'; he has projected his possibilities upon it, and it has acquired a sense and significance.

No doubt the most primordial understanding is of an everyday, practical character. It has often been argued that man's intellectual endowment was developed in response to his biological needs. To understand the world is, in the first instance, to be able to cope with it; to know one's way about, to know how to relate things to human concerns and to bring them into service, to know also how to avoid dangers. Such an understanding of the world projects a human frame of reference upon phenomena and categorizes them in accordance with this frame. We may call this a practical understanding as distinct from a theoretical one. A practical understanding may manifest itself simply in patterns of action, for instance, in the way we handle or manipulate things, though we may never put this into words and might find it very difficult to do so. For this reason a practical grasp of something may be much harder to communicate than some piece of theoretical understanding. It is much easier to grasp theoretically the teaching of a book on the principles of government written by a political scientist than to grasp the art of government from a great statesman. When we speak of 'art' or 'skill,' we have in mind a kind of practical wisdom that cannot be neatly formulated in propositions. But undoubtedly this is a genuine kind of understanding and a very important kind indeed. It consists in projecting oneself into the situation in such a way as to avail oneself of the possibilities it offers. Thus politics has been called the 'art of the possible.'

Theoretical understanding has been developed out of practical understanding, though theory and practice should not be absolutely opposed to each other. Clearly there is no practice worthy to be called an 'art' or 'skill' (whether it be hunting or agriculture or engineering or playing a game or governing a country) that does not involve some implicit theory or insight into the way things behave and are related in the particular field of activity concerned; and likewise there is perhaps no 'theory' so pure that it is entirely free of practical interests. The distinction of practice and theory may be relative, but it is nevertheless important and useful. As one moves from practice to theory, one moves from the particular to the general, from the concrete to the abstract, from the actual to the hypothetical, from the case where existential concern is at a high level to the case where it is diminished, perhaps almost to vanishing point. As this occurs, one also moves away from the projecting of categories related to practical concern to the more theoretical categories, such as the categories of understanding as described by Kant or to the concepts of natural science.

To the difference between practical and theoretical understanding corresponds another rather obvious difference between the existentialist approach to the problem of knowledge and the approach that has been characteristic of philosophical tradition. The tradition has taken scientific understanding as the norm and has seen the theoretical categories as indicative of the basic structure of understanding. The existentialists, on the other hand, have taken practical understanding as the most fundamental kind and have supposed that scientific understanding is derivative from it. Perhaps it is the imagination that links the two forms of understanding and plays different roles in each. It is clear that any kind of projecting of possibilities involves the imagination. In everyday understanding, the imagination is motivated by practical needs. In scientific understanding, the imagination also plays a major role, for instance, in the framing of hypotheses; but here it is motivated not by practical needs but by the desire to know.

Incidentally, the role of the imagination in knowing and the relation of existentialist to more traditional approaches to the problem of knowledge are treated in Heidegger's book on Kant, *Kant and the Problem of Metaphysics*. Heidegger claims that the eleven pages on the schematism of the categories in Kant's *Critique of Pure Reason* 'form the heart of the whole work.'[6] He claims that the imagination and the temporal nature of man are the fundamental conditions that make understanding possible; and, of course, temporality and imagination are precisely what we see in the activity of projecting possibilities and meanings and even the world itself.

To talk of projecting meanings is also to say that all understanding includes an act of interpretation. Whatever presents itself to us is seen 'as something' or heard 'as something,' and so on. We see a patch of color *as* a building on the skyline; we hear a noise *as* a jet-engine. To assign meanings implies that we already have a frame of reference (or several frames of reference) on which we 'place' the several objects that confront us in experience. In our discussion of the world we considered the same phenomenon in a somewhat different way when we noted that the existent tends to incorporate everything into his world (see above, p. 61). But in that connection we also noted that there are many 'worlds.' Now we may correspondingly claim that there are several ways of understanding—not only the practical and the theoretical ways, but also, let us say, the understanding that belongs to the artist, the historian, the theologian, and so on. Every understanding, insofar as it implies an act of interpretation, includes a pre-understanding, a way of looking at things and of conceiving things that determines how we grasp them. The pre-understanding itself may become an object of investigation, as we inquire how far its *a priori* categories are in fact adequate to grasping and interpreting the content of experience. In critical understanding, there must be a constant reciprocal interplay between the interpretative categories and the actual deliverances of experience. The conceptual apparatus that we already bring along is necessary if we are to incorporate the material of experience into the understanding; but the categories themselves must be flexible and have a capacity for revision if they are to be adequate to an expanding experience. It is in some such interplay that the progress of understanding takes place, and many examples of this could be furnished from the history of the natural sciences.

THE FORMS OF KNOWING

When we talk of 'knowing,' we imply that understanding has reached a level of adequacy that entitles us to be reasonably certain about its findings. I say 'reasonably certain,' for perhaps one never has absolute certainty. It may be the case that we use the verb *to know* more glibly than we should. How often do we really know that we know? However, ordinary usage does permit us to talk of 'knowing' when we may not have absolute certainty, and in this section we shall be discussing 'knowing' in the broader rather than the narrower sense.

There are various kinds of knowing, and these have been distinguished both in philosophy and in common sense. We have already touched on the distinction between practical and theoretical knowledge. More fundamental still is the difference between knowing a fact and knowing a person—a difference so deeply felt that many languages have separate verbs for expressing the two kinds of knowing. Self-knowledge is still another important kind of knowing.

In any theory of knowledge one or other of the ways of knowing is usually given a paradigmatic status. In the past mathematical knowledge was often accorded a priority, for it seemed that such knowledge possessed an exactness, clarity, and certainty superior to what is attainable in any other area of inquiry. However, it is now held by many philosophers that these characteristics of mathematical knowledge are due to its essentially tautologous character. At the present time the natural sciences are more likely to be regarded as providing the criterion for what may be counted as knowledge.

They provide the empirical element that mathematics itself lacks, but by bringing mathematical concepts to bear on their subject matter, the sciences are able to achieve something of that 'exactness' that seems to be implied when we talk of 'knowledge.'

But once again we find that the existentialists tend to move against the stream. For the existentialist the paradigm of knowing is not the objective knowledge of empirical facts sought by the sciences, but knowing persons. Such knowing may be either the subjective or introspective knowledge of self, or the knowledge of other persons gained through encounter with them. Perhaps in one sense self-knowledge could claim a degree of certitude unattainable elsewhere, for in this case there is an immediate and intuitive awareness. Yet on the other hand, knowledge of the self or of human persons generally is admitted to be one of the most difficult things to reach. And even if one does reach to it, does not such knowledge always have a somewhat vague and indeterminate character, as compared with the exactness of what we learn through the methods of the natural sciences?

Obviously, there are not only different kinds of knowing but also degrees of knowing. One's knowledge of another person (or of oneself) may be vague or it may be more precise, it may be shallow or it may be profound, just as one's knowledge of natural phenomena may be. We tend to judge the adequacy of both kinds of knowledge by the degree to which those claiming such knowledge are able to predict a course of behavior or action. One's knowledge of another person may be no less exact than, let us say, one's knowledge of the weather, but the two kinds of knowledge are arrived at in different ways.

What then is peculiar about the kind of knowing which the existentialist takes to be paradigmatic? The answer would seem to be that such knowing is characterized by participation. It is not attained by observing something external to oneself but by immersing oneself in that which is known. It is obvious that in the case of self-knowledge, one already has this kind of participation. But something similar is true in the case of knowing another person. There is a mutuality, a give-and-take involved in this. We do not get to know a person simply by observing him, though it would be foolish to rule this out altogether. Our knowledge of him begins to develop as he lets himself be known and as we in turn let ourselves be known by him. We know someone well, as we say, when this mutuality, a kind of participation in each other's being, has gone on for some time and a thorough understanding has been established.

The use of the word *knowing* in the Bible is very significant.

There too it is knowledge by participation and knowledge of the other person that have priority over knowledge of facts, knowledge that something or other is the case. To know God, for instance, is not primarily to know that there is a God (though this must be implied) but to stand in a relation to God such that one puts faith in him. Significant is the Old Testament idiom whereby the verb *to know* is used of sexual intercourse. 'Now Adam knew Eve his wife . . .' (Gen 4:1). Knowledge is related here to the union of knower and known. We may notice also that this idiom points to the bodily factor in knowing. Knowing belongs to being-in-the-world and being-with-others. It is not the isolated act of a pure thinking subject.

The existentialist stresses participation in the act of knowing. He is critical of that kind of knowing in which the knower strives for detachment from what is known, so that he may examine it in an external way. In this second kind of knowing, one aims at objectivity. The object is that which is placed over against me; subject and object stand face to face, each external to the other. In saying that the existentialist is critical of the kind of knowing that aims at detachment. I do not want to say that he does not recognize that such knowing has its own value. It is true that in some exaggerated instances existentialists have projected an anti-scientific image. Their protest is legitimate, however, when the abstract detached attitude appropriate to some sciences gets extended indiscriminately, and when it is claimed that only the 'objective' knowledge attained in this way has a right to be considered knowledge. The existentialist's protest is particularly needed when the object of the study is man himself. No doubt sociology, anthropology, and other studies that seek to make man an object of research, to be studied by methods essentially similar to those employed in the study of any empirical phenomenon, have their limited value. But the existentialist is surely correct in affirming that this abstract approach is incapable of reaching and understanding what is most distinctively human in man. This can be known only by our participation in human existence. All this was indeed clearly stated by Wilhelm Dilthey in the 19th century, but we have been slow to learn the lessons. Especially in the United States, sociology and other empirical studies of man are accorded a vastly exaggerated status, and as one 'survey' follows another it is scarcely surprising if people come to be regarded as something less than people.

Existentialists are agreed that knowledge of the human is not reducible to a general knowledge about empirical facts; and they are agreed further in stressing the primacy of human knowledge, that is to say, existential knowledge. They vary considerably among themselves as to how they wish to express this. Karl Jaspers insists that all our knowing is of the subject-object pattern, but he also recognizes the importance of what he calls the 'comprehensive' or the 'encompassing' (*das Umgreifende*). This cannot itself be an object; yet we are aware of it as the larger realm that includes both subject and object, and it includes the 'being in itself that surrounds us' and the 'being that we are.' To be aware of the comprehensive or encompassing is to be delivered from a narrowly objectifying relation to our environment, to transcend the subject-object gulf by participation.[7] N. Berdyaev seems to think of 'objectification' as not far removed from a fall of man. Following the anthropologist Levy-Bruhl he holds that man's earliest thinking did not objectify but remained in union with that which it knew in accordance with a *loi de participation*. But this participation was broken. 'The awakening and development of the conscious mind was accompanied by division and alienation. Man had to pass through a stage in which he subjected his thought and reason to a critique. To pass through objectification is the fate of spirit in this world.' But he thinks that we have now to return to a new mode of participation. Existential philosophy marks a new transition 'from the interpretation of knowledge as objectification to understanding it as participation, union with the subject matter, and entering into cooperation with it.'[8] Something like an echo of these views may be found in the writings of Marshall McLuhan, who holds that in the new electric age we are coming to the end of fragmentation and entering a time when something like the 'mythic consciousness' will again be important. What he calls the 'cool media,' such as television, are precisely those that involve the participation of the persons to whom they are addressed.[9]

It should be noted further that the existentialists make no sharp distinction between knowing, feeling, and willing. From Kierkegaard to Berdyaev it has been maintained that knowledge has its passionate and striving characteristics. This may become clearer when we study the affects (see below, Chapter Nine) and see how the notion of existence entirely abolishes the old-fashioned faculty-psychology. We should note too that while personal knowledge is taken as the paradigm by the existentialists, it is by no means utterly different from knowledge of empirical facts—indeed, if it were, it could hardly serve as a paradigm for all knowledge. Though there are differences of opinion on this point, most existentialists would agree with Michael

Polyani, who in his book *Personal Knowledge* argues that even the seemingly abstract and impersonal procedures of natural science are not without their personal factors. But this will become clearer in the following section on truth.

THE PROBLEM OF TRUTH

What is truth? Does it reside in the object? Or in the subject? Or in the relation between them? Or elsewhere? Traditionally, truth has been considered to be the agreement between a mental content (a judgment or an idea) and the fact in the world that the judgment or idea 'represents.' It will not surprise us, in view of the foregoing discussions of knowing and understanding, that the existentialist philosopher rejects this traditional conception of truth as inadequate. It may indeed describe one kind of truth, the kind at which abstract objectifying understanding is aimed. But—so it is argued—there is a more primordial kind of truth, a truth that belongs to the concreteness of existence.

Kierkegaard talked especially of the 'truth of subjectivity.' Perhaps his terminology was unfortunate. Is not truth, almost by definition, something objective? What is true for one person is surely true for all. How then is it possible to associate truth with subjectivity?

Kierkegaard's language is to be understood in terms of his protest against what he took to be the abstractness of 'objective' truth. The fullness of truth implies its inwardness. It is not something impersonal to be bandied about in propositions, but something to be inwardly appropriated. No doubt the religious influence in Kierkegaard's philosophy is also at work here. Jesus Christ had claimed, 'I am the truth' (Jn 14 : 6). What is this truth that is identified with a personal life? Certainly it must be something more concrete than the truth of propositions. Kierkegaard puts it this way:

> When the question of truth is raised in an objective manner, reflection is directed objectively to the truth, as an object to which the knower is related. If only the object to which he is related is the truth, the subject is accounted to be in the truth. When the question of truth is raised subjectively, reflection is directed subjectively to the nature of the individual's relationship; if only the mode of this relationship is in the truth, the individual is in the truth, even if he should happen to be thus related to what is not true.[10]

This does not mean that 'thinking makes it so' or that truth is to be identified with my private prejudice; but it does mean that truth in the fullest sense comes out of the inward depth of existence and is rooted in the openness of existence.

It is possible to criticize Kierkegaard's account of truth as too individualistic. This tendency is corrected in some of the later existentialist philosophers, notably Berdyaev and Marcel. They are as clear as Kierkegaard that truth has always a personal dimension, but they are better aware of the communal character of our knowing, that truth depends on a community of truthfulness. This has been specially brought out by Marcel, who found the teaching already expounded by the American idealist philosopher Josiah Royce, with his doctrine of a community of interpretation. A team of scientists pursuing research is constituted just as much by the bonds of personal truthfulness that guarantee the integrity of the research as by its quest for objective truths to be gained as a result of the research and then written down in textbooks. To the full notion of truth (if I may use the expression *notion* in a more or less Hegelian sense) there belong not just the propositions that may come at the end but the personal endeavors of freedom, fidelity, and struggle which lead to the truth.

The relations of truth, freedom, and the overtness of existence are explored in Heidegger's essay 'On the Essence of Truth.' One is in the truth so far as one is free; one is free so far as one is open to things as they are; one is open to things as they are so far as one lets them be what they are, not manipulating them but participating in their overtness. Heidegger keeps coming back to the Greek conception of truth as $\dot{a}$-$\lambda\dot{\eta}\theta\epsilon\iota\alpha$, literally, un-hiddenness. Truth 'happens,' as it were, when concealments are stripped away and when things emerge into openness. But this implies that truth is rooted in existence, in the *Dasein*, in 'subjectivity' (though Heidegger is careful to avoid this term of Kierkegaard). For the *Dasein* is the clearing in the opacity of being, man is the place where openness occurs, so that he is 'in the truth' (or in the untruth of concealment) in virtue of the very fact that he ex-sists.[11]

To sum up this chapter, one may say that existentialist philosophy impresses upon us the need to pay more attention than hitherto to the personal or existential factors in understanding, knowledge, and truth. If some philosophers of existentialist tendency have been led to exaggerated criticism of objectification and the abstractness of science, this may be excusable as they seek to restore a balance and to remind us that all understanding, knowledge, and truth occur only in the context of personal existence.

CHAPTER SEVEN

Thought and Language

THINKING

In the present chapter we shall still to a considerable extent be concerned with the problems discussed in the preceding one—that is to say, with the cognitive and intellectual side of existence. We have seen that existentialist philosophy lays great stress on the *process* whereby we come to understand or to know or to arrive at the truth. These things are not lying ready-made for our inspection. They have to be appropriated through personal endeavor. Thinking is the activity by which we come to know, and closely connected with thought is language, which might even be called thought's embodiment.

In its view of thinking, existentialism finds itself once more at variance with much of the philosophic tradition. In particular, there is a long tradition that thought and reality are one. It goes back at least to Parmenides: τὸ γὰρ αὐτὸ νοεῖν ἐστίν τε καὶ εἶναι; 'for thinking and being are the same.' The tradition continued to dominate Western philosophy and found perhaps its most systematic expression in the philosophy of Hegel; the real is the rational, it is absolute thought thinking itself. It was precisely against this philosophy that Kierkegaard raised his protest. Thinking and being, thought and reality, he tells us, are *not* the same. Reality bursts thought open.

We have already noted Kierkegaard's criticism of 'abstract thought': 'because abstract thought is *sub specie aeterni*, it ignores the concrete and the temporal, the existential process, the predicament of the existing individual arising from his being a synthesis

106

of the temporal and eternal situated in existence.'[1] Kierkegaard's complaint is precisely that thought separates us from reality and that its world is not the real world of existence. However, we should be careful to notice that Kierkegaard speaks explicitly of *abstract* thought. The existentialist polemic against what is taken to be a too narrow intellectualism is frequently misunderstood as an attack upon thought in general. It is true that in Kierkegaard, Unamuno, and others, we do come across extravagant statements that suggest that thought is being abandoned and that feeling and willing are to take its place.

But the main thrust of existentialism is in the direction not of abandoning thought (which would be an impossible project in any case) but of recognizing that it has many forms. The abstract thought criticized by Kierkegaard fails because it seeks to impose on reality a tidy pattern that belies actual existence. The trouble with such thought is not that it is thought but that it is abstract. It is not dialectical, as Kierkegaard understands 'dialectic.' Thus he himself develops the notion of 'paradox.' Paradox is not plain contradiction, which would be the rejection of thought. 'Paradox unites the contradictories,' not by resolving them in a rational structure but by letting reason and paradox become themselves reconciled in faith. 'Reason and paradox encounter one another happily in the moment; when the reason sets itself aside and the paradox bestows itself. The third entity in which this union is realized . . . is that happy passion to which we will now assign a name, though it is not the name that so much matters. We shall call this passion *"faith."* '[2]

Nevertheless, Kierkegaard does sometimes seem close to adopting an irrationalism, and this has provoked a reaction among other existentialists. Karl Jaspers is perhaps the philosopher of existence who has been most careful to respect the claims of reason and thought. Reason is, after all, a basic constituent of the human existent. While Jaspers would agree with Kierkegaard that reality goes beyond reason, he sees no divorce between them. On the contrary, there is some correspondence between our concepts and reality. They are both embraced within the 'encompassing,' which seems in this regard to take over the function that Kierkegaard assigned to the paradox. Jaspers certainly recognizes the limits of thought, and later we shall have to consider what he means by 'ciphers,' ideas by which we try to represent to ourselves realities that cannot be grasped by thought (see below, p. 115). But Jaspers has a very proper suspicion of irrationalism, romanticism, and emotionalism, of which, indeed, the 20th century saw a terrible manifestation in the Nazi phenomenon. The philosophy of existence, both because it is philosophical and because it is existential, must have regard for thought and reason. A perceptive commentator on Jaspers has expressed the matter thus: 'To reject the perversion of overweening intellectualism does not mean that we are to be precipitated into subjectivism and irrationalism. It would be foolish to condemn reason as such. Rather we must insist on the power and efficacy of a reason which is permeated by existence as the source of its truth.'[3]

Martin Heidegger has had much to say about thought and thinking. He understands thinking to be quite fundamental to human existence, but by distinguishing different modes or levels of thought he is able to argue that some thinking is much more fundamental than some other thinking. What he calls 'calculative' thinking he will hardly allow as thought at all. This is the everyday thinking by which we solve our practical problems, or again, it is the thinking of the natural sciences. Such thinking is done most efficiently by machines nowadays, and perhaps this is an indication that it is not the most typically human kind of thinking. Such thinking would need to be different from calculative thinking or from the click-clack of the computer. It would need to be a thinking 'permeated by existence,' to recall the phrase used in connection with Jaspers. Heidegger begins his book *What Is Called Thinking*? by declaring: 'We come to know what it means to think when we ourselves try to think.'[4] But the thinking that Heidegger chiefly stresses—he calls it by such names as 'primordial' and 'essential' thinking—is not only permeated by existence but also by being. It is our response to being, our meditative dwelling with reality. This is a different way of interpreting Parmenides' saying about the relation of thinking and being. Thought does not constitute reality; rather, being communicates itself in what is most truly called thought. This essential thinking has nothing of the busy, active character of calculative thinking. It is, on the contrary, passive and receptive. Heidegger called one of his books *Gelassenheit*, a word with a history in the German mystical tradition that goes back to Eckhart. The word is generally translated 'abandonment' or 'releasement,' but the title of the English translation of the book is *Discourse on Thinking*, and this is not entirely inappropriate since this 'releasement' is, in Heidegger's view, the highest level of human thinking.

These remarks on thinking as understood among some of the existentialists raise in turn the question of logic and so, in a new way, the question about irrationalism in existentialism and whether existentialism can in reality lay claim to be a *philosophy*. For logic, after all, supplies the rules for thinking. If the rules are set aside, how can it be claimed that people are still thinking or that what comes out of their alleged thinking is philosophy? We may have been correct in saying that Kierkegaard's paradoxes are not plain contradictions, but surely they are illogical. Whatever else we may expect from a philosopher, have we not a right to expect him to be logical? And if he abandons logic, then has he not abandoned philosophy? And may not similar objections be brought against most other existentialists? If Heidegger, for instance, especially in his later writings, wishes to commend some meditative quasi-mystical type of thinking, then he is quite entitled to do so; but should he not explicitly admit that he has given up philosophy? He does in fact say that 'the idea of "logic" gets dissolved in the vortex of a more primordial inquiry.'[5] But how can there be a more primordial inquiry that dispenses with logic, and how can it be philosophical?

Surely the answer to such questions is that just as there are several modes or levels of thinking, so there are several logics. Traditional philosophy has been dominated by one type of logic, but the time may have come for breaking its tyranny, and for recognizing that there are other ways of doing philosophy and that these have logics of their own. The existentialist today may get some help at this point from the logical analyst, and especially from the later Wittgenstein and his followers. For the analyst too is saying that there is a plurality of logics. There are many games, and each game has its own rules.

However, while I am not impressed with the critics who would argue that Kierkegaard, Unamuno, Heidegger, and others abandon philosophy and logic, and even thinking itself, one does have to acknowledge that the traditional logic belonged to a style of thought that had strictness and clarity, and that the thinking of the existentialist is in constant danger of becoming an undisciplined thinking, where passion and conviction take the place of demonstration and obscurity is passed off as profundity. It is therefore of the greatest importance that existentialist philosophers who claim to move beyond the traditional patterns of thought and logic should tell us as clearly as they can what they are doing and what their particular logic is.

LANGUAGE

Thinking is articulated in language. Whether any kind of thinking is possible without language is doubtful, for even our unspoken thoughts are put into words and sentences. It may be the case that

some kinds of contemplative thought need no words, and several of
the existentialists speak appreciatively of silence. It would seem,
however, that such silence comes only after speech. According to
Jaspers we reach this silence 'not by refraining from thought and
speech, but by carrying them to the extremes where they revert to
silence. In time, they will shortly make us speak again.'⁶ But apart
from the exceptional or extreme cases, all thinking implies language.
It is through language that thought becomes public and accessible,
and this is essential to our being-in-the-world.

There is considerable discussion of language in the writings of
existentialists, though it is scarcely with them the overriding concern
that it is among logical analysts. It may be worthwhile at the beginning of our discussion to ask about the difference between the existentialist's approach to language and that of the analyst. As I
understand it, the analyst is interested in the internal structure of
language, its logical syntax. He is interested also in the way language relates to the world; how words 'signify' and 'refer'; how
propositions can be meaningful; and what are the conditions that
they should be true. The interest of the existentialist is different.
He is much more concerned with language as a human or existential
phenomenon than with its internal structure or its relation to a
referend. Indeed, the existentialist fastens his attention primarily
on the spoken word, on talk or discourse, as the full human phenomenon. The tone of voice, the gesture, the facial expression—
these are characteristics that are irrelevant to logic, but they belong
to the full reality of language and are lost when the written or printed
word is substituted for talk.

The existential or human elements in language are always
present, though at some times more obviously than at others.
A mathematical formula printed in a textbook would present us
with a case where the personal or existential character of language
had been dimmed down almost to vanishing point. A political
speech, on the other hand, would be a case where the personal
aspects of language are evident. But the old-fashioned distinction
of language into informative and emotive was far too simple-
minded. Most of our language is a very mixed phenomenon, and
perhaps no language is entirely impersonal.

There seem to be at least two ways in which language is in-
separably linked to personal existence. First, all language is someone's language. Language does not spring up in a vacuum, it proceeds
from *homo loquens*. In fact, there is nothing more human than language, even when it takes the shape of an abstract formula. Second,

all language is addressed to someone. (I suppose this is true even when one is talking to oneself.) A primary function of language is to communicate.

We may say then that the existentialist is concerned with the existential analysis of language rather than with its logical analysis. His business is to probe these existential relations that make language possible and that in turn are made possible by language.

This means that the existentialist studies language primarily in the context of being-with-others. There are some very significant remarks on language on the opening page of Buber's *I and Thou*. He introduces the idea of 'primary words,' especially the primary words 'I-Thou' and 'I-It.' We noted already that these primary words are not isolated words, like 'I' and 'It' and 'Thou,' but combined words that already imply the context of our being-with-others-in-the-world. 'If "Thou" is said, the "I" of the combination "I-Thou" is said along with it.' Here we see the insistence on the personal dimension of language—that it is always communication. 'Primary words do not signify things, but they intimate relations. Primary words do not describe something that might exist independently of them, but being spoken, they bring about existence.'[7] These sentences illustrate the existentialist (or personalist) disinterest in referring in favor of what is taken to be the more fundamental function of language, as relating the speaker to the other person; and Buber also seems to assert that speech is not made possible by a pre-existing relation to the other but actually creates this relation. It was with a similar thought in mind that I wrote at the end of the last paragraph about 'existential relations that make language possible and that in turn are made possible by language.' However, I think it would be fruitless to ask whether being-with-others comes before language, or language before being-with-others; if 'being-with-others' is understood in a fully personal and existential sense, then we must surely say that being-with-others and language are equiprimordial. Lastly, Buber makes the point that 'I-Thou' language is spoken with the whole being and expresses the whole person, while 'I-It' language never does so. Language is self-involving to various degrees.

It seems to me that Buber's laconic sentences contain *in nuce* an existential analysis of language, and that while other existentialist writers have different emphases, they do not add anything essentially new to what is already contained in Buber's remarks. For instance, the early Heidegger (we defer for the moment a consideration of his later views on language) offers a fairly elaborate analysis of discourse as a fundamental *existentiale* in terms of expressing and communicating, but the main points of it are already adumbrated in Buber. Heidegger, however, does hold that some mode of being-with-others precedes language, and he also pays attention (as we must do shortly) to the relation of language to reality.[8] Sartre claims that 'language is not a phenomenon added on to being-for-others; it *is* originally being-for-others; that is, it is the fact that a subjectivity experiences itself for another.'[9] Sartre's discussion of language is introduced in the context of his remarks on seduction. To make the other love me, I must become for him a fascinating object, and this I achieve by language, in the widest sense. Sartre acknowledges that the primitive language is not necessarily seductive and that there are other forms of it. But 'language can be revealed entirely at one stroke by seduction as a primitive mode of expression.'[10] His tendency to dwell on inauthentic relations with the other forms a corrective to the somewhat idealized 'I-Thou' relation stressed by Buber, though, of course, the latter was well aware of the fragility of this relation and its tendency to deteriorate.

Any realistic account of language must take notice of its ambivalence. It can communicate, but it can also cover up and even deceive. What criteria are there by which we may judge the integrity of language? Here we may recall our earlier discussion of truth, and especially Heidegger's understanding of truth as $\dot{a}$-$\lambda\dot{\eta}\theta\epsilon\iota\alpha$, 'un-hiddenness' (see above, p. 105). He understands the relation of language to reality in terms of the making unhidden that which is talked about. Language is not a picture of reality, to be judged true if there is a point-to-point correspondence between the picture and the fact it 'represents.' The locus of truth is not in the proposition but rather in the reality itself. Language lets what is talked about stand out and be seen for what it is. Language successfully communicates when it lights up for two or more people their being-in-the-world and lets each see what the other sees. It is obvious that such an interpretation of language lays as much stress on the personal integrity of the users of language as on the logical strictness of the language itself.

But much language does not achieve this lighting up and communication. Kierkegaard wrote: 'How ironical that by speech man can degrade himself below dumb creation—he becomes a chatterbox.'[11] 'Idle talk' (*Gerede*) is Heidegger's expression for the kind of discourse that does not really communicate or disclose entities as they are. 'We do not so much understand the entities which are talked about; we already are listening only to what is said in the talk as such.'[12] This idle talk, so far from opening things up for us, really closes them off. The word gets passed along, it already contains an accepted interpretation of what is talked about, it even becomes authoritative, but it never fulfills the role of authentic discourse. Such idle talk is, of course, characteristic of the 'they,' the 'crowd,' or whatever name may be used, and helps to maintain its dominance. It prevents any original or creative encounter with 'the things themselves.'

The phenomenon of inauthentic talk helps to explain the existentialist's hostility to dogmatism and to views that are accepted simply on the basis of authority or their lengthy history within the tradition. In all such cases, language has been diverted from its true function—the words are passed along, but they are heard as words. The disclosure does not take place; we are not allowed to see or appropriate for ourselves the reality that the words are about. So the existentialist favors a return to the sources, an exposure to the way things are rather than to the way they are said to be. This does not mean an arrogant rejection of all tradition, whether in philosophy or theology or art; but it does mean a critical searching of the tradition, so that it communicates reality to us and is not allowed to pass itself off in place of the reality.

Although the existentialist analysis and critique of language is very different from logical analysis, the two approaches should be regarded as complementary rather than as rivals. Both of them recognize the first-class importance of language in human affairs and the ease with which language can become misleading and deceptive, so that it defeats its own purpose; and both of them, in different ways, offer guidelines for the proper use of language.

THE LIMITS OF THOUGHT AND LANGUAGE

We have alluded more than once in this chapter to logical analysis as a type of philosophy that has had a special concern with language. It is well known that many analysts have also been positivists. They have claimed that there are well-defined limits to what we can talk about or think about, at least in any meaningful way. I propose in this final section to ask whether the existential analysis of language also brings us to limits or whether it suggests ways whereby the impasse of positivism may be broken.

The whole existentialist understanding of man as the being who is constantly going out beyond himself certainly does not predispose toward accepting limits to what can be significantly said or thought.

I think most existentialist philosophers would agree with David E. Jenkins when he declares: 'I retain the belief that one of the challenges of being a human being is that we are faced with the opportunity of deciding what we ought to think. If men had accepted what their generation found thinkable, we should have had no science and precious little humanness.'[13] These sentences occur in the midst of a passage where he is protesting against ' "the modern world-view" as a final and decisive arbiter of what we, as men and human beings, can or ought to think'—a passage that can hardly fail to remind us of our discussion in the last section of the 'idle talk' of the 'they' that passes itself off as authoritative and already interprets the world for everyone before there is any encounter with 'the things themselves.'

Some existentialists are antimetaphysical, but I doubt if any of them could be called positivists. As we have seen, they do *not* agree with the proposition that thought and reality coincide. Reality breaks out beyond thought and it is precisely this 'beyond' that fascinates the existentialists and about which they want to say something. To put the matter somewhat differently, one might say that in treating language as an existential phenomenon, the existentialist has already moved away from positivism. For in language man expresses *himself*; but he is himself the self-transcending being, the one who already knows in himself the mystery of ex-sisting. His very nature is to go out beyond the limits of any given state in which he finds himself.

Of course, the pushing out of the frontiers of thought and language takes place in different ways and in different degrees with different philosophers. From the very beginning or our study we have been aware of the tension between those existentialists for whom man is an ultimate and those who relate their interpretation of man to an idea of God or Being. Even the first group, I have urged, are not positivists. However, it is only the second who are interested in trying to show how thought and language can reach out beyond the limits of sense phenomena and of existential self-awareness.

In an earlier discussion (see above, p. 111) we mentioned Heidegger's early views on language and promised that his later thoughts on the subject would come up for consideration later. In his early work, language (or rather discourse) was said to be an *existentiale*, a basic possibility of being belonging to the human existent. This is the typical existentialist view and forms the basis for the kind of analysis that has up to this point occupied us in the present chapter. But in his later thought Heidegger moves away from the existential and human aspects of language. We are told that man did not invent language and could not have invented it.[14] Before he can speak, man must be addressed by being. Language is the 'house of being'—and this is no mere metaphor formed by applying the familiar image of a house to being, for it is from thinking the essence of being that we may finally think what 'house' and 'dwelling' are.[15]

Although in *Being and Time* Heidegger had disavowed what he called a 'word-mysticism' (*Wortmystik*), it can hardly be denied that he moves in the direction of one in his later writings. Language is not only the house of being but increasingly takes over the character and functions once assigned to being itself. One obvious way in which Heidegger's *Wortmystik* shows itself is in his fascination with etymologies and the primordial meanings of words (and this is a fairly early development in his philosophy). We have already taken note of the way in which he related his understanding of truth to the Greek ἀ-λήθεια; many other Greek words are studied by him in the belief that the articulation of being evinces itself in these words. German words are also studied in a similar fashion. His belief is that 'along with German, the Greek language is (in regard to its possibilities for thought) at once the most powerful and the most spiritual of all languages.'[16] Heidegger's phenomenology of words as clues to the meaning of being can sometimes be very illuminating; but some critics have claimed that his arguments from the etymologies of words constitute the weakest part of his philosophy.

Heidegger's approach to language undoubtedly allows more scope to the symbolic and oblique uses of speech than does the view of language associated with logical empiricism. Though the mystery of being cannot be talked of in the literal language appropriate to the multiplicity of finite beings, nevertheless, if all language is the house of being and the gift of being, then there occurs in it some revelation of the character of being.

The question of the relation of language to the ultimate mystery of being is worked out also by Karl Jaspers. His treatment is in some ways fuller than that offered by Heidegger but is scarcely less elusive. He seems to recognize three levels of thought and language: 'Appearance is described and thought in concepts. Signs convey what I am and can be as myself. Transcendent reality, to be experienced by existence (*Existenz*) alone, is manifested in ciphers.'[17] A cipher (and Jaspers prefers this word to 'symbol') denotes 'the language of a reality that can be heard and addressed only thus and in no other way.' In this language Transcendence is thought of in terms of some intelligible entity, but if we take the language at all literally, we fall into superstition. 'Unless it remains an infinite, suspended, evanescent language, the objectivation of Transcendence will be superstitious. That is what superstition is: making an object of Transcendence.'[18] As examples of ciphers he gives the personal God, the one God, and the incarnate God. These all relate to Transcendence, but none of them conceptualizes Transcendence or gives us a literal idea of it. Would one say that these ciphers have cognitive content? In Jaspers' terminology, one would have to deny this, for all knowledge is said to be of the subject-object pattern. The ciphers certainly do not yield knowledge in this restricted sense. Yet they are not just empty symbols, quite unrelated to the Transcendence of which they speak. There is a constant conflict among the ciphers, and those that triumph presumably have more adequacy than those that are rejected. The ciphers cannot conceptualize or objectify Transcendence, but they evoke some notion of it. They take us beyond all ordinary thought, but they are themselves a kind of thinking.

Jaspers' teaching is complicated further by his belief that we can go even beyond the ciphers. He speaks of 'that striking paradox of a language to end language,' and what he has in mind are the contemplative explorations of the mystics. He is above all impressed by the Asian mystics, though among Europeans he mentions Meister Eckhart, who, as we have already noted, has affinities also with Heidegger. 'There is a marvelous power in these attempts to pass not only beyond reality but beyond all ciphers, to reach the unthinkable, unspeakable ground that bears us and encompasses all encompassing.'[19] As an illustration of a thinking (or, should we say, a product of thought or perhaps a non-verbal language) that goes beyond even the ciphers, Jaspers describes and analyzes the great Buddhist edifice called the Boro Buddor in Java. According to him, it 'combines images, symbols, spatial arrangements, and the pilgrim's movements in that space, into a thrilling visualization of Buddhist thought beyond all ciphers.'[20]

Here we have indeed come to the limits of thought, to the attempt to think the unthinkable. In the long run mysticism and positivism have certain affinities—they are both reduced to silence before that which can be neither thought nor spoken. The early Wittgenstein of the *Tractatus Logico-Philosophicus* seems clearly to have been part positivist, part mystic. Yet positivism and mysticism are also very different. The positivist gives up long before the mystic does. Probably the way one evaluates mysticism will determine the way one evaluates these more metaphysical thrusts of thought and language found in such existentialist thinkers as

Heidegger and Jaspers. Since I believe that thought, meditation, contemplation, prayer, philosophy, theology are all continuous (though, of course, differentiated), I believe that thought and language are capable of being extended in the directions that we have indicated in this section.

CHAPTER EIGHT

Feeling

FEELING AND PHILOSOPHY

What are usually known as the feelings, affects, moods, or emotions, have long been studied in philosophy. They belong so intrinsically to man's constitution that they cannot be overlooked in any attempt to give an account of who man is. From Plato and Aristotle down to modern times, philosophers have attempted to analyze man's emotional life and to relate it to his condition as a rational and moral being.

But the feelings have always been suspect. Philosophy, as rational reflection, is precisely an attempt to rise above passion and prejudice. The philosopher has usually distanced himself from emotion and has sought a dispassionate understanding of things. If he has admitted the emotions into the purview of philosophy, it is so that he can subject them to rational scrutiny. He would not acknowledge them to be a source of philosophical truth but would regard them rather as a distorting influence. They are to be understood so that their influence in deflecting thought from the rational norm may be, as far as possible, neutralized.

Of course, there have been exceptions to the generally suspicious attitude toward the emotions. Pascal acknowledged that the heart has its own reasons, and that these 'reasons of the heart' may justifiably overrule, at least on some occasions, the reasons of the intellect. Even philosophers of strongly intellectualist tendency have sometimes been impressed with the wholeness and immediacy of the kind of apprehension that comes in feeling, and have contrasted this with the fragmented apprehension of discursive thought. F. H. Bradley, for instance, considered feeling as the clue to the highest thinking of all, and perhaps on this account, in spite of all his brilliant reasoning, he has been described as 'ultimately an anti-intellectualist.'[1]

Generally speaking, however, one may say that philosophers have been interested in 'philosophy of feeling' only to the extent that this has meant a rational investigation into the passions. A philosophy of feeling in the sense of a philosophy determined by the feelings has usually been (like a 'philosophy of life') dismissed as something less than philosophy because it has seemed to sit lightly to the rigorous claims of truth.

With the rise of existentialism, however, the entire question of the feelings and their relation to philosophy has been reopened. I am not thinking so much of the extreme claims made for passion and the 'heart' by men like Unamuno as of the more sober treatment of the affects in such writers as Sartre, Heidegger, Ricoeur, Marcel, and others. It may well turn out that the phenomenology of the emotions provided by philosophers of existentialist tendency will prove to be one of their most valuable and lasting achievements. Existentialism is not, I would maintain, a mere philosophy of feeling in the sense that its convictions are molded by emotion more than by reason. In its best representatives one does not encounter raw emotion but emotion that has been long subjected to reflection. On the other hand, it is acknowledged that our feelings too are a way by which we reach philosophical truth. The feelings are not seen as antithetical to reason and thought but as a source of insights that can be disengaged and communicated through philosophical reflection. Moreover, these insights may be among the most profound and intimate available to us.

Existentialism is not a philosophy of feeling, but it does recognize that feeling has its place in the total texture of human existence. To take feeling in isolation would be to deal with an abstraction, but we have seen that a pure intellectualism is equally an abstraction. Probably we are all still too much influenced by old-fashioned 'faculty psychology,' and we think that the intellect, the emotions, and the will are separate activities of the 'soul' rather than merely distinctions that we make within the total content of experience. At any given moment this includes intellectual, emotional, and volitional elements, and these cannot be sharply marked off from each other. They belong within a living whole. What the existentialists say about the feelings cannot be taken in isolation but must be under-

stood in the context of their attempt to set forth a concrete philosophy
of human existence in its total range.

It has long been recognized that the passions are closely connected with the body and its changing states. When a man is angry,
there are physical symptoms. He may become red in the face, his eyes
flash, his voice is loud and hoarse, his body-posture is threatening.
In recent times the physical basis of the passions has been more
clearly explicated. Nowadays a psychological account of anger will
read very much like a physiological account. It will talk of hormones,
of the heartbeat, of the sympathetic nervous system, and so forth.
At least since the time of William James, it has been recognized that
an adequate account of the emotions cannot be given by some
speculative 'mental science' but must be sought rather in biology and
physiology.

The stress on the physical basis of the emotions is not in any way
an embarrassment to existentialism. We have already seen that,
for the existentialist, existence is understood as a being-in-the-world,
and that it is in virtue of having (or being) a body that man participates in a world. Thus man is understood as a psychosomatic unity,
and no existentialist account of the feelings would ignore what
might be termed their visceral aspect. However, an existentialist
account would certainly differ from a merely physiological one, or
from a psychological one insofar as this tended to be behavioristic.
For the existentialist, in his demand for concreteness, would have
to say that the behavioristic account is an abstract one. This is not to
deny that it has its uses, in certain given contexts. But it is to deny
that an empirical account of the emotions is a complete account.
To the outward observable phenomena that are open to observation
there must be added the inward experience, known only through
participation in emotional existence. The existentialist account of
feeling is not only concerned with the inward, subjective aspect
(as if this were something isolated in a vacuum) but with the bodily
or physical aspect. Again, however, it is the body as experienced by
an embodied person, not the body as a mere object for observation,
that enters into the existentialist point of view.

We have seen earlier in this book (see above, p. 70) that it is
through the body that we are in the world and participate in the
happenings of the world. Those feelings that are, in one aspect,
bodily (and therefore physical and worldly) events and, in another

aspect, inward experiences of the existent, are perhaps our most direct openings on to the world. The perceptions that we have by way of sense-experience, we have as spectators of the world; but through our feelings we are immediately participating in the world. Perception through the senses becomes the basis for an objective understanding of the world. I detach myself from the object, so that it stands over against me as object. But in feeling I am united to that which I feel, and both it and I are included in a whole. The kind of sense-perception that comes nearest to such feeling is touch. Significantly, to touch something is also to feel something and to stand in a peculiarly intimate relation to it.

Because through feeling I have a uniquely direct way of participating in the world, the feelings or emotions are, as it were, a kind of register of my being-in-the-world. The language used by some existentialists brings this out very clearly. Heidegger speaks of *Gestimmtheit*—that is to say, being 'attuned' to the world. Ricoeur uses a similar metaphor when he talks of *tonalité*, as if one had to adjust to the 'pitch' of the world. The same writer uses the word *atmospheric* in relation to the feelings. The atmosphere is that which envelops us, and also that which we breathe; there is a sense in which we 'breathe' in the world through the feelings and are merged into the world as the environment in which we live and move and have our being.

Are there emotions that are not founded in the body? One may at least say that some feelings are more directly and obviously bodily and worldly than others. The esthetic feeling aroused by the spectacle of the starry sky seems more closely tied to the physical than the esthetic feeling aroused by contemplation of the mathematical elegance of Copernicus' theory of the heavens. To mention another example, Kant claimed that the feeling of respect, to which he assigned considerable importance in the moral life, is a rational feeling distinct from those passions that are tied to bodily experience. Admittedly, there are feelings and emotions that appear to be much more loosely correlated with bodily happenings than, let us say, fear and anger. Yet it would seem that even the most sophisticated feelings are rooted ultimately in our being-in-the-world or, to speak more adequately, in our being-with-others-in-the-world. Respect, for instance, implies our existence in a moral community. Moreover, this 'rational' passion is clearly akin to passions of a more obviously 'emotional' sort—to reverence, admiration, awe. Paul Ricoeur says of respect that it is rooted in 'something like a disposition of desire for rationality' and is thus 'like the Cartesian generosity which is at once action and passion, action of the free will and emotion in the depths of the body.'[2] Feeling seems to lie somewhere between the mere life-processes of the body, of some of which we are barely conscious or even unconscious, and the conscious exercise of rational thought. In Plato's tripartite division of the soul, the 'heart' (θύμος, the spirited part or seat of the feelings) is distinguished both from the desires of the body and from the reason and is said sometimes to work with the one, sometimes with the other (*Republic*, 440–441).

If our account of the feelings is, up to this point, correct, so that it can be acknowledged that they 'attune' us to the world and that at least the more sophisticated feelings are close to reason, then the possibility that feeling may yield some genuine insights having philosophical interest cannot be dismissed out of hand. It could even be the case that this intimate relation to the world through feeling could disclose to us truths concerning the world such as would be quite inaccessible through that mere beholding which characterizes our observation of the world through the senses.

But are we perhaps talking nonsense? Are not the fleeting moods and feelings that come and go in our minds simply 'in our minds' and no more? How can these elusive affects reveal anything about the nature of the reality beyond ourselves? Nothing seems more subjective than feeling. I feel a pain in my tooth, let us say, and this toothache is purely private to myself, though a really bad toothache may exclude almost anything else from the field of consciousness. However, a toothache has certainly some objective reference. It is brought on by the physical condition of the tooth, which happens to be at one and the same time a part of my body (and so a part of *me*) and a part of the physical world. But let us take another example. I might say, looking at charred trees on a blackened hillside after a forest fire, 'What a sorry sight!' What can this mean? Is there anything sad or sorrowful about the hillside? Or am I being misled by language? We apply words like *sad* and *sorrowful* to things we see in the world, but do not these adjectives properly apply to ourselves? It would seem to be not the hillside that is sorry but myself when I look on it, and I am simply projecting my own feelings upon what I see. Yet the matter is not quite so simple as this either. When I saw the same hillside a month ago before the fire, when the trees were green and there was a lot of wildlife about, I would not have dreamed of calling it a sorry sight. To say that the sorrow is in my mind rather than in the hillside can scarcely mean that the presence or absence of sorrow in my mind has nothing to do with the actual state of affairs 'out there.' It is true, of course, that we are all to some extent 'moody,' and that moods of elation or depression may come unexpectedly upon us, so that the very same landscape may seem to us one day to be joyful and the next to be mournful. People whose moods are very changeable and unpredictable we call *temperamental*. To a more than ordinary degree, they project their inward feelings both on the world and on other people. In extreme cases—for instance, in paranoia—this projecting of feelings becomes pathological and distorting. But the very fact that we are able to recognize pathological cases implies that there is a norm. The fact that feelings can be misplaced is an attestation that certain feelings are appropriate to certain situations.

Feelings, then, are not just 'in my mind.' They are correlated with what is outside of my mind. In the language of phenomenologists we may say that feelings are 'intentional,' that is to say, they are directed upon actual states of affairs. The fact that feelings are sometimes quite inappropriate (or disproportionate) to the states of affairs toward which their intentionality is directed is no argument against the claim that in normal cases the feelings do in fact 'attune' us to the real state of affairs—indeed, the possibility of entertaining the 'wrong' feeling implies the normal case. All that this means is that we may be in error concerning how we feel about something. Equally, we can be in error about what we perceive with the senses. But the possibility of hallucination assumes that normal perception is veridical.

Someone might say: 'I feel mad about the way the government is handling this matter, but perhaps it is wrong for me to feel that way.' His anger or indignation is intentional, that is to say, it is directed toward an actual state of affairs, the conduct of the government. Furthermore, this anger or indignation is not some arbitrary or purely subjective feeling, but is supposed to be appropriate to the government's action. This action is of such a kind as to be worthy of exciting indignation. However, the speaker also acknowledges that he may be mistaken in feeling the way he does. Here we may notice that we use the word *sensibility* for the capacity to entertain the 'right' feelings. The person who has sensibility is indignant in the face of injustice, compassionate in the face of suffering, and so on. But his sensibility implies also a sensitivity. He has, as we say, the 'feel' for what is going on. He is 'attuned' to the world around him (including the world of human affairs), and he makes the appropriate emotional responses.

If we think of the feelings as 'intentional' and so as directed upon states of affairs in the world, we must also think of this relation as reciprocal. It is surely significant that the feelings or emotions have been traditionally called *passions* or *affections* or *affects*. These three terms all seem to suggest that the subject of such feelings is a passive recipient. The feelings are induced in him by circumstances outside of himself (or, in some cases, by inward factors over which he has no control). Feelings arise and pass away, and we can neither generate them at will nor banish them at will. Insofar as feelings are in fact aroused in us by states of affairs in the world (including our bodies) then again this points to the inadequacy of thinking of the affects as merely subjective. They are reflections of or responses to objectively occurring events. However, we are not purely at the mercy of external events as to how we feel. We learn to master our moods, at least within limits.

All of these considerations bring us back to the point made by Plato and noted earlier in our discussion, that the feelings (the 'heart' or θύμος) lie somewhere between the blind instinctive processes of the body and the conscious activities of thought and reason, and that the feelings may sometimes operate in the service of the one, sometimes of the other. Thus we think of some feelings as 'primitive,' of others as relatively sophisticated. The former are closer to instinct, the latter to thought and reason. I suppose blind unthinking rage would be an example of the more primitive type of feeling, while respect and moral indignation would illustrate the sophisticated type of feeling. But it is not always easy to make the distinction. Sexuality, for example, can sometimes be primitive, but, as we have seen in an earlier chapter (see above, pp. 85 ff.), a truly human sexuality is no mere bodily instinct but a highly sophisticated existential phenomenon.

In place of such traditional words as *feeling, emotion, affect, passion*, and the like, Heidegger prefers to use the expression *Befindlichkeit*. It is hard to find any satisfactory English equivalent. The English translation of *Sein und Zeit* has 'state of mind' for *Befindlichkeit*; but although this gets the general idea well enough, it fails to bring out the notion of 'finding' implied in the German word. '*Wie befinden Sie sich?*' is the common German expression for 'How are you?' or 'How do you do?' Literally, it means 'How do you find yourself?' *Befindlichkeit* is literally 'the-way-one-finds-oneself.' A feeling or emotion is the way one finds oneself in a given situation. It is the way one is 'tuned in.' The kind of insight, disclosure, or knowing that belongs to the-way-one-finds-oneself is not the objective understanding one has of a thing that is presented to the senses, but neither is it merely subjective. It is an insight into a situation to which the person who finds himself in that situation himself belongs. The expression *situation* is itself a very flexible one. It may refer to some relatively limited group of circumstances, or it may be expanded almost indefinitely. Indignation would normally be a feeling related to some quite specific situation, whereas such a mood as boredom has a vagueness about it and is related to 'things in general.' The question arises whether there may be a mood or feeling (or perhaps more than one) relating to man's total situation in the world. This question will occupy us later in the chapter. For the present we simply note that through the feelings we participate in situations, and that these situations are disclosed or opened up to us in that reciprocal interplay of intention and affection that we have seen to be characteristic of feeling. It is this kind of disclosure that is of interest to the existentialist philosopher, and he includes such disclosures among the data of his philosophizing. In allowing that feeling has this disclosive property, he may permit himself to talk of 'ontological' feeling. To philosophers of the older schools, such an expression might seem to verge on the scandalous. But if indeed we are to philosophize in terms of our total being-in-the-world, then feeling too affords a clue to that circumambient being in which our existing is set.

Some remarks of Paul Ricoeur may be profitably noted at this point. 'Feeling,' he writes, 'is wholly itself only through that consciousness of being already in, through that primordial *inesse.* . . . Whatever being may be, feeling attests that we are part of it: it is not the entirely-other but the medium or primordial space in which we continue to exist.'[3] These sentences summarize very well the ideas we have considered in the last few pages.

We have talked indifferently of feeling (in the singular) and of the feelings, passions, or affects (in the plural). Strictly speaking, feeling is an abstraction. We know only fairly specific feelings. How specific our feelings are may be seen from the fact that ordinary language, at its pre-philosophical and pre-psychological levels, has an extraordinary range of words for describing the range of feelings and the nuances of mood. Fear, alarm, dread, apprehension, consternation, dismay, terror, fright, panic, horror, trepidation are all closely connected feelings; but each word makes its own subtle distinction within the general family of 'fearful' emotions.[4] We have already mentioned 'sensibility' as the characteristic of the emotionally perceptive person, but even in our everyday being-with-another there is considerable measure of sensibility and the ability to discern and describe the varying shades of emotion. Furthermore, it is apparent also that the emotions generally described as 'fear' have close links with others. Shyness, awe, reverence, even Kant's respect, have elements of fear; but this series tends to pass over into admiration. On the other hand, fear, especially as regards its physical basis, is close to anger; here we meet again a whole range of distinctions— rage, fury, indignation, resentment, sullenness, irritation, annoyance, and so on.

To classify the feelings in families and to explore the many subtle differences among them can be no part of our task in this book. We have already noted indeed that some feelings may be classed as 'primitive' and others as 'sophisticated,' but clearly there are much more interesting ways of trying to classify the feelings.

But while we must refrain from any detailed attempt to order the feelings in respect of their affinities and differences, there is a broad kind of distinction that will have some importance for our subsequent discussions. This is the distinction that may be made between 'negative' and 'positive' emotions. By the former I mean such emotions as fear, anger, hate, disgust, and the like. They all disclose situations we are 'already in,' so to speak, but where we do not really belong and we want to extricate ourselves or change the pattern of the situation. By 'positive' emotions I mean, for instance, love, joy, confidence, and the like. They evince a sense of 'belonging' and place a favorable interpretation on the situations that evoke them.

The distinction is important because most existentialists claim that there are some fundamental feelings that are specially disclosive of being, and the question then arises whether these fundamental feelings are of the negative or positive kind. Actually, we get different answers, and in this matter too the division of existentialists into two great camps becomes obvious. For some, such feelings as anxiety, boredom, nausea even, are the primary 'ontological' feelings, and they 'light up' the human condition in its grimmer aspects; man is not 'at home' in the world, which has an uncanny and even threatening character. For others, joy, hope, and what Ricoeur calls the feeling of 'belonging' are important. It should be noted that the difference here is by no means to be equated simply with the difference between an atheistic and a religious existentialism. Anxiety plays a major role in the thought of Kierkegaard, the greatest of the Christian existentialists, while joy is by no means absent from the philosophy of his great atheistic counterpart, Nietzsche. Admittedly, these two are the most paradoxical of all the existentialists. However, they warn us against oversimplifications.

On the whole, it has been 'the tragic sense of life,' as Unamuno called it (*el sentimiento trágico de la vida*), that has been prevalent among the existentialists; and the attempt to redress the balance and to encourage a more hopeful sentiment has come later and is less pronounced. Thus we shall consider first of all anxiety as a fundamental ontological affect, and this is probably most typical of existentialism as a whole. But so that our account may be a fair one, we shall also take note of the different, more positive tendencies to be found in some writers.

ANXIETY

The English word *anxiety* is perhaps the best expression to translate the German *Angst* and its cognates. *Anxiety* is the word used in the English translation of Heidegger's *Sein und Zeit*. It must be acknowledged, however, that it is not altogether a satisfactory translation. It suggests too much day-to-day anxieties of ordinary life rather than the rare and subtle emotion that the existentialists wish to designate by the German word *Angst*. Heidegger's translators remark in a footnote that *uneasiness* or *malaise* would be in some ways more appropriate translations.[5] However, they stay with *anxiety*, and I shall do the same. *Anxiety* is certainly a preferable translation to either *dread* (found in English translations of Kierkegaard) or *anguish* (found in Hazel Barnes' translation of Sartre's *Being and Nothingness*, where indeed the English term does in fact correspond very closely to the French *angoisse*). The objection to 'dread' is that in English usage it suggests something very much like fear, and all the existentialists are agreed that when they talk of *Angst* they do not mean fear. 'Anguish' is better, but in ordinary usage it suggests acute pain; and while anxiety is certainly painful, it is not the notion of pain that is of chief interest in philosophical discussions of *Angst*.

Although I am using one word, *anxiety*, to denote a phenomenon discussed by several existentialist philosophers, we should be clear that the word does not have precisely the same meaning in every writer who uses it. Anxiety (*Angst, angoisse*) is somewhat differently understood by Kierkegaard, Heidegger, and Sartre. However, there is also close kinship among them, and the two later writers explicitly acknowledge the derivation of the idea from Kierkegaard. Heidegger says: 'The man who has gone furthest in analyzing the concept of anxiety . . . is Søren Kierkegaard.'[6] Sartre, contrasting the descriptions of anxiety in Kierkegaard and Heidegger, claims that they 'do not appear to us contradictory; on the contrary, the one implies the other.'[7] He then goes on to expound his own interpretation.

All of these writers are agreed that anxiety is, in a special way, revelatory of the human condition. For Heidegger, it is the *Grundbefindlichkeit*—the basic way in which one finds oneself. To see in anxiety a fundamental clue to the understanding of human existence implies, of course, the phenomenological and existential approach to feeling as outlined in the earlier parts of this chapter, and there distinguished from the psychological and empirical approach to feeling. The discussion of anxiety will serve as an illustration of the existentialist interpretation of feelings generally. It will provide confirmation for the point forcibly made by Sartre in these words: 'For the phenomenologist, every human fact is, in essence, significative. If you remove its signification, you remove its nature as a human fact. The task of a phenomenologist, therefore, will be to study the signification of emotion.'[8] Over against this is another point of view: 'For the psychologist, emotion signifies nothing, because he studies it as a fact, that is, by cutting it away from everything else. Therefore, it will be non-significative from its beginning; but if every human fact is really significative, the emotion studied by the psychologist is, by its nature, dead, non-psychic, inhuman.'[9]

Since the existentialist ideas on anxiety have their provenance in Kierkegaard, it will be appropriate to begin by considering what he said on the subject. His most extended discussion is found in the book known in English as *The Concept of Dread*. This is a difficult book, and the concept that emerges is by no means clearcut. But perhaps this is inevitable, for anxiety has a subtle and elusive character that thought can scarcely grasp.

The notion of anxiety is introduced in the context of a discussion of the origin of sin. What makes sin possible? The discussion is in terms of the Genesis narrative of the fall of man, but Kierkegaard understands this story as one that describes an event or development in the life of every human being—the passage from innocence to sin. What makes this event possible is the prior condition of anxiety. This primordial anxiety is described in at least three ways. 1) It is inherent in the state of innocence. Already in dreaming innocence there is something like an instability, an uneasiness, a presentiment that disturbs the tranquillity of bliss. 'This is the profound secret of innocency, that at the same time it is anxiety.'[10] The illustration that Kierkegaard uses is the awakening of sexuality and of sensuality in the individual. There is a malaise, a premonition that finally issues in the sensual act, and so in the loss of innocence and a changed quality of existence. This is a leap, not to be described analytically but known only in experience. 2) Anxiety is also linked to freedom. Again, it is a kind of instability prior to action. It is described as the 'vertigo' or 'dizziness' of freedom. For freedom means possibility, and to stand on the edge of possibility is rather like standing on the edge of a precipice. To use a different metaphor (it is mine rather than Kierkegaard's, but I think it gets the point), one might say that freedom is by its very nature pregnant with possibility; and it is the stirring of possibility in the womb of freedom that is experienced as the primordial anxiety. 3) Kierkegaard associates anxiety with man's peculiar constitution as body and soul, established in spirit. In the very way he is constituted man is subject to a tension, and this tension is anxiety. The human task is to accomplish the synthesis of body and soul, and this task is from the beginning anxiety-laden. Anxiety is a peculiarly human phenomenon. An animal knows no anxiety, for its life is purely sensual; an angel likewise knows no anxiety, for his life is that of the pure intellect. But man, con-joining sense and reason, body and soul, lives in the shadow of anxiety.

This last point leads us to notice that although up till now we have been thinking of anxiety as the presupposition or precondition for sin, it is also, in Kierkegaard's thought, the effect of sin. For fallen man lives amid ever deepening anxiety. This is not fear, which always relates to some definite state of affairs in the world. Anxiety is not directed to any concrete object but is, as one commentator on Kierkegaard has expressed it, 'a complex of presentiments which, though nothing in themselves, develop themselves by reflecting themselves in themselves.'[11]

This brief summary of Kierkegaard's teaching on anxiety con-firms my remark that his concept is by no means clearcut. Indeed, it may not even be entirely self-consistent. But this untidiness is perhaps inseparable from reflection on the concrete phenomena of existence, and no one will deny the profundity of some of Kierkegaard's in-sights. But a final inconsistency has to be added. Up till now, the idea of anxiety has been presented in a fairly negative way—it is the precondition of sin and also the characteristic of man's fallen existence. Yet, like many later existentialist theologians, Kierke-gaard is willing to assign a positive role to anxiety as a propaedeutic to faith. To endure anxiety is to have one's eyes opened to the reality of the human condition, and so to see the need for grace.

When we turn from Kierkegaard to Heidegger, we find significant differences in the treatment of anxiety. The claim is made, however, that the phenomenon of anxiety offers 'one of the *most far-reaching* and *most primordial* possibilities of disclosure.'[12]

The discussion of anxiety is closely linked to Heidegger's analysis of 'falling' (*Verfallen*), and although this falling is not to be simply identified with traditional ideas of the fall of man, there are (as we shall see later) some connections, and it is significant that Heidegger relates anxiety to falling, just as Kierkegaard had related it to the origin of sin. In Heidegger's view, what happens in falling is that the existent flees from himself. He may lose himself in the inauthentic being-with-others which is called the 'they' or again in the busy-ness of his concerns with the world of things. Yet this very fleeing from itself suggests that the *Dasein* has in some way been already confronted with itself.

The flight connected with falling is quite different from a flight arising from fear. Fear is always fear of some definite being within the world. But what we are concerned with now is flight from oneself. 'That in the face of which one has anxiety is being-in-the-world as such.'[13] Again, he says: 'That in the face of which one is anxious is completely indefinite. Not only does this indefiniteness leave factically undecided which entity within the world is threatening us, but it also tells us that entities within the world are not "relevant" at all. Nothing which is ready-to-hand or present-at-hand within the world functions as that in the face of which anxiety is anxious.'[14]

Thus we do not know what makes us anxious and we cannot point to anything. That which arouses anxiety is nothing, and it is nowhere. Yet also, we are told, it is so close as to be oppressive and stifling. It is not this or that particular thing, but rather the world, or being-in-the-world. Thus the mood of anxiety offers something like a total disclosure of the human condition.

Heidegger also declares that in anxiety the entities within the world tend to 'sink away.' The existent understands that he cannot find himself in the world, and he is thrown back upon himself in his unique freedom and possibility. 'Anxiety brings *Dasein* face to face with its *being-free-for* (*propensio in* . . .) the authenticity of its being.'[15] In our everyday being-in-the-world and being-with-others we are able to tranquilize ourselves and escape the radicalness of the human condition. But anxiety jerks us out of these pseudo-securities. We are made to feel 'uncanny' and 'not at home.'

In subsequent analyses Heidegger relates anxiety to the notions of finitude and death, but for the present we shall not pursue these themes. We do note, however, that just as Kierkegaard saw anxiety as a propaedeutic to faith, so it seems to receive a positive evaluation in Heidegger. Anxiety awakens us from our illusions and false securities. It confronts the individual with his responsibility and the call to grasp his authentic being. It is said, indeed, to be a rare phenomenon in human experience, because it is for the most part quenched and kept under by the evasive flight from ourselves, characteristic of falling. But though rare, the pure ontological anxiety is of first-class importance, and it is through their exposure to it that men are summoned out of falling into authentic existence.

Very closely connected with anxiety in Heidegger's analysis is the phenomenon of care (*Sorge*). This is one of the broadest characteristics of human life; it is a life of care and a life of caring (the ambiguities of the word and of its Latin equivalent, *cura*, are deliberately exploited in Heidegger's discussion). Care is a complex phenomenon. It involves the forward thrust of the existent into his possibilities in tension with the factical conditions and limitations that he already brings with him, and to these are added his present 'falling.' The Heideggerian understanding of care as the structure of man's everyday being-in-the-world seems to me to correspond roughly to the Kierkegaardian thought of anxiety as the constantly deepening and proliferating accompaniment of the fallen life.

'Kierkegaard describing anxiety in the face of what one lacks characterizes it as anxiety in the face of freedom. But Heidegger . . . considers anxiety instead as the apprehension of nothingness.'[16] So Sartre distinguishes between the two accounts of anxiety that we have just outlined, though, as we have already noted, he considers these accounts to be complementary rather than contradictory. Sartre's judgment of the difference is, I think, substantially correct. Kierkegaard stresses freedom in his view of anxiety, though not omitting finitude; Heidegger stresses finitude, though not oblivious to freedom. It will now be useful to consider Sartre's account of the matter and see whether he succeeds in accomplishing any synthesis.

His analysis is in fact conducted in terms of a subtle dialectic between freedom and nothingness. He begins with Kierkegaard's idea of anxiety as the vertigo of freedom. This is not fear, which has to do with something happening to me from outside. Anxiety arises rather because 'I distrust myself and my own reactions.'[17] In other words, there is a profound ambiguity in freedom—hence the paradoxical expression that we are *condemned* to be free. A nothingness slips into my action. I am not the self that I will be, or I am it in the mode of not being it. 'Anxiety is precisely my consciousness of being my own future, in the mode of not-being.'[18]

This is anxiety in the face of the future, and there is a corresponding anxiety in the face of the past. 'It is that of the gambler who has freely and sincerely decided not to gamble any more and who, when he approaches the gaming table, suddenly sees all his resolutions melt away.'[19]

Freedom, then, is by no means a simple freedom, but one that is 'instigated and bound by nothing.' It is in the exercise of this freedom that I experience anxiety. I can avoid anxiety by seeking refuge in conventional patterns of action and conventional scales of value, but I do this only at the price of falling into 'bad faith.' Like Kierkegaard and Heidegger, Sartre sees anxiety as something to be endured, not evaded.

These analyses of anxiety all see in it a clue to the being of man, and this being is moreover revealed as essentially paradoxical, if not absurd. At the very center of existence is an unresolved tension between freedom with its possibilities and finitude with its restrictions and its threat of nihilation. Unless we face this fundamental irrationality of the human condition, these thinkers would tell us, we are evading the truth of our own being.

Are we to accept this reading of human existence? Can anxiety be given the key role that is assigned to it by existentialist thinkers? Does not the granting of such a role commit us to an essentially tragic and even pessimistic understanding of man and the world? Before we can answer these questions, we must see whether there are alternatives to anxiety as the basic affect.

There is an interesting passage in Heidegger's *Introduction to Metaphysics*. Talking of the question of being and claiming that 'each of us is grazed at least once, perhaps more than once, by the hidden power of this question,' he goes on to say:

> The question looms in moments of great despair, when things tend to lose all their weight and all meaning becomes obscured.... It is present in moments of rejoicing, when all the things around us are transfigured and seem to be there for the first time, as if it might be easier to think they are not than to understand that they are and as they are. The question is upon us in boredom, when we are equally removed from despair and joy, and everything about us seems so hopelessly commonplace that we no longer care whether anything is or is not.[20]

The passage is interesting because alongside the mood of anxiety in which everything sinks to nothing, Heidegger seems willing to admit two other moods having ontological significance—boredom and joy.

Boredom had been already discussed by Kierkegaard in connection with the esthetic stage of life, and he saw this mood as one that leads to a radical questioning of the meaning and value of life. However, we shall not pursue the question of boredom, for this, like anxiety, is a negative mood, or at least an indifferent one.

More interesting is the possibility that joy may be considered an ontological affect. For if joy is our clue to the way things are, our privileged participation in being, whereby being is disclosed to us, then does not this contradict the view that anxiety is the 'basic way in which one finds oneself' (*Grundbefindlichkeit*) and is not this conflict one that can hardly be resolved?

We may illustrate the nature of the conflict by pointing to a sharp contrast between Heidegger and Ricoeur. Heidegger, as we have seen, is willing to assign an ontological dimension to the feeling of joy, but he clearly attributes primacy among the affects to anxiety. If we do feel at home in the world and have a sense of belonging, then this is not primary. 'That kind of being-in-the-world which is tranquilized and familiar is a mode of *Dasein's* uncanniness, not the reverse. From an existential-ontological point of view, the "not-at-home" must be conceived as the more primordial phenomenon.'[21] But Ricoeur turns the argument the other way round. He wishes to claim that joy and the feelings of belonging are primary. He writes:

If being is that which beings are not, anxiety (*angoisse*) is the feeling *par excellence* of ontological difference. But joy attests that we have a part of us linked to this very lack of being in beings. That is why the spiritual joy, the intellectual love and the beatitude, spoken of by Descartes, Malebranche, Spinoza and Bergson, designate, under different names and in different philosophical contexts, the only affective 'mood' worthy of being called *ontological*. Anxiety is only its underside of absence and distance.[22]

Here we appear to witness something like a head-on collision. Heidegger takes anxiety to be the basic ontological mood, with feelings of being 'at home' secondary and even illusory. Ricoeur sees joy as the primary, even the only, *ontological* mood, with anxiety its derivative.

Is there any way of resolving the difference or of deciding between the opposing points of view? Or is it perhaps finally just how one feels about things? We would be reluctant to accept this second possibility, after all we have said about the disclosive power of feeling and that we are dealing with more than just arbitrary and subjective states of mind.

It will not do either to say that the positive emotions have primacy over the negative ones, for this would simply beg the question. The point at issue is whether being or reality has such a character as would inspire positive emotions of joy, hope, belonging, the sense of affinity and being at home, and the like; or whether it is so alien that the most basic clue to its character is anxiety or the indifference of boredom or perhaps even the nausea of which Sartre has so brilliantly written in the novel *La Nausée*.

Ricoeur provides a possible clue in the course of his discussion. He asks: 'Does not the clash of anxiety and beatitude argue against the very idea of ontological feeling?' And he replies: 'Perhaps this clash has no further import than the distinction between the *via negativa* and the *via analogiae* in the speculation on being.'[23] We may remember at this point how traditional religious language has spoken both negatively and positively about God. It has recognized his wrath and his otherness as well as his love and his closeness. At least there may be a possible solution along such lines. On the other hand, it may be that there is a fundamental ambiguity and even a dualism in being itself—and we shall find that the atheistic existentialists come very close to dualism. However, the further discussion of these difficult problems must be deferred until the chapter on existentialist metaphysics (see below, p. 190 ff). For the present, it is enough that we have seen how the existentialists have developed a new and interesting approach to the problem of the feelings, and how they have sought to incorporate these existential phenomena into their total philosophy.

CHAPTER NINE

Action

THE EXISTENT AS AGENT

After two chapters on the intellect and one on the feelings, the time honored division of man's psychical life into intellection, affection, and volition would seem to call for a chapter on will and action. We have already indicated, however, that the old-fashioned faculty psychology has no significance for existentialism. Man exists as a whole. He cannot be pieced together from thought, feeling, and will. These are abstractions from the whole. It would also be absurd to suppose that one can first form a picture of the human existent, and then let the existent get into action; for the very conception of man in existentialism turns away from all static ideas and sees him in action from the first. At an early stage in this book it was indicated that the existentialists agree with John Macmurray's view of the self as agent rather than with the traditional understanding of the self as subject (see above, p. 94). Sixty years before Macmurray another philosopher of existentialist tendency, Maurice Blondel, had made action his central category; and in his book *L'Action* Blondel had worked out a new dialectic in which the comprehensive category of action embraces but certainly does not abolish thought. Thus, in the present chapter we are not bringing in a new dimension of existence in addition to those already explored. We are simply aiming to make more explicit the understanding of the existent as agent, an understanding that has been present to the whole argument up till now. We are not being so naive as to suppose that man's inner life can be neatly divided into thinking, feeling, and willing. Rather, we see action as an inclusive concept, by considering which we shall gain a clearer understanding of many of the matters already discussed in greater or less degrees of isolation.

We can find more justification for placing this chapter in the position assigned to it by recalling Kierkegaard's teaching about the stages of life (see especially *Either/Or* and *Stages on Life's Way*). The stages are not really stages but progressive deepenings of life, in which what went before is taken up into a richer texture. It will be remembered that in Kierkegaard's scheme the ethical stage or life of action comes after the esthetic stage, which is primarily the stage of feeling and enjoyment. A passage from his *Journals* expresses in autobiographical form something like the transition from the esthetic to the ethical:

> I have looked in vain for an anchorage in the boundless sea of pleasure and in the depth of understanding; I have felt the almost irresistible power with which one pleasure reaches out its hand to the next; I have felt the sort of meretricious ecstasy that it is capable of producing, but also the *ennui* and the distracted state of mind that succeeds it. I have tasted the fruit of the tree of knowledge and often delighted in its taste. But the pleasure did not outlast the moment of understanding and left no profound mark on me.[1]

As against the certain aimlessness of the life described in these sentences, he has this to say:

> What I really lack is to be clear in my mind *what I am to do.* . . . What would be the use of discovering so-called objective truth, of working through all the systems of philosophy and of being able, if required, to review them all and show up the inconsistencies within each system; what good would it do me to be able to develop a theory of the state and combine all the details into a single whole, and so construct a world in which I did not live, but only held up to the view of others; what good would it do me to be able to explain the meaning of Christianity if it had no deeper significance *for me and for my life*; what good would it do me if truth stood before me, cold and naked, not caring whether I recognized her or not, and producing in me a shudder of fear rather than a trusting devotion?[2]

The existentialist, then, insists on action, for only in action does existence attain concreteness and fullness. However, it is clear from the quotations taken from Kierkegaard (and the same point could be established for the other leading existentialists) that action is not mere function or mere activism. For the existentialist, action properly so-called is intensely personal and involves the whole man. It includes both thought and passion. Were thought, passion, and inward decision lacking, there would be nothing worthy of the name of action. Thus, in spite of the premium that the existentialist places upon action, existentialism is not the same as pragmatism. Action is not to be identified with the outer act, nor is it to be measured in terms of the 'success' of such an act (see above, p. 16).

If there is a sense in which it would be true to say, from an existentialist point of view, that man is what he does, this sense is certainly very different from the understanding of man sometimes denoted by the expression *functional man*. It is true that both this conception and the existentialist one attempt to get away from substantial and static categories to ways of thinking that are more dynamic and more appropriate to man as a living, changing being. But the notion of functional man must be judged hopelessly abstract, and presumably it could be nothing else, in view of its origin in empirical sociology. Man is more than the tasks he performs and the roles he plays. He is the unity of a *person* who *expresses himself* in all these activities or, perhaps better expressed, *makes himself* in these activities His actions are more than empirically observable deeds, for in them he is both projecting and realizing an image of personhood.

Few thinkers of recent times have taught a more consistently dynamic view of man than has Gabriel Marcel, yet he has also been the most relentless critic of the 'functional man.' 'The dynamic element in my philosophy,' he has written, 'taken as a whole, can be seen as an obstinate and untiring battle against the spirit of abstraction.'[3] Functional man, reduced to a factor in the empirical social reality, is deprived of mystery, dignity, personhood, and eventually of humanity itself. The overcoming of this error is to be accomplished not by trying to go back to a static view of man but by developing a richer and more adequate understanding of what human action is. If man is fundamentally the existent, the one who goes out from himself and transcends himself, then action is to be understood in terms of this mystery of self-transcendence. Man is not merely functional man, he is better described as *homo viator*. (This title of a book of Marcel's essays is peculiarly expressive of his understanding of the human condition.)

The reluctance of some existentialists to use such traditional words as *will* in the description of human action is, I suspect, due at least in part to the danger that such an expression will suggest the abstraction of a *tertium quid* which gets added to thought and feeling.

Action is not an abstraction of this kind. In action properly so-called, the whole man acts, and therefore the concept of action embraces within itself the whole mystery of human existence.

FREEDOM

Action implies freedom, and there can be few themes, if any, nearer to the heart of existentialism than freedom. The theme is present in all the existentialist writers. It is prominent in Kierkegaard, for whom to exist and to be free are almost synonymous expressions. The interest in freedom, or rather the passion for freedom, is not confined to any particular variety of existentialist. Surely two of the greatest apostles of freedom in the 20th century have been the atheists Sartre and Camus, for the atheism of existentialism is very different from that deterministic atheism that flourished in the 19th century. Sartre is just as insistent as Kierkegaard that freedom and existence are indistinguishable. One does not first exist and then become free; rather, to be human is already to be free.

However, it is in their discussion of freedom that the existentialists become most elusive. We know, of course, that existentialists generally are agreed that the human reality outstrips the power of analytic thought and bursts out of imprisoning categories. If we are genuinely open to the fluid dynamic reality that we call *existence*, then our accounts of it will always be untidy and incomplete. Nowhere is this more true than when we try to talk of freedom. And although we have cited both Kierkegaard and Sartre for the view that human existence and freedom are one and the same, this identification does not deliver us from the attempt to deal specifically with the problem of freedom. It may be rhetorically permissible to identify freedom and existence, but for philosophy the problem is to clarify the distinction implicit in the use of these terms.

But how can we talk at all of freedom or try to conceptualize it? However we try to grasp it, it seems to elude us. However precious we may esteem it, by its very nature it is insubstantial and fleeting. Thus, for Sartre it is established by an act of negating—the negating of the in-itself of being, so that there may come into existence the fragile freedom of the for-itself, which is precisely without being and in search of being.

Rather than attempt to extract a concept of freedom, however untidy, from existentialist philosophy at large, I shall concentrate attention on the reflections of one writer in particular. The choice is Nikolai Berdyaev, whose thoughts on freedom seem to me to have been especially profound and perceptive. I shall draw chiefly on the section entitled 'Freedom' in *Christian Existentialism*, Donald A. Lowrie's excellent, quasi-systematic anthology of Berdyaev's work.[4]

Berdyaev is voicing the opinion of existentialists in general when he turns away from traditional arguments to establish the freedom of the will. 'The question is not at all that of freedom of the will, as this is usually stated in naturalistic, psychological or pedagogical-moralistic usage.' The difficulty in these traditional arguments was that they attempted to objectify freedom, to treat it as an object that could somehow be perceived, investigated, and either proved or disproved from the outside. For the existentialist (as for Kant) freedom is not to be proved, but is rather a postulate of action. It is already there as a condition of our existing (including our thinking). 'To understand an act of freedom rationally is to make it resemble the phenomena of nature.' But such phenomena belong to a 'secondary' world. Freedom must be already there before we can even think of such a world.

In speaking of this freedom that is prior to the phenomenal world, Berdyaev's language becomes metaphysical and even mystical. Yet surely he is right in seeing freedom as itself a mystery, so that one can speak of it only in some such language as he uses. To stress the priority of freedom he often says that freedom has the primacy over being. Such language is paradoxical, but it makes sense in the context of Berdyaev's philosophy.

> An ontological system recognizing the absolute primacy of being is a system of determinism. Every objectivized intellectual system is one of determinism. It derives freedom from being; it appears that freedom is determined by being, which in the last analysis means that freedom is the child of necessity. Being is thus ideal necessity, with no possibility of outburst; it is complete and absolute unity. But freedom cannot be derived from being; it is rooted in nothingness, in non-being, if we are to use ontological terminology. Freedom is baseless, neither determined by nor born of being.

He can also say that freedom 'proceeds from the abyss which preceded being . . . the act of freedom is primordial and completely irrational.'

Of course, some of the words used in the sentences quoted are notoriously ambiguous—*being* and *rational* are obvious examples. But allowing for that fact, we can acknowledge that Berdyaev is going to the root of the mystery of freedom. Freedom is indeed 'meontic,' a nothing rather than a something, a possibility rather than an actuality. It cannot be grasped by thought but only known through the exercise of freedom; and perhaps even then it is only in those rare moments of the experience of anxiety in the face of freedom that we perceive something of that abyssal and primordial character of freedom so much stressed by Berdyaev.

However, although Berdyaev's emphasis is on the primal and irrational (perhaps one should better say prerational) nature of freedom, he introduces another notion that helps to correct the tendency to represent freedom as utterly arbitrary. He reminds us that St. Augustine spoke of two freedoms, which he designated respectively *libertas major* and *libertas minor*. 'And in truth,' writes Berdyaev, 'we see at once that freedom has two different meanings. By freedom is meant either the primordial irrational freedom which precedes good and evil and determines choice between them, or the final, reasonable freedom, freedom in good and truth, which is to say that freedom is understood both as the starting point and the way, and also as the end and the aim.' This distinction between the freedom that is prior to action and the freedom that is subsequent to it can hardly fail to remind us of the very similar distinction that we met in Kierkegaard and some other thinkers between the primordial anxiety that comes before the exercise of freedom and the subsequent anxiety or care that accompanies man throughout his life.

Furthermore, just as anxiety was linked to the problems of sin and evil, so is freedom. For freedom is in itself an ambiguous phenomenon. As Berdyaev sees it, freedom (in both its forms) is involved in a dialectic whereby it can easily pass over into its opposite. The primordial freedom can pass over into anarchy. 'It gives rise to the tragedy of the world process.' The second freedom has also its dialectic. It can lead to 'compulsion and force in truth and good, to forced virtue, to a tyrannical organization of human life.' Even Christianity, which ought to enable the highest freedom, has constantly been tempted to deny or pervert it. Freedom seems to contain in itself the seed of its own destruction, so that the mystery of the origin of freedom runs together with the mystery of the origin of evil. 'The tragedy of the world process is that of freedom; it is born of the inner dynamic of freedom, of its capacity of changing into its opposite.' In striking this tragic note, Berdyaev is of course at one with many of his fellow existentialists.

But even if freedom has its inevitable risk and tragedy, Berdyaev and the other existentialists are passionately insistent that freedom is to be preserved and increased. And the reason for this is clear.

If freedom is almost identical with existence itself, there is no humanity without freedom. Freedom may be dangerous, but there is no human dignity without freedom, and the risk of increasing freedom must constantly be taken. Berdyaev rightly links freedom with creativity. The highest reach of humanity is creativity, a sharing in the power of God the Creator. 'Creativity is the mystery of freedom. Man can indeed create the monstrous as well as the good, the beautiful, and the useful.' But again, despite the risk, his creativity must be given scope as that in man which is distinctively human and in the free exercise of which the self-transcendence of the existent takes place.

These remarks bring us to the question of political freedom. Camus' book *The Rebel* is perhaps the great existentialist manifesto in this regard and one of the most sensitive and perceptive analyses of the modern West that can be found. But Berdyaev shares the same passionate spirit of rebellion against everything that diminishes human life. 'Freedom needs resistance and struggle. . . . The ancient taboos surround man on every side, cramp his moral life. And to liberate himself from their power, man must feel himself inwardly free, and only then can he struggle externally for freedom.' And the goal of this struggle is the creativity that is truly human. 'Man's liberation is not only *from* something, but *for* something. And this *"for"* is man's creativity.'

In spite of his passion for freedom (or, some would say, because of it), Berdyaev reveals that aristocratic sympathy that runs through the existentialists generally. The masses, he claims, do not value. freedom. They are content with the routine patterns of existence. For this reason they are peculiarly exposed to the dangers of dictatorship, founded on demagogy. 'Education to freedom is something still ahead of us, and this will not be achieved in a hurry.'

Although I have based this exposition of the existentialist understanding of freedom almost entirely on the work of Berdyaev, I think it would be fair to say that he gives a specially eloquent presentation of a position that is shared by most of the existentialist philosophers. I should add that in order that the exposition might be as widely representative of existentialism as possible, I have deliberately omitted Berdyaev's teaching about the relation of freedom and Christianity (except for one brief reference). For in this matter of freedom, as in so many others that have come to our notice, there is finally a parting of the ways among the existentialists. All acknowledge the risk and tragedy of freedom, and all cherish freedom. But for the atheists among them, tragedy and even absurdity have the last word, whereas the Christian existentialists believe that hope and creativity will prove stronger than the negative forces. We shall have to face the significance of this conflict, but for the present we simply note once more that the conflict is there.

Existentialist writings abound in allusions to decision, choice, commitment, engagement, resoluteness, and the like. We may say that these are the existential phenomena in which action and freedom are brought most sharply and intensely into focus. If we found it necessary to reject or at least to qualify profoundly the idea that a man is his deeds, for fear that this might be misunderstood as the abstraction of functional man, we might agree that there would be less objection to saying that a man is his decisions, for this notion of decision certainly includes the inwardness and the pathos of action.

I deliberately mention the pathos of action, for decision is never simply self-fulfillment. It is also self-renunciation. To decide for one possibility is *ipso facto* to renounce every other possibility that was open in the situation. Thus we strike once more against the tragic element in human existence. For the existentialist the human existent does not fulfill himself by, let us say, a gradual expansion of his capacities and an enlargement of his powers over a broad front. He fulfills himself rather by decisions that may be painful because of what they cut out of his life. In other words, the stress on decision means a corresponding stress on the intensiveness of life rather than its extensiveness. Every decision is a decision against as well as a decision for; and every decision limits the range of possibilities that will be open for future decision.

Decision brings the existent face to face with himself in a way that must stir anxiety. Thus most of us hate to make decisions of any magnitude. We avoid them or we postpone them as long as we can. For if to decide is on the one hand to thrust forward into a new level of existence, it is on the other hand to take the risk of cutting oneself off from the other possibilities that were open. It is to pledge or engage one's future, and since no one can foresee the future, such an engagement is always freighted with risk and attended by anxiety.

In *Either/Or* Kierkegaard explores the nature of decision with special reference to three cases that are familiar to most people— marriage, friendship, and vocation. Unlike the many trivial decisions that we make from day to day, the three cases mentioned have lasting consequences for the whole life of the individual who makes the choices.

Marriage—and Kierkegaard, of course, is thinking of the Christian conception of marriage—is a lifelong union of two persons who commit themselves to each other 'for better or for worse,' a relationship that utterly transcends any temporary mood or infatuation. But whether this relationship can be realized must still remain in doubt at the time the commitment is made. Kierkegaard's own inability to go through with his marriage to Regina Olsen is perhaps the best commentary on the seriousness of the existential choice involved in marriage—though we may remember that Kierkegaard's breaking of his engagement was due to his making what he took to be a still more serious commitment.

Friendship, as Kierkegaard understands it, is again a permanent relationship. A friend is different from a chance acquaintance, however pleasant and agreeable the latter may be. A friend must be chosen, and the number of friends must be limited, for we can form relationships in depth with only a small number of people. Again, we see that decision for must also be decision against. We may know a large number of highly attractive and agreeable people, but as far as true friendship in depth is concerned, we must choose only a very few from this large number.

In Kierkegaard's own case, it was his vocation that demanded of him the most serious and anxiety-laden decision of all. (Later we shall have to ask about the morality of such decisions, but we leave this aside for the present.) In deciding to respond to the peculiar destiny that, as he believed, God had marked out for him, Kierkegaard had also to decide to renounce the possibility of marriage. His was a particularly poignant case, yet any serious vocational decision presents similar issues. To choose a vocation is at the same time to renounce a great many other possibilities.

It is true that nowadays the seriousness of decision of which Kierkegaard wrote will scarcely be understood by many people. The Christian ideal of marriage has been rejected by many, and thus the decision to marry loses its seriousness if there is the implicit provision that a change of partners may be effected after a few years. Whether friendship has so greatly deteriorated is doubtful, though possibly the mobility of modern society makes more difficult the development of permanent friendships at the deeper levels. The ideal of lifelong vocation is probably the one that has declined most. The changing of jobs and the need to retrain for new jobs has become part of the modern economy. Even the religious life is thought by some nowadays to be something in which one might engage for a time, rather than take lifelong vows. Kierkegaard, of course, makes a distinction between a mere job and a vocation. But this may once again reflect an aristocratic tendency in existentialism that is not particularly relevant to an age of mass-existence (whether we like such mass-existence or not). For in such an age the kind of choices of which Kierkegaard wrote just may not be possible for the great bulk of mankind.

Let us agree that there is a dilemma here. The seriousness of decision as we learn about it in Kierkegaard must rightly be considered as belonging to the most human core of our existence—the most profound, the most tragic, the most glorious. But whether Kierkegaard's treatment of these themes is relevant to changed social conditions is doubtful. To say this is not necessarily to be critical of Kierkegaard. One might rather be critical of the kind of society in which existential seriousness has apparently diminished.

Yet the matter cannot be left there. Perhaps there are new areas of existential seriousness today. Are people making decisions, just as binding, permanent, and anxiety-laden, in matters other than marriage, friendship, vocation? Or has the notion of the 'permanent' commitment, so prominent in Kierkegaard, declined, so that we live now in the era of the provisional and the pragmatic? Is total or permanent commitment something *passé*? It is important, however, that we should not be misled by Kierkegaard's stress on permanence. He does indeed wish to make the point that an important decision or commitment engages us well beyond the moment in which it is made and has to be maintained through changing circumstances and changing emotional states. But he does not for a moment think that this decision is taken once and for all and that the initial anxiety of the decision can then be left behind. On the contrary, the decision has to be continually reaffirmed in the continually changing situations of life, and these new decisions (or reaffirmations of the original decisions) will be just as serious and anxiety-laden as the original decision itself. Perhaps they may be even more so, for one will have deepened one's understanding of what that original decision involves.

Of course, no decision worthy of the name could be purely provisional in the sense that we can simply drop it if it has become inconvenient. It is of the very nature of decision that it implies some kind of leap, as Kierkegaard called it—a leap beyond the immediate situation so that we have committed ourselves for circumstances that have not yet become clear. Marcel and Sartre use the expression *engagement*. It is man's very nature to 'engage' himself, to pledge himself for the future. He makes promises, he supports policies, he marries, he makes friends, and so on. Marcel sees fidelity as a basic human virtue, making genuine community possible.

In the long run, however, what is really chosen is *oneself*. It is out of its decisions that the self emerges. A self is not given ready-made at the beginning. What is given is a field of possibility, and as the existent projects himself into this possibility rather than that one, he begins to determine who he shall be. It is in this context that the question of permanence versus provisionality must be considered. A unitary self, as distinct from a series of unconnected acts, can emerge only if there is a constancy of policies and commitments. Fidelity and loyalty are due not only to others but to that image of humanity that one is seeking to realize in actual existence. On the other hand, there are times when loyalty degenerates into mere stubbornness or even fanaticism. A man may make a firm and permanent vocational commitment, let us say; yet as a rational being he must remain open to the possibility that he will some day see things differently. We must remember too that the full content of the commitment is not grasped at the beginning but only unfolds itself as one engages with it. Thus, it would be possible to visualize that a person might commit himself permanently and sincerely to the religious life, and yet, in the light of subsequent experience and changing theological emphases, he might finally decide that his vocation lies elsewhere. In such a case, however, it would still be a question whether he had abandoned the fundamental commitment or whether he supposed that he had found a better way of implementing it. A simpler case would be that of someone who made a vocational commitment that because of circumstances had to be superseded. One thinks of a young man who decided to devote his life to fighting the once dreadful scourge of tuberculosis. But in a few years the disease in question had been pretty well brought under control, and he had to look for a new field for his talents. But although the direction of his work shifted, the basic commitment to the cause of health remained.

The cases we have mentioned have brought us to the borderline of ethics, and we shall have to pay fuller attention to these matters in subsequent discussions.

The emphasis placed on decision often leads the existentialists to a corresponding depreciation of action in which the element of conscious, even agonizing, decision is not apparent. Habit and custom, traditional and routine ways of doing things, are criticized as falling below the level of truly human action. Again, this type of criticism goes back to Kierkegaard. What specially angered him was to see Christianity itself reduced to a conventional institution. It had been absorbed into the folk customs, so that to become a Christian was commonly understood to mean that one had been baptized in infancy, grown up in the Church, been confirmed at the appropriate age, and so on. This conventionalized Christianity—or 'Christendom,' as Kierkegaard called it—he regarded as an apostasy, for it took away all true decision and all the anxiety and deep seriousness of the leap of faith. Later existentialists have criticized in a similar fashion the pressures of the mass society that through the press, advertising, television, and so on, molds the lives of people in stereotyped ways and produces a world of conformists, made to pattern. In such a world the very possibility of choice and decision is almost taken away. The decisions have already been made for us, and all we are expected to do is to conform to them and so reinforce them. In this situation the existentialist calls for a radical awakening and conversion. The first thing to do is simply to choose choice, to exercise the power of decision that has been so seriously eroded. Not so much the content of the decision as simply its quality as a personal act, fully and intensely appropriated by the agent, is what matters.

That this demand for responsible personal decision in the face of all the influences that militate against it and that make for a mindless conformity has considerable justification, no one will deny. At the same time there can be an existentialist excess in these matters. There is a place for habit, custom, and tradition. These need not be deadening influences if they are intelligently taken over and applied. No doubt I do act in 'bad faith' when I deliberately avoid facing an honest decision and follow the conventional pattern of behavior in order to be spared the anxiety that comes when one is, in Kierkegaard's famous phrase, thrown into seventy thousand fathoms. But it would be absurdly romanticist and individualist to suppose that one must be always agonizing over decisions or to hold that only something done as the result of a fully conscious and intense decision can be reckoned as a truly human action. The individual accumulates some wisdom as he goes along, and he will surely acknowledge that the community has a wisdom too, embodied in its rules and customs.

Action should not be defined too narrowly and the existentialist view of action easily becomes exaggerated. But, apart from such exaggerations, we can acknowledge that it is in action, including thought, freedom, and decision, that man is most truly and fully himself.

CHAPTER TEN

Finitude and Guilt

THE FACTICITY OF EXISTENCE

The last chapter, gathering together some of the earlier analyses, has suggested that we see the full dimensions of a human existence when we consider man in action; and stress was laid on such positive characteristics as freedom, creativity, and the power of choice. But this positive characterization has taken place against a more somber foil, at which we have hinted from time to time, and we have not been left unaware of a tragic element intertwined in the very roots of existence. Whether or not we accept that anxiety is the most fundamental of the affects, it cannot be denied that it is a very important one at least. We have seen that anxiety accompanies the exercise of freedom, and that even acts of decision, where man seems most free and creative and responsible for his destiny, have their negative and tragic aspects.

Human freedom is never an absolute freedom. It is hedged about and limited in innumerable ways. Tragedy has been defined in various ways. One of the many ways of defining tragedy sees it as a clash between the aspirations of human freedom and creativity with a cosmic order that is stronger and defeats man. Tragedy and limitation are part of what it means to be human, and the time has come to consider these notions more closely and to integrate them into that understanding of human existence developed in the preceding pages.

Existentialists use the word *facticity* to designate the limiting factor in existence. *Facticity* (the word has been coined to translate the German *Faktizität* and French *facticité*) does not mean the same as *factuality*. When we say that something is factual we are pointing to an objective state of affairs observable in the world. Facticity, on the other hand, might be called the inner side of factuality. It is not an observed state of affairs but the inward, existential awareness of one's own being as a fact that is to be accepted. No one has chosen to be. He simply finds himself in existence. We discover ourselves, so to speak, as free existents in the midst of a world of things. We did not put ourselves in that world. There is almost surprise, even shock, that we find ourselves there as a fact to be reckoned with. As Austin Farrer once expressed it: 'The loneliness of personality in the universe weighs heavily upon us. To put it somewhat quaintly, it seems terribly improbable that we should exist.'[1]

The factical is the given, and above all, the givenness of our existence. That *we are here* is, if you like, an inexplicable brute fact. Man has indeed formed beliefs about his origin and his destiny, or has claimed to have received revelations concerning them. Some of the beliefs may be true and some of the revelations may be valid, but these are matters of faith. The only thing we *know* beyond doubt is that we *are*. Where we have come from or where we are going remains a mystery. We may have our beliefs or aspirations, but the plain given fact is simply that we are and have to be.

However, it is not just human existence in general that is a factical given. My existence, your existence, his existence, her existence are in each case characterized by facticity. We may recall from the introductory discussion of the concept of existence that a basic characteristic of it is 'mineness' (see above, p. 51). I discover not just that I exist, but that I exist as this particular 'I.' I cannot exchange my existence for the existence of another. I am I. This sentence is no doubt a tautology, yet it also expresses a mystery— the inexplicable fact that I just happen to be this particular person and no other. I have this particular body; I am of this particular race and color; I have this particular heredity, this particular intelligence quotient, this particular emotional make-up, and so on. Futhermore, I have been born into this particular historical situation in this particular society, and all kinds of forces are operating in the situation and in the society to shape my life and to limit what I can become. The decisions of people whom I never knew and who never knew me —decisions taken, perhaps, long ago—are shaping events in which I am today being caught up. And when I begin to take decisions myself in such limited areas as are open to me, then each decision determines, to some extent, what choices will remain open in the future.

Facticity may be considered as the opposite to possibility. In earlier chapters, we have been mainly concerned with possibility, with the open horizons of being into which the existent projects himself. But the horizon is never an unlimited one, and there is never an absolutely open future. I never start from scratch, nor do I ever have before me a *tabula rasa*. I am always already in a situation, bringing to it capacities that are already fixed within fairly narrow limits. Thus, when one speaks of possibility, one must have in mind factical possibility. There are no free-floating possibilities, or possibilities that exist in a vacuum, if one may so speak. Possibilities occur only in actual situations, and this is to say that they are already limited by the situational element. The expression that 'politics is the art of the possible' is a recognition of the limits of possible action in a given situation; but one might equally well say that existence is the art of the possible.

Martin Heidegger has used the expression *thrownness* (*Geworfenheit*) as a somewhat vivid metaphor for man's factical condition. Man is thrown into existence, each one is thrown into his own particular existential situation. From the human point of view, it is rather like the throw of a dice. Just as you may throw a three or a six, so in life you may come up American or Vietnamese, white or black, affluent or destitute, ill-natured or good-natured, intelligent or stupid. There is no known reason why the throw should be one way rather than another. (This is not to say that there may not be some reason; perhaps there is a divine providence that determines these matters, but this is an article of faith, not something that can be shown philosophically.) As we see it from the purely human point of view, we all start out as different people with different endowments in different situations, and there is as little assignable reason for the differences as there is for the dice turning up one number rather than another.

Human possibilities, therefore, whether we are thinking of the human race as a whole or of individual existents, are always set in a framework of facticity. This framework may vary considerably. In some cases it is a very broad framework, allowing a wide range of choice. In other cases it is so narrow as to be stifling. But it is always there, and it always holds the threat of tragedy and the frustrating of possibility.

Existence never escapes from the tension between possibility and facticity. On the one side man is open and projects his possibilities;

on the other side he is closed by the factual situation in which he already finds himself. Understanding and imagination open up to us the field of possibility; the affects disclose to us the already prevailing situation. The tension is experienced in all kinds of ways. The rational will directs itself upon a worthwhile goal; but irrational appetite supervenes to divert us elsewhere. To quote Austin Farrer again: 'Choice is exercised by us, appetite comes upon us.'[2]

Facticity makes plain to us the radical finitude of human existence. Finitude can be described in various ways, and in later parts of this chapter we shall consider some of the most significant aspects of human finitude. Facticity, however, is one basic way of describing finitude. To exist factically is to be there, that is to say, to occupy a particular situation and to see everything from the perspective of that situation. We have already taken note that in virtue of being a body, man has a particular situation and viewpoint in the world. Not only the individual but the race has always its situation. Each generation has its particular viewpoint. 'Primal finitude,' writes Paul Ricoeur, 'consists in *perspective* or *point of view*. It affects our primary relationship to the world which is to receive objects and not to create them. It is not exactly synonymous with "receptivity" itself, which consists of our openness to the world. It is rather a principle of narrowness or, indeed, a closing within the openness.'[3]

To some extent, of course, during his history and above all during his recent history of technological advance, man has overcome some of the limitations on his existence. He has harnessed powers that vastly exceed the power of his own body; and he has even, in the age of electric immediacy, overcome some of the disadvantages of perspective and brought everything into a closeness and accessibility. If, as Ortega y Gasset once argued, to be God is to occupy all points of view simultaneously and harmonize them,[4] then perhaps man with his electronic devices is advancing beyond the more obvious limitation of his being-there. But clearly his radical facticity and finitude are in principle not able to be overcome and will remain permanent characteristics of the human condition.

DEATH

We have begun this discussion of finitude by talking about perspective and point of view. We do not grasp things all at once as a whole, but *seriatim* and from one point of view out of an infinite number of possible points of view. However, it is not just the point of view that constitutes our finitude, but equally the fact that the view is limited. It penetrates a certain distance and then stops.

This holds for our existence in time. When we look back, our memory embraces perhaps some decades but becomes increasingly vague and finally breaks off; and we assign to that blank beyond memory our 'birth,' our coming into being, for there was a time when we were not. Looking forward, we anticipate various events, but we know also that somewhere along the line we shall have no more part in the events of the world. Just as there was a beginning to our histories, so there will be an end—death. But whereas the beginning, as past event, can be assigned a date, we cannot assign a date to the future event of death. We can be sure that there will be such a date, but from our present point of view we cannot tell whether our actual existence will extend as far as our anticipations for the future or whether it might even extend beyond them.

The theme of death has figured rather prominently in the writings of the existentialists. Some critics have seen in this fact (and also in the attention paid to anxiety) an evidence that there is a kind of morbidity in the existentialist outlook, a preoccupation with the weakness and mortality of man rather than with his strength. We may very well concede that sometimes preoccupation with death is morbid, but possibly the so-called 'healthy' attitude to death (which in fact means ignoring it) is equally morbid, that is to say, unhealthy and escapist. No account of human existence claiming to be in the slightest degree realistic can fail to say something about death as a universal characteristic of such existence. Psychologists have been learning in recent years of the very profound influence that the anticipation of death has upon people who perhaps never say anything about it. This also illustrates the contention of the existentialists that death is not simply the termination of life, not just an event that comes along at the end of the story, but itself enters very much into the story. Biologists too are telling us that awareness that he is going to die is one of the characteristics that allows man to exist as man and not merely as animal. According to Theodosius Dobzhansky such death-awareness is one of the basic characteristics of mankind as a biological species.[5]

Of all the existentialist philosophers, Heidegger is the one who has carried out the most detailed study of the existential meaning of death and incorporated it into his philosophy of existence.[6] We shall attempt to summarize his thoughts on the subject.

The question of death comes up in connection with another question, namely, how does one grasp the human existent as a whole? If the very nature of existence is that it 'goes out' into the new, so that at any moment the existent is unfinished and on his way to some new possibility of being, then is it not impossible ever to see him in his totality? The question then is whether death may not permit us to view the *Dasein* in its totality. For death sets a term to existence. *Dasein* is 'finished' at death and no longer 'ex-sists' in the sense of going out into the new. Yet it might be wondered whether *Dasein* is not so thoroughly finished at death that it becomes impossible to grasp the *Dasein* altogether, for death finishes *Dasein* in the sense of abolishing existence rather than completing it.

At this point, however, we must notice that death can be studied and understood in more than one way. From the point of view of existentialist philosophy, death must be considered existentially, that is to say, as it enters into existence and is inwardly appropriated by the existent. This in effect means that empirical studies of death have little relevance here. We can observe death in others and we can attempt to set forth certain criteria for determining when death has taken place. But in these cases we see death only from the outside, as it were. And how could it be otherwise? For if we ourselves were to experience death, then we could say nothing about it and would have no understanding of it, for the simple reason that we would in fact be dead! Is it not absurd even to imagine that one could arrive at an existential understanding of death?

There is a further difficulty. One may indeed speak of death as the 'end' of human existence, but in what sense is it an end? It does not seem to be an end in the sense of a goal or fulfillment. It is true that in a very few cases—Christ and Socrates would be classic examples—death comes as the appropriate culmination of life. But more often death appears as the violent cutting off and interruption of life; or it may delay its approach until long after a man's powers have broken down, so that 'clinical' death, so to speak, comes along months or even years after the death of the man's personal being. But if death is the 'end' in the sense of a mere stopping or cutting off, how can it have any existential significance in showing us existence as a whole?

Heidegger's way of dealing with these difficulties is to shift attention from death as the once-for-all observable fact at the end of life to the existent's inward awareness that his being is a being-toward-death. Though the precise moment of clinical death is uncertain and lies somewhere in the future, death is already present as a certain possibility—indeed, one may say as the most certain of all possibilities. In the mood of anxiety, I am aware of living in the face of the end; the existence that is mine is a precarious existence and at any time it may vanish into nothing.

Heidegger relates death to care, and it will be remembered that care constitutes the everyday being of the *Dasein* (see above, p. 60). We have seen that care itself is a complex phenomenon—it arises from the tension between the forward thrust of possibility into the future and the facticity of the situation into which the existent is already thrown, together with the 'falling' into the world and the 'they.' Death can be understood in relation to these three moments of care.

First of all, with respect to possibility and the future, death is seen as the supreme possibility of human existence, the one to which all others are subordinated. All our possibilities are, so to speak, spread out in front of death. There is a kind of hierarchy of possibilities, with death occupying the key position. Clearly, death is different from the other possibilities. As Heidegger expresses it, death is 'the possibility of the impossibility of any existence at all.'[7] Death is the last possibility of all, the possibility that makes impossible any further possibilities whatever.

To talk of death as a possibility, as we have just been doing, raises some problems. We have indeed acknowledged that death is a possibility of a unique sort, insofar as it means the end of possibilities. But is it not so unique that it should not be called a *possibility* at all, at least in the Heideggerian sense of the word? For Heidegger, a possibility is a mode of existence which the *Dasein* can choose and into which he can project himself. Presumably in suicide one chooses death as a possibility to be actualized, but Heidegger is clear that he is not advocating suicide. Actually, it will only be in the next chapter where we discuss authentic existence (see below, p. 113 ff.) that it will become plain what can be meant by reckoning death among the possibilities of existence. But even at the present stage of the argument, we can see that one may either accept death as qualifying all one's possibilities, or else exclude it from consideration as long as possible. Tolstoy's famous story *The Death of Ivan Ilyitch* illustrates the point rather well. For everyone except Ivan (and even for him up till the moment when he becomes aware that he is mortally ill) death is a most inconvenient and disagreeable subject, not to be thought about or talked about. For Ivan, it becomes a theme of engrossing importance, coloring everything else. I am not, by the way, suggesting that Heidegger recommends the morbid brooding over death that might seem to be implied here. He explicitly rejects such brooding, just as he rejects suicide. What he does ask for is an *anticipation* of death, a realistic inclusion of the death-factor among our projects and the way we evaluate them.

Death as ultimate possibility also raises the problem about conceiving existence as a whole. Although we have conceded that death is not an 'end' in the sense of a goal or fulfillment, it is a limit to existence. To become aware of death and to accept mortality is to become aware of a boundary to existence. Awareness of such a boundary does enable one to think of existence as a finite whole. The precise bearing of this for Heidegger's thought is something that we shall again leave to the next chapter, but clearly there is a great difference in existential attitude between the man who lives in the face of an end and the man who systematically excludes the thought of death, or seeks to do so.

Next we must ask how death is related to the second constitutive moment in care, namely, facticity. Possibility is directed to the future, to the 'not yet'; facticity, on the other hand, concerns what has been, the 'already'. From the very beginning of life, the human existent is already in the situation of mortality. He is always old enough to die. Death is one of the most inexorable 'givens' of the human condition. It is true that man has been able to do much to reduce mortality, and it is conceivable that with the advance of medical science people will live longer and the effects of senescence be greatly reduced. But no one seriously believes that death can be eliminated, or even that its elimination would be desirable. People usually want to postpone death, but death and temporal finitude are so much a constitutive part of humanity that an unending human life would be a monstrosity. Death is and will remain part of the factical human condition.

Care implies, in the third place, 'falling,' absorption into the instrumental world and into the impersonal collectivism of the 'they.' This shows itself in the everyday attitude to death, which is one of flight and avoidance. Throughout the ages men have shunned the sight of death and the mention of death, and they have devised innumerable ways of assuring themselves, when the reality of death inevitably confronts them, that death does not really change anything and that after death it will be business as usual. In contemporary America the attempts to deprive death of its reality are just as frantic as they ever were in any culture. On the one hand there are the funeral customs—the embalming of bodies, the expensive caskets designed to delay as long as possible decay and decomposition, soft music piped into the tombs. Then there is the deep-freezing of bodies, in the hope that one day medicine will have discovered a cure for the victim's disease, and there can take place a joyous (?) resurrection.

It is, of course, natural to fear death or to be anxious in the face of death. But this is very different from constructing a vast cultural illusion (to say nothing of a highly profitable industry) to help us forget about death or to persuade ourselves that it is unreal.

As we shall see later, Heidegger, by a remarkable *tour de force*, claims that death, honestly accepted and anticipated, can become an integrating factor in an authentic existence. Whether this paradoxical approach to the question of death is successful, the reader can decide for himself.

Among other existentialists, however, death is seen as the great surd of existence, the final proof of the absurdity of both men and the universe. Camus and Sartre are just as insistent as Heidegger on the need to face death as a reality, but it is the reality that shows the indifference and equivalence of all things in the long run. This need not produce an attitude of despair even if it excludes any ultimate hope. With Camus it produces not despair but rebellion. 'Human insurrection is a prolonged protest against death.'[8] For Sartre death has no special importance in itself—it is just the final absurdity, neither more nor less absurd than life itself. Death comes along 'into the bargain,' as he expresses it.

Death, then, is the great symbol of human finitude, perhaps of human absurdity. Yet it should not be supposed that those existentialists who place death in the center of their philosophizing are on that account nihilists. Heidegger, as we shall see, finds a way from death to authentic existence. Camus is inspired by death to 'metaphysical rebellion.' A just comment is made by the Catholic writer, Arthur Gibson:

> His atheism stemmed from a clear-eyed observation of a mad world, a cruel world, a blind world, an absurd world, wherein he found many human beings carefully avoiding the precious mortality that distinguished them by its presence in them from all inanimate nature, and by their knowledge of it from the animals. He urged on man a rebellion moderated by equilibrium and guaranteed in its moderation by the supreme relativizer, death.[9]

TEMPORALITY

Continuing our discussion of the finitude of existence, we come to the subject of temporality. That man is a creature of time, that he comes into being and passes out of being, has long been a theme for poets; and the transience of human life is one of the most poignant aspects of finitude.

Although we are now turning explicitly to temporality, the theme has been implicit in the earlier discussion. Birth and death mark the beginning and the end of every human existence, and the existence itself is the stretch of time between these boundaries. Furthermore, the phenomenon of care has a temporal basis. We have seen that care is constituted by possibility, facticity, and falling, and each of these has a temporal reference. Possibility is primarily future in its reference, facticity has to do with the 'already' of the given situation, while falling implies absorption in the present.

Successiveness is itself the mark of a finite experience. Man does or enjoys or knows only one main thing at a time. His experience is, so to speak, linear. In the course of his life, his several powers and capacities reach their pitch at different times and are never all present together.

But human experience is something more than successiveness, and the existent is more than the sum of the instants through which he lives. The temporality of existence is of a peculiar kind. What makes care possible and so existence possible is precisely a transcending of the successive instants so that man lives rather in a series of 'spans' and there is even what we call his 'lifespan.'

There is a major difference between man's relation to time, and the way in which a thing or an animal relates to time. There is a sense in which they are all in time; they pass through the successive instants of time; they all have a past, a present, and a future. The thing, however, simply endures through a succession of instants, at any one of which its past and its future are external to its present. But in the case of the existent past and future are intrinsically related to the present. We never catch the existent in a knife-edge present, so to speak. By memory the existent has brought his past with him into the present; and by anticipation and imagination he has already laid hold on his future and projects himself into it.

We would not *exist* (in the sense in which the word is used in this book) if we lacked this peculiar kind of temporality whereby we transcend the now and unite, to some degree, the past, present, and future. I say 'to some degree,' for the kind of unity that is achieved is variable. Indeed, at the extreme (perhaps pathological) end of the scale, human existence may come close to passing over into the now-centered mode of being characteristic of the thing or animal. (The animal is 'care-free.') For the thing or animal, the present only is real; the past is no longer and the future is not yet, and this means in effect that they are unreal. Only the now has reality. Perhaps we would say the same about the past and future of the human existent, but we would say it with a difference of meaning. In the case of the existent, the past and the future may be real in a manner that lets them live, as we sometimes say, in the present. To be constituted by the temporality of care is to be ahead of oneself in possibility, that is to say, to ex-sist into the future; it is to be already there, in a factical way, as having brought what has been into the present and, in the tension of these, it is to be falling into the present world of concern.

The radical finitude of our temporality, then, is experienced not just in successiveness but in the tensions among the dimensions of temporality. There is a quest for a wholeness of experience or an immediacy of fruition that would gather up in itself past, present, and future. This could also be described as the quest for the eternal understood as a wholeness quite different from the unending successiveness of the 'everlasting.'

However, in typical finite experience the dimensions of temporality lack such wholeness and are usually in a state of imbalance. One or other of the three dimensions of temporality has come to have undue predominance.

The first type of imbalance is that in which there is an exaggerated stress on possibility and on the future. The will dwells exclusively on what is ahead, but in so doing it gets converted from genuine willing (the action of the total self) to mere wish or velleity. There are many variations in such imbalance. Some of them are relatively harmless, such as the impractical idealism of youth. In an adult person an irresponsible idealism or utopianism can be cruel and mischievous. Much more serious, however, is a retreat into a world of wish-fantasy. Action becomes impossible and is replaced by a mere toying with unrealistic possibilities than can never be actualized. All genuine willing must take account of *factical* possibility, that is to say, of possibility that is open in the particular situation. Of course there never is a radically open future. It is always closed off to some᾽ extent. At no time does the human agent stand before pure possibility· The illusion that he does, perhaps arising out of a fear to accept the past, can result only in an unrealistic and impractical mode of existence in which action has been, in varying degrees, stifled and overcome by fantasy.

Preoccupation with the past produces its corresponding disorder. Where there is massive awareness of the given situation and of what has been, this may produce something like a paralysis of all genuine willing. Again, there are many forms to be observed. The situation may have induced acute anxiety, preventing any decision that would expose the agent to radical change and novelty; thus there is no act of will that breaks into the future, but rather an attempt to find security in the routines and rituals of the past. Or again, this situation may be one in which there is a burdensome sense of guilt, leading in turn to a dull indifference in which, because everything appears hopeless, there is no point in willing anything. Or it may be that the given takes over entirely, and the person concerned acts compulsively from urge, instinct, addiction, or whatever it may be. In all these cases a genuine future and genuine possibilities have been cut off, so that action is rendered impossible.

There is also the imbalance of the present, and probably this is the commonest case of all. Also, this is obviously the case in which a truly human 'existence' tends to be lost in a way of being like that of the animal or even the mere thing. This dwelling in the present has, like the other cases, various ways in which it manifests itself. Always, however, it is typical of the man who, in common parlance, has no will of his own—the irresolute man, the man of bad faith, the scattered man, to use expressions found in existentialist writers. He may have fallen into the 'they,' so that he lets everything be decided for him by the prevalent opinion. Or he may have become enslaved in an apparatus or a system, so that everything that he does is determined for him by circumstances. Or he may have subscribed to some authoritarian code or institution. But it is unnecessary to elaborate further.

By introducing the notion of imbalance, the present discussion, which began by considering finitude, has moved toward the concept of guilt. Finitude would seem to be the condition of the possibility of guilt, though, of course, finitude is not itself guilt. But guilt seems to be a tragic inevitability. The possibilities for imbalance are so great that the disordering of existence can hardly fail to happen. So we turn now to the direct consideration of guilt and alienation.

GUILT AND ALIENATION

Existentialism is not necessarily a pessimistic philosophy, but its adherents have been realistic in acknowledging the disorder of human existence. To exist is to project oneself into the future. But there is always a lack or disproportion between the self as projected and the self where it actually stands. This discontinuity in existence has been noted from Kierkegaard to Ricoeur. One may call it a flaw or fault, not so much in the sense of a fault calling for blame as in the sense in which the word is used by geologists, that is to say, to express a radical break or discontinuity.[10] The gap is between existence and essence, or between facticity and possibility, or between the self one is and the self that is projected. But this kind of flaw is not yet a moral flaw, but rather the kind of finite being that makes morality possible. The case is similar with Heidegger's notion of falling. He takes care to explain that this is an ontological possibility and that he is not making an ontical pronouncement on man's actual condition. Man is so constituted that he stands in the possibility of falling, that is to say, of a disproportion or a failure to measure up to the stature of his possibility. Nietzsche was clear that the flaw or imperfection in the way man is constituted, the fact that he is unfinished, not only makes possible the deterioration of man but is equally the ground of the possibility of his advance toward superman.

There is therefore something like a tragic conception of guilt among the existentialists. From the very way he is constituted as a finite being who is also free, man is placed in the possibility of guilt, and his 'rising' seems to be inseparable from his 'falling.' In Heidegger the very notion of guilt receives a strange, premoral, and ontological sense. In German, the word *Schuld* can mean either 'guilt' or 'debt.' In his interpretation of guilt[11] Heidegger makes much of the notion of *Schuld* as debt or lack. In his very being, man is characterized by a nullity or lack of being, and it is upon this basis of nullity that he must take up responsibility for his being.

The notion of alienation also appears in the literature of existentialism and adds a further dimension to the understanding of guilt. Of course, the idea has played a considerable role in the thinking of modern times, even before the advent of existentialism. It was prominent in the thought of both Hegel and Marx, though it already had different forms in each of these men. F. W. Dillistone remarks:

> For Hegel the estrangement was to be found within the very structure of life universal. For Marx, it was to be found within the structure of man's conditions of labor which compelled him to be alienated from his work, from himself, and from his fellow men. The answer to man in his predicament Hegel sought through a philosophical system, corresponding to the dialectical process of the Universal Mind. Marx, on the other hand, sought it through a revolutionary change in man's economic conditions

which would make possible a complete harmony between man and his work.[12]

It is interesting to note that these remarks of Dillistone are taken from a book dealing with atonement, for any recognition of alienation at once raises the question of the healing of the break, and existentialism is no exception in seeking to go beyond the fact of man's alienation to find ways of attaining wholeness.

For the existentialist, alienation is understood chiefly in inward terms. It is the existent's alienation from his own deepest being. He is not himself but simply a cipher in the mass-existence of the crowd or a cog in the industrial system or whatever it may be.

How far is this alienation comparable to the religious idea of sin? Actually some Christian theologians have seen a considerable resemblance between the two. Paul Tillich, for instance, has used the idea of existential estrangement to elucidate the traditional concept of sin, though, as Paul Ricoeur has shown in his masterly study *The Symbolism of Evil*, alienation or estrangement is one among several images that are implicit in the Biblical idea of sin. An apparent difference between the Biblical and existentialist ideas is that sin is alienation from God whereas existential alienation is precisely what that phrase expresses—alienation from one's own being. Certainly the atheistic existentialist would not be willing to identify alienation with sin in the traditional religious sense. Yet even in atheistic existentialism (and perhaps this is more apparent in its literary than in its systematic forms) there is something like a sense of cosmic alienation, a not being at home in the world, reminiscent, as we have seen, of such earlier forms of belief as Gnosticism (see above, p. 27 f.).

But in spite of finitude, alienation, and even sin, man quests for his true life. Existentialism in most of its forms is not just a cold analysis of the human condition but itself a passionate quest for authentic existence. Our next step is to consider the various ways in which true selfhood is to be sought.

CHAPTER ELEVEN

In Quest of Authentic Existence

THE PROBLEM OF A TRUE HUMANITY

By the very way humanity is constituted, one seems driven to talk of a 'true' humanity (and presumably also of a 'false' humanity). For if man has not a nature or essence that is simply given, but rather 'makes' himself what he becomes by his own deeds and decisions, then it would seem that he can either become what it is in him to become, or fail to become it. One is reminded at this point of an expression that was used in the context of the idealist philosophies of an earlier time: *Werde was du bist!*—'Become what you are!' But such language seems to suppose that there is already some kind of blueprint, as it were, that has now to be unfolded. Such an idea would be unacceptable to some of the existentialists at least. They maintain that to call man the 'existent' is precisely to hold that there is no blueprint. Man must decide who he will be, and more than this, each individual must decide the question for himself. Each one's existence is his own, characterized by a unique 'mineness.' There is no universal pattern of a genuine humanity that can be imposed on all or to which all must conform. Indeed, to impose such a pattern or to demand conformity would mean to destroy the possibility of a genuinely human existence for the persons concerned. They become truly themselves only to the extent that they freely choose themselves.

We have already taken note of the existentialists' use of the word *authentic* (see above, p. 53). Existence is authentic to the extent that the existent has taken possession of himself and, shall we say, has molded himself in his own image. Inauthentic existence, on the other hand, is molded by external influences, whether these be circumstances, moral codes, political or ecclesiastical authorities, or whatever.

But do these considerations not lead us into a complete relativism and individualism? If everyone is unique and is to determine who he will become, have we not abandoned any idea of a true humanity, and perhaps even any idea of morality that could be universally binding? Are we not going to end up with a chaos in which everyone 'does his own thing,' to use the current expression, and does it without regard to anyone else? And is this not an exaggerated liberty, which has become sheer license?

It must be said first of all that the existentialist criterion of an authentic existence is a formal rather than a material one. This is not entirely the case—we shall see that in various ways the content of such an existence is not just a matter of indifference. Nevertheless, the notion of authenticity has to do primarily with formal considerations. It is the form or shape of an existence that is the measure of its authenticity—the extent to which it has achieved a unity rather than being scattered, the extent to which it exercises freedom rather than being determined by the prevailing public tastes and standards. Sartre has written: 'You are free, therefore choose—that is to say, invent. No rule of general morality can show you what you ought to do; no signs are vouchsafed in this world.'[1] By his concept of abandonment Sartre means that there is no God who establishes values or sets an ideal of humanity toward which each man must strive. Each must invent his own values, and he exists authentically insofar as he strives to realize values that really are his own. But then, as Dostoevsky said, if there is no God, everything is permitted.

Actually, we shall see that the rejection (or at least the suspension) of conventional morality is typical of existentialists, including some Christian existentialists, and we shall have to ask about the meaning of this. However, no major existentialist philosopher has taught that everything is permitted. Even if the criterion of true selfhood, genuine humanity, authentic existence, or whatever it may be called, is a formal one, some material principle is always introduced. In Sartre's own case, the control is exercised by his notion of responsibility. As he understands it, the anguish of a choice arises from the fact that, in making the choice, I am committing not only myself but, in a certain manner, all mankind. 'The existentialist frankly states that man is in anguish. His meaning is as follows: when a man commits himself to anything, fully realizing that he is not only choosing what he will be, but is thereby at the same time a legislatoi deciding for the whole of mankind—in such a moment a man cannot escape from the sense of complete and profound responsibility.'² This anguished responsibility is brought on by the question of whether the concept or image of man which I choose for myself is one that I can choose for all. This sense of responsibility would seem to exclude some choices, such as the choice to be a sheer ruthless egoist or, perhaps, the choice to be a fascist. For presumably I could not be responsibly myself in making such choices.

However, there is some confusion in Sartre's thinking on these matters. If man is fundamentally (as Sartre claims) the desire to be God and if the other is seen as an obstacle to that desire, then what basis is there for introducing this somewhat Kantian principle that I ought to be able to universalize my commitments? Is Sartre smuggling in some principle or value that I do not invent and that is prior to me? We may note the following sentence: 'Who can prove that I am the proper person to impose, by my own choice, my conception of man upon mankind?'³ It seems to me that the word *proper* badly needs clarifying in this sentence. How does such an evaluating term manage to insinuate itself into the discussion? Sartre, of course, goes on to say that no one can offer the proof required. Each person has to bear the risk of his own decision. But on his own premises there is no risk, and it is senseless to talk of being a 'proper' person or (as he also does) of 'having a right' to legislate for others. Or rather, it would be senseless if one *really* accepted a moral nihilism. Sartre does not, and the question must arise whether he himself is not finally in bad faith and a victim of the self-deception he deplores.

Camus is clearer about the self-contradictory character of nihilism. 'I proclaim that I believe in nothing and that everything is absurd, but I cannot doubt the validity of my own proclamation, and I must at least believe in my protest.'⁴ Even more striking is the affirmation that supplies content to the nature of the protest, when Camus tells us that rebellion in man is his refusal to be treated as an object.⁵ To refuse to be treated as an object is to affirm oneself as a person, and that is to affirm the dignity (worth or value) of personal being. In a truly absurd or godless world, persons would be just as absurd and worthless as anything else.

The formal character of the existentialist conception of authentic existence receives content in another way. Among the basic structures of existence is being-with-others (see above, p. 75 ff.), and we have seen that no one can be a self apart from other selves. Hence no image of authentic existence can lack a social dimension. Sartre has to import his Kantian principle because he lacks any adequate doctrine of the social character of existence. But if the basically communal structure of existence is admitted, then it is clear that there can be no genuine humanity or authentic selfhood that is purely ego-regarding or that is anti-social in the way that fascism is. No one could be truly himself in projecting such images, for these very images are images of a crippled and defective existence.

In saying this, I am of course implicitly denying the Sartrean view that man starts from nothing and invents his values and his images for himself. It seems to me, on the contrary, that already with existence there is given an image or goal of existence—not, indeed, a detailed model or pattern, but a basic awareness of the direction of human fulfillment. This is conscience, and to the discussion of conscience we now turn.

CONSCIENCE

Conscience has a somewhat ambiguous status among existentialist philosophers. The reason for this is that the term *conscience* itself can be understood in a number of ways. 'Conscience' may mean a person's awareness of the moral code accepted in his society, together with the feelings of discomfort or satisfaction that he may have as he either breaks or keeps the rules expressed in the code. But it is also the term we use for the kind of moral conviction that will sometimes lead a person to reject the accepted standards of his society in response to what he believes to be a more deeply founded imperative. Existentialists tend to be critical of conscience in the first of the two senses and to hold that only the second is important.

The clash between the two levels of conscience is dramatically presented by Kierkegaard in his consideration of the story of Abraham and Isaac in the book *Fear and Trembling*. The command of God comes to Abraham to lay his son upon the altar and slay him in an act of human sacrifice. By what Kierkegaard calls a 'teleological suspension of ethics,' Abraham is ready to go against his moral principles and his human feelings to obey the command. He is ready to set aside the 'universal,' that is to say, the generally accepted standard of what is right, in order to carry out the duty uniquely laid on him as an individual before God. We may say that Abraham is tempted to commit murder. 'But what is a temptation? Ordinarily, a temptation is something which tries to stop a man from doing his duty, but in this case it is ethics itself which tries to prevent him from doing God's will. But what then is duty? Duty is quite simply the expression for the will of God.'[6] It is clear, however, that we are not to think of the will of God as entirely external to the person who obeys it. Abraham decided to sacrifice his son 'for God's sake and so, what is absolutely identical, for his own sake.'[7] What we have here is a conflict of consciences, or a conflict between different levels of conscience. The conscience that reflects the 'universal' ethic is superseded by that conscience which is both the command of God and the individual's own deepest self-awareness. 'What is at stake in the book,' comments George Price, 'is Abraham's self, his struggle *to be*, to exist as the individual he knew he ought to be. And Abraham must always forge his own categories. He is therefore the paradigm for any and every individual who finds himself at the frontier of ethics.'[8] The expression 'the individual he knew he ought to be' puts very clearly what I called the second sense of conscience.

The mention of Abraham as the paradigm for any individual at the frontier of ethics reminds us, of course, that Kierkegaard had his own struggle of conscience, which was settled in the same way as Abraham's. I refer to his projected marriage with Regina Olsen. He was engaged, and had taken upon himself a moral commitment to marriage. We have seen already that Kierkegaard took very seriously such a commitment (see above, p. 143). But he chose to break off the engagement, to set aside conscience in the first sense and the 'universal' ethical principle. He did this in response to what he believed to be God's will for him; but this will was also his vocation, so one can equally say that he did it in order to be himself.

I shall not for the moment comment on the 'teleological suspension' of ethics until we have seen some comparable examples from other existentialists.

Nietzsche goes beyond Kierkegaard in visualizing not merely the suspension of conventional moral obligation but its outright supersession. The commonly accepted morality is like the 'old broken tables' of the law, and as yet there are only half-written new tables. 'When I came to men,' says Nietzsche's Zarathustra,

> I found them enthroned upon an ancient arrogance; all thought that they long had known what was good and evil for man. All speech concerning virtue seemed to them an old stale thing, and he that wished to sleep soundly spake of 'good and evil' ere bedtime. This sleep I broke when I taught that none *yet knoweth* what is good and evil—unless it be that he is a creator! But a creator is he that createth man's goal and giveth earth its meaning and its future: it is he that first maketh good and evil to be.[9]

The traditional morality sought to preserve human life and invoked

God as its guarantor. But now God is dead, and it remains to man to fashion a new morality that will not, like the morality of the mob, simply maintain things as they are but will look to the superman of the future.

> The most anxious ask today: 'How is man to be preserved?' But Zarathustra, alone and first, asketh: 'How is man to be *surmounted*?' The superman is my care; *he*—not man—is my first and only care: not my neighbor, nor the poorest, nor the greatest sufferer, nor the best. . . . Today the petty folk are become master: they all preach submission and humility and cunning and diligence and consideration and all the long etcetera of petty virtue. Whatsoever is womanish, whatsoever is slavish, and especially whatsoever is of the mongrel mob—these will now be the master of all human fate. . . . Surmount me these masters of today, O my brethren—these petty folk; *they* are the greatest peril to the superman![10]

Here man as he is, and his moral standards, are frankly scorned. Nietzsche's care is for the superman who will surmount man as he is. Again, I withhold comment for the present.

Heidegger affords material for a third illustration. About the 'public conscience,' as he calls it, Heidegger asks: 'What else is it than the voice of the "they"?'[11] This kind of conscience simply reflects the commonly accepted standards of right and wrong. The true conscience, or the conscience at a deeper level, functions precisely in delivering us from the voice of the 'they.' 'Conscience summons *Dasein*'s self from its lostness in the "they".'[12] Only when he stops listening to the voice of the 'they' can the existent truly hear the call of conscience. From where does the call come? It comes from the depth of one's own being. It is the call of the authentic self, struggling to be born. To what is the call addressed? It is addressed to the inauthentic or fallen self, the self that is dominated by the 'they' and entangled in concerns that have come to determine it rather than to be determined by it. What is the content of the call? There is no content. 'The call discourses in the uncanny mode of *keeping silent*. And it does this only because, in calling the one to whom the appeal is made, it does not call him into the public idle talk of the "they," but calls him back from this into the reticence of his existent potentiality for being.'[13] So again we meet the formal character of the existentialist notion of an authentic existence. There is no universally prescribable content. Each must seek to realize his own potentiality for being.

With these examples before us, what we are to say of the existentialists' tendency to despise conventional morality, and of their claim that there is a deeper level of conscience that demands our obedience before anything else? I think we can only reply that there is a true insight in this position, but that its application is extremely perilous.

The true insight consists in this, that there never would have been any ethical creativity or progress in human history unless sometimes men had defied the tribal code or the conventional morality in the name of some deeper voice of conscience. There have been occasions in history when men have had to say, 'We must obey God rather than men!,' or in a more humanistic language, 'Humanity compels us to go against what the majority find right!'

The peril consists in the fact that no individual conscience ever speaks with complete purity. Indeed, we all know how easy it is to manipulate conscience. To think again of our examples, were Abraham and Kierkegaard right in believing that they knew God's will, and in believing that it suspended the ethical imperative? An appeal to 'God's will' can be made the excuse for the most outrageous kinds of conduct. Leaving aside the case of Abraham, which comes out of a distant cultural milieu, how do we esteem Kierkegaard's own action with respect to his engagement? Was he right to follow a higher vocation, or was this really an egoism? And if every individual claimed the right to set aside his ordinary moral obligations for the sake of the ultimate demands of his own authentic selfhood, surely we would soon find ourselves in moral chaos. The case is even more acute when we turn to Nietzsche. Who is the superman who can set aside the morals of the 'petty folk'? Even if Nietzsche is sometimes too simply and cavalierly represented as the father of the Nazis, there is enough in common to cause one to question very deeply the attitude to morals that we find here.

But then there is another side to the problem. If we agree that the existentialists' attitude to conventional morality is an extremely perilous one, we need not be surprised if we receive the reply that all human existence is an extremely perilous business and that the frightful risks of challenging the accepted morality sometimes have to be taken. If there is the danger of moral nihilism, there is equally the possibility of moral advance.

It seems, in fact, that one is faced with a choice. One can play it safe, as it were, accepting the conventional standards of morality and acting accordingly. This need not be bad faith, for one may have genuinely approved these standards and have interiorized them, so that they are not just externally imposed. But to do this is to run

the risk of stagnation. It could result in what Karl Jaspers, who is
far from an extremist, called 'the tranquillity of the cultured, bour-
geois Christian world that spoiled its own freedom and lost touch
with its origin.'[14] The other choice, which would surely be taken
with much existential anxiety, would be to challenge the conventional
code at some point and seek innovation. The risk then would be not
moral stagnation but the possibility of moral dissolution. However,
there is a risk in both cases, and unless the second kind of risk is
sometimes taken, there will never be any moral advance. Perhaps
in our own era of change the second kind of risk, the one that
most of the existentialists seem to advocate, is specially appropriate.
But we may get further light on this if we next consider in more
detail some of the ways in which authentic existence is supposed
to be attained.

<h2>THE ATTAINMENT OF SELFHOOD</h2>

In the analyses carried out in the preceding pages there has gradually
been building up the picture of the conflicts and tensions that inevitably attend the dynamic reality of human existence. On the one
hand we have seen man exercising freedom, will, decision, creativity,
setting goals and striving for their attainment; he appears as a
being possessed, as Schleiermacher expressed it, with a 'sense and
taste for the infinite.' On the other hand we have seen him in his
'thrownness,' a being of care and temporality, finally abandoned to
death, so that his taste for the infinite is anchored to a radical
finitude. We have seen him in his essential sociality as a being-
with-others, capable of love and community; but we have also seen
that this being-with-others is usually swallowed up in the inauthentic
collectivism of the 'they,' and that many of the great existentialist
thinkers (we except Buber and Marcel) have thought it necessary to
stress the individual's need to extricate himself from the crowd in
order to be fully himself. We have also seen that man is a being of
conscience, aware of a destiny to be fulfilled. But against this is to
be set his guilt and alienation.

In all this welter of conflicting tendencies, does anything make
sense? Are we to write off human existence as fundamentally absurd?
Or are we to say that although existence is a paradox and although
(as we have acknowledged early in the inquiry) existence cannot be
neatly understood by rational thought, it is not just meaningless
and its disorders can be overcome within a dynamic wholeness?
Man never gives up the quest for wholeness, and we have seen that

even the most extreme among the existentialists seem to stop short of a doctrine of sheer absurdity and of nihilism.

However, just as there are profound conflicts and tensions in existence itself, so there are great differences among the existentialists as to how the threatening and destructive tendencies in man can be overcome. By and large we strike once more upon the difference between atheistic existentialists on the one hand and religious existentialists on the other. But this is only a very broad and approximate kind of division. Some religious existentialists are just as despairing of the human condition as are atheistic ones. But despair is a difficult stopping place. Certainly the Christian existentialist believes that he passes beyond it, and the atheist too looks for at least a partial salvation. Perhaps somewhat more useful than the division of existentialists into atheistic and Christian is the division into those who believe in grace and those who do not. I use the expression *grace* for the idea that there is a saving or healing power that comes from beyond man and that overcomes his alienation with reconciliation and wholeness. Some Christian existentialists would assert that the human situation, considered in isolation, is just as hopeless and absurd as their atheistic counterparts claim. They deny that man has either the wisdom or the power to set his own existence in order. Only by a divine condescension could this happen. On the face of it, this might seem like an abandonment of some of the fundamental tenets of existentialism and a new form of 'bad faith.' But the existential Christian who talks of the need for grace will not usually deny the reality of human freedom, and he will try to correlate his understanding of grace with man's free decision in faith. There are, on the other hand, non-Christian existentialists who do not believe in grace but claim that man, through his free obedience to his conscience and its call, can attain to wholeness and authentic selfhood. Thus they preserve the autonomy of existence. But there are always borderline cases. For instance, Heidegger in the relatively early work *Being and Time* sets before us a picture of autonomous man striving to be himself out of his own resources; but in his later writings he can talk of the 'grace' of being, and commends a mode of thinking and listening that has its passive as well as its active aspects. Jaspers too, while denying the need for some special gracious act directed by God toward man, recognizes that there is a kind of grace in existence itself.

But even among the differences, there is something in common. Whether it is conceived as autonomous or empowered by grace, an act of will or decision seems to be at the center of every existentialist idea of human wholeness. It is such an act that, so to speak, pulls the self into a coherent unity. To gather up the whole self into a concentrated act of will is really and authentically to become oneself and to be rescued from the scattering and dissolution of the self in trivial concerns and in the crowd. The central role of the will seems to be equally important whether one is considering Kierkegaard's Christian faith or Heidegger's secular resoluteness. 'Christianity in the New Testament has to do with man's will, everything turns on changing the will, every expression (forsake the world, deny yourself, die to the world, and so on; to hate oneself, to love God, and so on)—everything is related to this basic idea in Christianity which makes it what it is—a change of will.'[15] For Heidegger too, will has a totality about it. He does not use the traditional terminology of will and willing very much, preferring to speak of 'resoluteness,' but in two passages where he explicitly discusses will and willing he insists that the will is not a kind of building brick for the construction of a self, but that 'in the phenomenon of willing the underlying totality of care shows through.'[16]

It will, I think, be helpful to give brief accounts of how Kierkegaard and Heidegger respectively understand the attainment of true selfhood. These accounts come from very different areas of the existentialist spectrum, one appealing to faith and grace, the other considering man in his autonomy. Yet however different they are, they show some fundamental family resemblance.

For Kierkegaard there is no human and no rational solution to the dilemma of existence. There is no human solution, for man's finitude and his sinfulness make it impossible for him to effect his own salvation; there is no rational solution, for the paradox of existence cannot be reconciled in rational categories.

The only answer to the paradox of human existence is a still greater paradox—the absolute paradox of Christianity, and above all, the paradox of the Incarnation, God's gracious condescension to man. In Kierkegaard's view, there is no rational defense or explication of Christianity. Lessing had said that the contingent truths of history cannot afford a basis for eternal truths of reason, and from the standpoint of reason he was right. In the line of Tertullian, Kierkegaard holds that Christianity is an offense to reason. It is to be embraced by an act of will in spite of reason. This is the 'leap' of faith.

It is also the 'moment' before God—the moment in which eternity impinges on time. This does not mean that the believer is delivered from time and its conflicts, but it does mean that there is a dimension of eternity in his life. As Martin J. Heinecken has expressed it, 'the individual in his existence as the synthesis of time and eternity is constantly still on the way, in the process of becoming what in another sense he already is, constantly riding the crest of the wave of decision.'[17]

Thus for Kierkegaard authentic existence is attained in the moment before God, which is also the moment of self-knowledge; in the act of willing Christ which is also the act of willing oneself. 'I *will* one thing only, I will belong to Christ, I will be a Christian!'[18] It is willing one thing, which is also the highest, the paradox of Christ and the Christian life, that confers what Kierkegaard calls 'purity of heart'—an existential integrity and authenticity.

In contrast to the Kierkegaardian view, for Heidegger it is not the 'moment before God' but rather the 'moment before death' that is decisive. Death is not merely a negative phenomenon. To anticipate death with resoluteness is to find a certain wholeness in it. It sets a boundary to my existence and so makes possible a unity of existence. Furthermore, as that possibility that is above all my own and that I must take upon myself, death sets me free from the 'they.'

I have advisedly used the expression 'moment before death' in connection with Heidegger's view in order to exhibit both the resemblance and the contrast to Kierkegaard's 'moment before God.' Both expressions have eschatological overtones. But the eternity beyond time of which Kierkegaard speaks is, in Heidegger, made a kind of eternity within time. It is the moment in which my past, present, and future are gathered into the unity of the resolute self.

This brief discussion of true selfhood as envisaged by Kierkegaard and Heidegger reminds us again that existentialism does not supply a content, or rather it permits many contents. But it is concerned more with the intensity and passion of our decisions than with their actual content. It is this, in a way, that realizes a kind of infinity or eternity in the midst of time. Kierkegaard seems very close to Heidegger when he writes: 'The temporal is a snail's pace, spreading out in time and space; the eternal is the intensive which hurries to meet death.'[19]

If we may borrow the expression of Paul Tillich, it is an 'ultimate concern' that finally gathers up the many proximate concerns of life and brings a unity and wholeness into existence. The content of this ultimate concern may differ greatly from one person to another. We have seen reason to believe, however, that some possible contents are excluded, for if these are taken as ultimate concerns, they prove to be dissolving rather than unifying (see above, p. 164).

This fact is obscured so long as one is thinking primarily of the individual existent, but it becomes obvious as soon as we take the social dimensions of existence seriously. We have now to widen our horizons, in order to consider existence in the context of history and society.

CHAPTER TWELVE

History and Society

FROM INDIVIDUAL EXISTENCE TO THE HISTORY OF MANKIND

Up till now our analyses have been directed mainly toward the phenomena of individual existence. It can hardly be denied that the mainstream of existentialism, beginning with Kierkegaard's high valuation of the individual, has had an 'individualist' bias, and it is difficult, if not impossible, to lead existentialism out of this bias and at the same time not to fall into that dehumanizing collectivism against which existentialism has been an entirely justified protest.

Yet we have from time to time insisted that no adequate existential analysis can neglect the social dimensions of existence; and we have seen that even among those existentialists who have in fact shown an individualistic bias, there are present, at least in embryo, themes that could be developed toward a better understanding of that social context within which all existence has its setting. In particular, we have noted that all existence is being-with-others (see above, p. 75 ff.); and, furthermore, it is being-in-the-world (see above, p. 56 ff.), where the 'world' is understood in human terms as, shall we say, the theatre in which the activities of the self are carried out.

We have now to develop more adequately our account of the social dimensions of existence, and we shall do so by means of a consideration of history. In taking this route, we shall be following the path chosen by many of the existentialists as they have tried to break out of personal and interpersonal categories to a consideration of larger groups or even of mankind as a whole in his solidarity.

Whether this can be done adequately, given the existentialist starting-point, is a question that must be deferred for the present (see below, p. 186).

We have already seen that radical temporality is one of the most basic characteristics of individual existence. Man is temporal through and through. We can now extend that understanding of existence by asserting the radically historical character of man. He is historical through and through. When we speak of *history* rather than of *temporality*, our attention is directed toward a wider stream of time and becoming, one in which all men are caught up together.

The radically historical character of human life and thought—in a word, of existence—was stressed in the later part of the 19th century by a group of thinkers who would not usually be termed existentialists. Best known among them was Wilhelm Dilthey (1833–1911), and his influence on contemporary existentialist thinking about history has been very great.

He claimed, on the one hand, that history is a human phenomenon and that the study of history must therefore be accounted a human science. In saying that history is a human phenomenon, one is pointing to the difference between 'history,' properly so-called, and 'process' or mere 'occurrence.' Process and occurrence are natural events, describable in terms of natural causality. But historical events are different. They are 'caused' by human agency—it may be by ambition, aggression, hunger, fear, deliberate decision, and so on. Of course, sometimes natural events enter into the course of history too. A sudden storm could affect the outcome of a naval engagement as much as the skill and courage of the seamen. An event of this sort, however, is made historical precisely because it intermeshes with events originating from human agency. And here we may notice the mixed character of history. It is on the one hand human creation, arising from freedom and decision; and it is on the other hand the product of circumstances, which provide the factical situations in which human decisions must be made. Expressing the matter in another way, we could say that the long process of evolution, both cosmic and biological, was natural process, describable in terms of those 'laws of nature' or regularities that the natural sciences discover; but with the emergence of man, a new factor enters, the historical factor, in virtue of which man's inner life is now externalizing itself in action and taking a part in shaping the world. But there is not a complete transition from the natural to the historical, and despite the increasing 'hominization' of the world, there presumably never will be. Just as on the level of individual existence, freedom is qualified by finitude in its several manifestations, so on the level of the history of communities and nations, policies initiated by human decisions have to be adapted to (and may even conflict with) sets of events over which there is no human control. And although human control over nature is increasing at a spectacular rate, it can never be an absolute control.

If the phenomena of history are to be distinguished from the occurrences or processes of nature, it would seem clear that the method of studying them must also be different. Dilthey insisted that the study of history must be included among the *Geisteswissenschaften* or 'human studies.' Pointing out that much had been written on the foundation and methods of the natural sciences, he claimed that the human sciences had been neglected. Too often, in fact, there has been an attempt to impose on the human sciences the methods that are really appropriate only to the natural sciences. But the kind of observation from outside that is appropriate to the natural sciences must be replaced by a kind of knowledge by participation in the case of the human sciences. 'Mankind, if apprehended only by perception and perceptual knowledge, would be for us a physical fact, and as such it would be accessible only to natural scientific knowledge. It becomes an object for the human studies only in so far as human states are consciously lived, in so far as they find expression in living utterances, and in so far as these expressions are understood.'[1] This kind of knowledge by participation we recognize as typical of the knowing stressed in existentialism and discussed in an earlier chapter (see above, p. 101). Although the terminology is not Dilthey's, we may say that his doctrine is to the effect that history must be studied existentially. It is no accident that Heidegger, in one of his major discussions of history, frankly acknowledges his debt to Dilthey.[2]

Incidentally, not only Dilthey but other writers outside of the explicitly existentialist tradition have developed views of history that have a decidedly existential quality about them. Among such writers may be mentioned Ernst Troeltsch (1865–1923), whose views are close to those of Dilthey himself; Benedetto Croce (1866–1953), leader of the type of historical idealism that flourished in Italy; and R. G. Collingwood (1889–1943), a British philosopher of idealist tendency who drew upon both German and Italian sources and whose posthumous work, *The Idea of History* (1946) continues to be influential. The fact that similar ideas about history can be found over such a wide spectrum of philosophers is a warning against labeling them 'existentialist' in too narrow a sense, and is indeed a warning against any restrictive use of labels in discussing philosophical ideas.

A further consequence of recognizing the radically historical character of human existence is to acknowledge that philosophy itself takes place in history. Its pronouncements are therefore relative to historical situations. To say this is to renounce the idea of eternal or timeless truth, and of any all-embracing system of thought that might claim to express such truth. In some writers, we find a historicism so extreme that they are even prepared to say that mathematics and science are relative to particular histories and cultures. Whether the argument should be pushed so far is debatable. But a metaphysic, even one that is existentially based, can do no more than describe the shape of the real as seen in a particular historical context. However, this understanding of the relativism of philosophies accords well both with the existentialist doctrine of truth (see above, p. 104 f.) and with the recognition of the finitude and facticity of human existence; for even the conscious criticism of historical perspectives and cultural presuppositions could never attain to that degree of objectivity and universality in which things could be viewed *sub specie aeternitatis.*

In this brief introductory section I have set out the frame of reference within which the existentialist discussion of history takes place. But clearly there is room for many sharp differences, and here as elsewhere existentialism turns out to be a very diversified phenomenon. In the next section we shall consider some actual examples of existentialist views of history.

CONFLICTING THOUGHTS ON HISTORY AMONG EXISTENTIALIST PHILOSOPHERS

Kierkegaard did not write very much on the subject of history. Indeed, he explicitly remarks more than once that his interest lies in the individual rather than in the history of the race, and that it is in the individual that salvation takes place, not in history. The fact that he never broke out of individualism has remained significant for the whole subsequent development of existentialism.

Nevertheless, there are at least two ideas in Kierkegaard that reappear (though in altered guise) in later existentialist reflection on history.

The first of these is the idea that history tends to be a neutralizing process, in which everything that is great and distinctive gets watered down and rendered harmless. 'History is a process. Only on the rarest occasions is a tiny drop of idea added to it. And the process consists in transforming this idea into twaddle—for which sometimes centuries and millions multiplied by trillions of men are required (and this is carried out under the pretext of perfecting the idea which has been added).'[3] This idea of history, so untypical of the 19th century, can be seen on the one hand as a revulsion against the Hegelian idea, in which history is understood as the unfolding and progressive enrichment of spirit. It is to be seen on the other hand in relation to Kierkegaard's understanding of Christianity. The great event in all history was God's condescension to man in the incarnate Christ. In a sense, this is all the history one need know, and yet it is not history in the sense of something past, but a contemporary truth. In a well-known passage Kierkegaard added that the disciples who lived at the time of Jesus and had every opportunity to know the details of his life did not enjoy any advantage over those disciples of nineteen centuries later. 'If the contemporary generation had left nothing behind them but these words: "We have believed that in such and such a year God appeared among us in the humble form of a servant, that he lived and taught in our community, and finally died," it would be more than enough.'[4] In the centuries since that event, Christianity has suffered the fate of having been turned into history. This was the transition from 'Christianity' to 'Christendom,' from an existential saving reality to a collective historical phenomenon in which the saving reality has been voided of power.

> In Christ, God offered to enter into relation with the human race. But what did the human race do? Instead of entering into relation with God, they transformed it into the *history* of how God in Christ entered into relation with the apostles, or the *history* of how God in Christ entered into relation with men. In brief, instead of entering into a relation with God, they have turned it into a historical matter which they repeat in diluted form from generation to generation. . . . The confusing factor which has produced 'Christendom' . . . is that, in the course of time, each generation, instead of beginning with the New Testament, has begun with 'our fathers' faith,' with holding fast to our father's faith. Always this knavery of bringing in history and the category of the human race instead of ideality and the single person, which is the Christian category.[5]

This is strong language, yet there is a second idea which we must also take into account and which somewhat modifies Kierkegaard's teaching. This is the important notion of *repetition*. There is an authentic repetition, as well as that mindless repeating 'in diluted form from generation to generation,' mentioned in our last quotation. And although Kierkegaard rejects all notions of progress and perfectibility, there is a form of repetition that holds out the promise of a completion in Christ. This repetition is compared with recollection, as known to the Greeks, but with a difference: 'Repetition and recollection are the same movement, only in opposite directions; for what is recollected has been, is repeated backwards; whereas repetition, properly so-called, is recollected forwards.'[6] Admittedly, this is a very obscure statement. The idea seems to be that a primordial state of existing is repeated, in the sense of being restored, through the act of faith made in the moment of decision. Abraham and Job are instanced as men who achieved such repetition or restoration. Once again, it will be noticed that Kierkegaard's discussion is related to the individual, and history is, indeed, precisely the way in which that primordial fullness of being gets lost in the first place, to be finally restored in repetition. But although Kierkegaard thinks of repetition in relation to the individual, I have introduced the concept in this discussion of history for two reasons. One is the importance of the idea of repetition (though, for the most part, differently understood) in later existentialist writers, notably Nietzsche and Heidegger. The other is the affinity between Kierkegaard's notion and the idea of repetition in early Christian thought, where it had a definitely historical and universal reference. The incarnation of the divine Word was understood as a repetition or recapitulation of the work of the Word in creation; and it was likewise believed that in the end all things would be restored to fullness of being in God. This idea, developed especially by St. Irenaeus, describes on the cosmic-historical scale what Kierkegaard has restricted to individual experience.

From Kierkegaard, we pass to Nietzsche, and to some very different ideas. Yet there are still important resemblances. Nietzsche too sees history as a story of decadence, a falling away from the great into the trivial and finally into nihilism. Christianity, in his view, has played a leading role in bringing about the debilitation of humanity. Yet, on the other hand the theory of evolution is also influential with Nietzsche. Beyond the flatness and triviality of conventional society, beyond even nihilism, lies the possibility of the superman and of a higher mode of being.

There is an interesting discussion of history in Nietzsche's famous essay 'The Use and Abuse of History.'[7] Already in the opening quotation from Goethe a strongly existentialist approach to the theme is announced: 'I hate everything that merely instructs me without increasing or directly quickening my activity.' We study history not for the sake of accumulating interesting information about the past but because 'we need it for life and action.'

Nietzsche then goes on to delineate three ways in which we may relate to history—the monumental, the antiquarian, and the critical.

It is in the case of the *monumental* understanding of history that the relation to life and action is clearest. The monumental moments of history have been those in which, as Nietzsche expresses it, the conception of man has been extended. There has been a new glimpse of the possibilities of humanity. The monumental is the rare, the classic, the great, that which surpasses the average level. Men contemplate these rare moments of history not merely in order to admire the past but because such knowledge gives courage and illumination for the present. 'It is the knowledge that the great thing existed and was therefore possible, and so may be possible again.'[8]

The *antiquarian* attitude to history is that of the man who reverences the past. Assuredly, he finds in it a certain stability. But there is the danger that everything ancient will be venerated equally, just because it is ancient. In the antiquarian attitude, there is neither the perspective nor the interest in present possibility that we have noted in the monumental. At its best, 'it only understands how to preserve life, not to create it.' At its worst, 'the horrid spectacle is seen of the mad collector raking over all the dust heaps of the past.'[9]

The *critical* way of looking at history serves as a corrective to both the monumental and the antiquarian ways. 'Man must have the strength to break up the past . . . . He must bring the past to the bar of judgment, interrogate it remorselessly, and finally condemn it.'[10]

Nietzsche does not identify himself with any one of these three approaches to history. All three can be put to service, and any one of them in isolation can degenerate. But there is another side to the matter. If the past can be illuminating for the present, it is equally true that the present must illuminate the past. 'You can only explain the past by what is highest in the present.'[11] Only the man who experiences something great in himself can penetrate the great events of the past. But here we return again to Nietzsche's critique of his society. Though the 19th century assembled an unprecedented quantity of historical data, its mediocrity of spirit prevented a genuine understanding of history. As with Kierkegaard, so with Nietzsche, it will be the gifted individual who will 'think himself back' to his true needs.

The idea of 'thinking oneself back' suggests something like 'repetition.' But Nietzsche's final idea of repetition is quite different. It becomes the notion of eternal recurrence. In the last resort, to understand history is to be stripped of all comforting illusions, and to know that what has been will be again and that what will be has already been. History is compared to an hourglass; the sand runs through from one half to the other, then the hourglass is turned over and the sand runs back. The neck between is the 'moment.' The moment is also compared to a gate, from which one long lane runs back and another forward. 'Must we not all have been here before? And must we not return and run down that other lane out before us, down that long terrible lane—must we not return eternally?'[12]

How seriously are we to take this doctrine of eternal recurrence? Is it really part of an existentialist understanding of history, or is it rather a metaphysic of history? It is true that Nietzsche does try to advance scientific considerations in its favor—and the theory of an oscillating universe still has its advocates among scientific cosmologists. But the roots of Nietzsche's doctrine are essentially existentialist. The symbol of the eternal return may be understood as the expression of the finitude of existence. God is dead, and man has taken over; but in spite of the promise of the superman, there can be no escape from the endless reshufflings of the finite: 'All goeth, all returneth; eternally rolleth the wheel of being. All dieth, all again blossometh; for ever runneth the year of being. All breaketh, all is joined anew; for ever this same house of being buildeth itself. All things separate, all things greet one another again; for ever the ring of being remaineth true to itself . . . . The center is everywhere.'[13] If freedom, autonomy, and hope appear in Nietzsche's understanding of history, they are finally overcome by tragedy and *amor fati*.

In Heidegger's treatment of history we meet themes that have already been encountered in our discussion of Kierkegaard and Nietzsche, but now these themes occur in a different configuration. After surveying some of the different meanings that have been attached to the word *history*, Heidegger makes the point that the *Dasein* or human existent is himself the theme of history.[14] *Dasein*, constituted by temporality, is the *primary* historical; the world is the *secondary* historical, and it is so because the world has always an existential dimension (see above, pp. 56 ff.). 'With the existence of historical being-in-the-world, what is ready-to-hand and what is present-at-hand have already, in every case, been incorporated into the history of the world.'[15] Even nature is incorporated into history, to the extent that it is the scene of *Dasein's* actions, as battlefield, cultic site, and the like.

Since *Dasein* is the primary historical entity, it follows that Heidegger's understanding of history is, so to speak, his understanding of the *Dasein's* existence writ large. That existence, as care, is constituted by the threefold temporal structure of what-has-been (facticity), the future (possibility), and the present preoccupation (falling). It is pulled together into a unity, an authenticity, by a resolute projection upon the *Dasein's* fate (death). 'Resoluteness constitutes the loyalty of existence to its own self.'[16] The inauthentic man is the irresolute man, and according to Heidegger such a man has no fate. Bearing this analysis in mind, we can now see the outlines of Heidegger's understanding of history. 'If fateful *Dasein*, as being-in-the-world, exists essentially in being-with-others, its historizing is a co-historizing and is determinative for it as *destiny*.'[17] The notion of 'destiny' (*Geschick*) has played a considerable and sometimes ominous part in the history of German philosophy. Its use in Heidegger is somewhat complicated, and we shall meet it again in a slightly different usage. But in the present context we may think of destiny as standing in the same relation to a society or a group of people living at the same time as fate (*Schicksal*) stands to the individual *Dasein*. Just as the individual's possibilities are always factical, qualified by what has been, so the future of any social group lies in a historical context. To give an example used by Heidegger himself, a generation has its destiny, and every individual of that generation shares in its destiny.

Just as there can be authentic and inauthentic existing on the part of the individual, so there can be authentic and inauthentic history on the part of a people. Inauthentic history means drifting along at the mercy of events. Authentic history (or, better, authentic historizing) means laying hold on the factical situation and advancing into the destiny that it leaves open. It is at this point that we meet Heidegger's understanding of repetition, which is very different from Kierkegaard's. The *Dasein* goes back into what-has-been and hands down to himself the authentic possibilities which he finds there and which are repeatable in the moment. This does not mean that one either uses the past as a mere example, or is restricted to or enslaved by the past. On the basis of his temporality and historicality, *Dasein's* repetition is a kind of 'fetching again' the possibility of the past. (Something like this active sense is present in the German word *Wiederholung*.) On the other hand, the repetition is also a disavowal of the past as such. There is a reciprocity between past and present, and certainly not just a slavish copying of the past.

It is because of the basic formal or structural similarity between history and the individual existence that the study of history is possible. Like Dilthey and Nietzsche before him, Heidegger claims that it is in virtue of our participation in—or even our constitution by—history (*Geschichte*) that we are able to develop a scientific interest in history (*Historie*) and to become historiographical and historiological.

But because history is therefore an existential study, Heidegger is constrained to turn around two common assumptions about history. He claims first that history is concerned not with facts but with possibilities, that is to say, not with reconstructing events or chains of events in the past but with exploring the possibilities of the *Dasein* that have been opened up in the course of history; and he claims further that history is interested not in the past but essentially in the future. It fetches from the past the authentic repeatable possibilities of existence in order to project them into the future.

These remarks can hardly fail to suggest a relation with Nietzsche's views on the 'monumental' type of history. There is a connection, and not only with the monumental type of history, but with Nietzsche's threefold division of history, which Heidegger sees as already adumbrating the threefold constitution of the *Dasein*. Any authentic study of history, it is claimed, must unite the three possibilities factically and concretely. I shall quote in full a paragraph in which Heidegger interprets the complicated relation between Nietzsche's view and his own.

As historical, *Dasein* is possible only by reason of its temporality, and temporality temporizes itself in the ecstatico-horizontal unity of its raptures. *Dasein* exists authentically as futural in resolutely disclosing a possibility which it has chosen. Coming back resolutely to itself, it is, by repetition, open for the 'monumental' possibilities of human existence. The historiology which arises from such historicality is 'monumental.' As in the process of having-been, *Dasein* has been delivered over to its thrownness. When the possible is made one's own by repetition, there is adumbrated at the same time the possibility of reverently preserving the existence that has-been-there (*Dagewesen*), in which the possibility seized upon has become manifest. Thus, authentic historiology, as monumental, is 'antiquarian' too. *Dasein* temporalizes itself in the way the future and having-been are united in the present. The present discloses the 'today' authentically, and of course as the moment of vision. But insofar as this 'today' has been interpreted in terms of understanding a

possibility of existence which has been seized upon—an understanding which is repetitive in a futural manner—authentic
historiology becomes a way in which the 'today' gets deprived
of its character as present; in other words, it becomes a way
of painfully detaching oneself from the falling publicness of
the 'today.' As authentic, the historiology which is both monumental and antiquarian is necessarily a critique of the 'present.'
Authentic historicality is the foundation for the possibility of
uniting these three ways of historiology. But the *ground* on which
authentic historiology is founded is *temporality* as the existential
meaning of the being of care.[18]

We have seen that alongside Nietzsche's doctrine of the three
types of history one had to set his view of world-history with its
tragic culmination in the notion of eternal recurrence. In the case of
Heidegger too, the early doctrine of history expounded in *Being and
Time* must be brought into relation to some of his later teaching.
This is not indeed so pessimistic as what we find in Nietzsche, but
it does lay more stress on the idea of destiny. To put the matter in
another way, the early teaching stresses that history is above all a
human or existential phenomenon; the later teaching, in the case of
history as on other topics, stresses rather the role of being as such.

In *An Introduction to Metaphysics* we find Heidegger in the
manner that is typical of the philosophers of existence disavowing
any doctrine of progress, and suggesting rather that history is a
flattening and a qualitative decline. Commenting on a chorus of
Sophocles in which man is depicted as taming the animals, ploughing
up the earth, building cities, and so forth, Heidegger remarks that
this must not be interpreted 'as a narrative of man's development
from the savage hunter and primitive sailor to the civilized builder
of cities.' He continues:

Such a notion is the product of ethnology and psychological
anthropology. It stems from the unwarranted application of a
natural science—and a false one at that—to man's being. The
basic fallacy underlying such modes of thought consists in the
belief that history begins with the primitive and backward, with
the weak and helpless. The opposite is true. The beginning is
the strangest and mightiest. What comes afterwards is not
development but the flattening which results from mere spreading
out; it is inability to retain the beginning; the beginning is
emasculated and exaggerated into a caricature of greatness, taken
as purely numerical and quantitative size and extension. That
strangest of all beings (man) *is* what he is *because* he harbors

such a beginning in which everything all at once burst from superabundance into the overpowering and strove to master it.[19]

The 'overpowering' is being, the non-human or trans-human environment in which human existence has its setting. More and more, Heidegger seems to stress the part that being itself plays in history—for this is not some timeless being, in the sense of the old fashioned metaphysics, but being in a dynamic sense. The notion of *Geschick*, 'destiny,' acquires a new sense. The word is derived from the German verb *schicken*, 'send,' and Heidegger also exploits its similarity to *Geschichte*, 'history.' W. J. Richardson has suggested the word *mittence* as a suitable translation. He writes:

Being discloses itself to and in its 'there,' but since it is being that holds the primacy, being is conceived as sending itself into its 'there.' We may speak of this self-sending as proceeding from being and call it a 'self-emitting,' or, if we may be permitted a neologism to designate a completely new concept, a 'mittence' (*Geschick*) of being. We may speak of it too as terminating in the 'there,' and therefore call it a 'committing' or 'commitment' (*Schicksal*) of the 'there' to its privileged destiny as the shepherd of being.[20]

If Richardson is correct, what we seem to have in some of Heidegger's later writings (the essay 'Der Spruch des Anaximander' has a crucial discussion) is a speculative attempt to consider the historical concepts of *Geschick* and *Schicksal* no longer existentially (from the side of man) but ontologically (from the side of being). In the course of history being withdraws itself or discloses itself to the 'being-there' of the privileged ontological entity, the *Dasein*. Thus there are different epochs of history, differentiated according to the different ways in which being discloses (or conceals) itself. These variations are the mittences of being and are experienced as the destinies of different generations. 'Out of the epoch of being comes the epochal essence of its mittence, in which is authentic world history. The epochal essence of being belongs within the hidden time-character of being and betokens the essence of time which is thought in being.'[21] This is an obscure doctrine, which has obviously moved away from the existential analysis of history found in *Being and Time*, and it will become more intelligible only after we have discussed the subject of existential metaphysics (see below, p. 190).

Jaspers is another philosopher of existence who has had interesting things to say about history. Early in this book we took note of his theory of an 'axial age' in world history, set forth in his book

The Origin and Goal of History. The axial age was the period around 500 B.C. when men in different parts of the world began to reflect with a new seriousness on the questions of their own existence. But the ultimate origin and the final goal of history remain hidden. In accordance with his finitude man lives out his history without knowledge of its ultimate context. 'Historians cannot investigate history's origin—how it came to begin—nor its goal, and whether it has any goal. Their science stands amid historic reality, always at the present, at a particular moment in time, open at both ends. That science itself is history, a part of its own object.'[22]

But although history as science works within limited horizons, men do in fact try to get a wider vision. They are not content with just an unending stream of events, without beginning or goal to confer meaning. Thus they represent history under the ciphers of history. Like other ciphers (see above, p. 116), the ciphers of history are not to be taken literally or objectified. They are an oblique, evanescent way of referring to that which cannot be directly grasped. Among the ciphers of history Jaspers counts all those myths and metaphysics of history which attempt to set forth its total character: the idea of progress, the doctrine of eternal recurrence, divine providence, eschatology, and so forth. Ciphers bring perspective and orientation into the multitude of events discovered by historical science. They are said to encourage seriousness and action beyond what would be possible if we understood history as simply a point-less stumbling from one event to another. On the other hand, a continuous struggle goes on among the ciphers of history—as among all ciphers—as now one, now another elicits an existential response and illuminates or fails to illuminate man's path.

Such are some of the currents and cross-currents in existentialist thinking about history. There is agreement that no merely external supposedly scientific account of history is adequate, and that history can be known only through engagement in it. There is agreement too in rejecting any easy, irresponsible doctrine of progress. But beyond this limited core of agreement, we meet differences paralleling those that we have encountered at many other stages of our inquiry already. Is history essentially made by man, or do forces of fate and destiny (perhaps tragic forces) bend the shape of history in spite of human effort? Does history move toward a goal, or does it repeat itself in endless cycles? Is there meaning and hope, or funda-mental absurdity? These differences will appear in their sharpest form when we come to the question of metaphysics.

EXISTENTIALISM AS SOCIAL AND POLITICAL CRITIQUE

We have seen how the problem of history has moved the focus of the existential analysis away from the individual to society. We have seen also that among existentialists the interest in history is not primarily an interest in the past but an attempt, through study of the human possibilities revealed in history, to find our way in the present and the future. The very meaning of existence is to project or transcend into the future. Thus, at the end of this chapter on history, it would seem perfectly fair that we should direct to the existentialists some questions of a social and political nature concerning the present state and the future prospects of the world. What bearing does existentialism have upon the technological revolution, the population explosion, space exploration, the arms race, and all the other things that are going on in the closing decades of the 20th century?

Some critics of existentialism might reply that it has no bearing upon these great issues at all. They would say that it is essentially an individualistic and personalistic philosophy, perhaps even in those forms where it seeks to develop an understanding of the interpersonal, and that when one has to consider nations, corporations, labor unions, political parties, and the like, existentialism is seen to be completely irrelevant.

I shall not deny that there is considerable force in this criticism. We have seen in several of the foregoing discussions how influential the category of the individual has been in existentialist thought. Yet, when we consider the matter further, we have also to acknowledge that several leading existentialists have been deeply involved in political controversy—Unamuno, Berdyaev, Sartre, Camus, to mention only a few. After all, there need not and should not be a disjunction between the individual and the communal poles of human well-being. It may be worth recalling that St. Augustine, who had some affinities with the existentialists of later times, was profoundly conscious of the mystery and the pathos of individual existence; yet his greatest work was a study of history in terms of the interaction of the two cities. An ideal human society, if we could envisage it, would be one in which social structures promoted the highest degree of individual development, and, conversely, one in which the promotion of individual fulfillment did not disrupt the cohesion of the social structure.

In what follows we shall briefly consider two questions. The first concerns the bearings of existentialism on contemporary society; the second concerns the political implications (if any) of existentialism.

1. If the vast and increasing number of human beings inhabiting our planet today are to survive (to say nothing of having a full life), then a far more tightly organized social structure is required than was sufficient in times gone by. There was a time when the province, the small town, the village even, were the natural social units, and within these small units, more or less personal relations were possible between individuals and groups and helped to shape the social structure. But now, in Marshall McLuhan's phrase, the world itself is a large village. However, it is such a large village that the kind of personal contacts once possible are no longer possible. Now vast organizations, governmental and commercial, national and international, are shaping the lives of all of us. Above all, planning is necessary in this kind of world, and it is a planning that can scarcely be done in any but an impersonal way.

Some point to the gains that technological society has brought— the conquest of disease, hunger, poverty, the opportunities for education and development. Others point to the threats—to ecological imbalance, to the depredation of the earth's resources, perhaps especially to the danger of depersonalization and dehumanization. I shall not rehearse these stale arguments, either pro or con. We are faced with a highly ambiguous situation. But the point is that this situation cannot be escaped. It is part of the facticity of contemporary existence.

Existentialists are sometimes accused of escapism and lack of realism. It is said that they want to turn the clock back, and that they have a romantic nostalgia for the 'simple' life of a rural type of society. There may be some justification for these charges, but the situation is more complicated and the question has to be taken further. After all, we have already seen that the 'instrumental' view of the world put forward by some existentialists could be interpreted as a philosophical charter for technological exploitation (see above, p. 62). It is not the technological society as such that the existentialist rejects, but the narrowing of human life which an exclusive preoccupation with its external conditions promotes.

The existentialist is on firm ground when he points to the growing extent of alienation that is appearing in the contemporary world, among the young, the intellectuals, the artists, the underprivileged. To some degree existentialism is the voice of this alienated group, for on the basis of its own account of history, it must be seen as itself a historical phenomenon (see above, p. 176). It brings to expression a profound undercurrent of the contemporary mind.

The existentialist critique of society is not therefore to be dismissed as merely romantic aberration. It is rather a prophetic voice, seeking to enhance the sense of the humanity of man and to guard it against further erosion. It looks not to the pre-industrial past of an agricultural society but to the possibility of a post-industrial (perhaps automated) society of the future in which the values and dignities of life will be rated higher than they are at present.

2. We turn now to the question about the political aspects of existentialism. Does this type of philosophy ally itself with any particular political ideology, or does it generate an ideology of its own?

Both of these questions must be answered in the negative. Just as we have seen that the existentialist concept of an authentic existence does not imply adherence to any particular ethical ideal and can be achieved in a variety of ways, so we find a wide variety of political affiliations among those who may be called existentialists. Heidegger was for a brief time a Nazi, but Jaspers consistently opposed the Nazis. Sartre has been attracted to Marxism, but it would be hard to find more penetrating and damaging critiques of Marxism than have come from Berdyaev and Camus. Their critiques are all the more telling because these men too have felt the attraction of Marxism. If existentialism does not ally itself with any particular brand of politics, neither does it generate an ideology of its own. Indeed, the very idea of an ideology would suggest a form of heteronomy or bad faith. If existentialism pointed to any political creed, it would be to the absence of government, to anarchy. But no one except a fanatic would advocate anarchy. In a perfect world, perhaps civil institutions would be unnecessary. But in an imperfect world, almost any government is better than none.

Does this mean then that existentialism is apolitical, and that to the adherents of this philosophy, political arrangements are a matter of indifference? I do not think so. But it would seem to me that the existentialist attitude to politics might be similar to that which Johannes Metz has recommended to the Christian in his concept of a 'political theology.'[23] According to Metz, the major function of the Christian in politics is a critical one. He advocates no ideology of his own and he does not identify himself with any actual ideology, but by means of his social critique he seeks to maintain and enlarge the conditions for a genuinely human existence.

I think it can be claimed that this is what many existentialists have done. They are not individualists in the sense of being indifferent to social and political arrangements, but they remain free to criticize every political movement that needlessly restricts human freedom and diminishes human dignity, every system that sets the abstraction of the system itself above the concrete well-being of the persons whom the system is supposed to serve.

This is the essential point in the existentialist critique of Marxism. 'For Marx,' claims Berdyaev, 'class is more real than man.'[24] The comment of Camus is similar: 'To the extent to which Marx predicted the inevitable establishment of the classless city, and to the extent to which he thus established the good will of history, every check to the advance toward freedom must be attributed to the ill will of man .... Marxism in one of its aspects is a doctrine of culpability on man's part and of innocence on history's.'[25]

Likewise fascism in its many forms sets up the abstraction of the state against concrete human existence. In political philosophy as in other branches of philosophy, the existentialist sees his task as that of fighting against every distorting abstraction. The notion of the corporate personality of the state is such an abstraction. It is a fiction and must not be valued above the real personalities of the citizens.

Thus, although existentialism is not identified with any one political system, it has inspired a political critique that seeks to defend human dignity against all political encroachments.

CHAPTER THIRTEEN

Existentialist Metaphysics

METAPHYSICAL DIMENSIONS OF EXISTENTIALISM

The status of metaphysics varies greatly from one period of history to another. There are times when an explicit interest in the problem of ultimate reality is strong, and then metaphysical thinking flourishes. But at times when people are more agnostic or positivistic in their outlook, such thinking languishes and may even be declared impossible. Yet it seems doubtful whether the proscription of metaphysics can be taken with complete seriousness, for even those who deny the possibility of metaphysics often appear to entertain a crypto-metaphysic of their own.

It is nowadays recognized that there is more than one kind of metaphysics, and that some metaphysics may be immune to criticisms that are very damaging to others. Speculative metaphysics of the traditional sort may be regarded as an attempt to extend reason beyond the empirical phenomena of the world so as to grasp the supposedly supersensible reality underlying these phenomena. This was the most ambitious type of metaphysics and the kind that Hume and Kant had in mind when they made their criticisms. These philosophers did not bring an end to metaphysics—there continued to be vigorous metaphysical speculation in the 19th century—but they did put a large question mark alongside the enterprise, and it is in disrepute with many persons today. However, there are more modest kinds of metaphysics. These are descriptive rather than speculative. They set out to describe the most general categories under which we have an understanding of our world and they explore the most general conditions of experience. Some philosophers who deny the possibility of speculative metaphysics are willing to allow that what I have called the more 'modest' kinds of metaphysics are legitimate exercises. Kant himself, while criticizing rational metaphysics, did not hesitate to use the expression *metaphysics* for his own critical exploration of the general conditions of experience.

Just as there are ambiguities in the meaning of *metaphysics*, so we find ambivalences in the existentialist evaluation of this type of philosophical inquiry. As far as speculative metaphysics is concerned, existentialists tend to share the distrust that most contemporary philosophers feel in the face of this high-soaring exercise of reason. At an early stage of our inquiry we saw that the existentialist denies the competence of thought to grasp the concrete realities of existence and to fit them into some comprehensive rational system. Kierkegaard's existentialism was called forth precisely in protest against what he took to be the overweening metaphysical system of Hegel, and later existentialists have remained anti-metaphysical in this sense. But existentialists are not positivists, and if they are distrustful of rational metaphysics, it does not follow that they reject all metaphysics, The very fact that human existence is the theme of existentialism leads into questions of a metaphysical kind, for the existentialist denies that this existence is an objectifiable empirical phenomenon. Rather, he agrees with St. Augustine that man is an abyss. There is in existence an inexhaustibility and a transcendence, and to probe into these in any depth is to engage in some kind of metaphysical inquiry. We have seen too that, for the existentialist, the existent cannot be abstracted from his environment, so that to raise the question of man is also to raise the questions of the world, of time, of history, and of man's relation to these.

Some existentialists frankly use the expression *metaphysics* for those parts of their philosophies that discuss the larger questions concerning man's place in the world, though they may distinguish between the kind of metaphysics that they affirm and the traditional kind. Other existentialists avoid the word *metaphysics* or even deliberately reject it, but we may find them substituting for it some other word, such as *ontology*, and engaging in a type of inquiry akin to metaphysics.

Among those who are willing to use the word *metaphysics* is Berdyaev. He acknowledges indeed that Kant showed the illegitimacy of rationalistic metaphysics. But he claims that 'it is precisely Kant who makes existential metaphysics a possibility.'[1]

What is here called 'existential metaphysics' Berdyaev can also call 'metaphysics of the subject,' to be contrasted with 'metaphysics of the object.' But the expression *metaphysics of the subject* is misleading, because we might be tempted to understand 'subject' as 'thinking subject,' and Berdyaev wishes to assert that metaphysics is a work of the whole man. 'The pursuit of a metaphysics which is completely scientific in form, of metaphysics as a strict and objective science, is a will o' the wisp. Metaphysics can only be the apprehension of spirit, in spirit and through spirit. Metaphysics is in the subject, which creates spiritual values and makes a transcending act, not into the object but into its own self-revealing depth.'[2] The last sentence also makes clear the inevitability of metaphysics, in the sense intended by Berdyaev; for the human existent is not exhausted by any objectifying empirical description but has dimensions which can be explored only in a metaphysical inquiry.

For most of his career Heidegger has made ontology the center of his task. His study of the existent has been seen as a way toward the problem of the meaning of being. In some of the earlier writing Heidegger seems scarcely to distinguish between 'ontology' and 'metaphysics.' Thus, in *Was ist Metaphysik?* the question of nothing is taken as an illustration of a metaphysical question and is also shown to be inextricably bound up with the question of being. But eventually Heidegger came to distinguish the ontological inquiry from metaphysics, and to speak of the 'overcoming' of metaphysics. As he understands it, metaphysics has been concerned with beings rather than with being as such; furthermore, it has failed to attain the level of a truly ontological thinking.

Jaspers dislikes the expressions *metaphysics* and *ontology*, but he has his own kind of metaphysics, which he calls by the clumsy name of *periechontology*. 'Ours is not an ontological search for a world of objective definitions, but a periechontological one for the source of subject and object, for their relations and interrelations.'[3] The theme of periechontology is the encompassing, that realm which embraces both subject and object. Because this is the encompassing, obviously it cannot be an *object* of study. Yet it is obvious too that although Jaspers does not call his enterprise *metaphysics* or *ontology*, his concern with the encompassing has the kind of ultimacy that is characteristic of metaphysics. His philosophy has also been compared to a kind of secular theology, and certainly the notion of 'philosophical faith' plays an important role in it.[4]

One could find 'metaphysics' or 'ontologies' in most of the other leading existentialists. One must agree with the comment of

Ronald Grimsley: 'The movement which began as a vigorous attack on Hegelian metaphysics is, therefore, metaphysical in another sense, since the dethronement of a predominantly conceptualizing rationalism in favor of an "existential" approach which accords greater importance to the testimony of affective experience is intended mainly as a way of impelling man towards a new awareness of being.'[5]

We must now consider in more detail the shape of an existentialist ontology.

FROM EXISTENCE TO BEING

I have said in the last section that because man is an inexhaustible abyss and because moreover he is unintelligible apart from his environment in the widest sense, the existential analysis leads into the borders of ontological reflection. But there is a recognizable path in several of the existentialist philosophers. The starting-point is existence in its total range, rather than the reason or intellect as such. Furthermore, it is existence in its critical situations or at its limits, where these limits and even what lies beyond them are lit up or disclosed. Thus, as we have learned in an earlier chapter (see above, p. 125), the existentialist can even talk of 'ontological emotions,' of moods or attunements in which the existent has become subtly aware of his total situation. It is in such situations that he claims his ontological insights, his vision of being.

But what is one to say about such insight or vision? Does it, for instance, have cognitive status? I have already argued that no sharp division can be made between feeling and understanding. But certainly the kind of metaphysic or ontology reached along the existential route, even if it is in some sense a kind of knowing, does not have the cognitive status belonging to our assertions concerning ordinary matters of fact. The existentialist would doubtless claim some 'truth' for his ontological vision; it does imply some disclosing or unveiling. But it is not a truth that is provable, and presumably the only kind of testing to which it could be subjected would be to ask others to participate in the vision or follow the road leading to it, and then learn whether they reach the same ontological insight. But this seems to suggest in turn that ontological language is not a language that describes but rather a language that evokes. It brings the other to the point where, it is hoped, he can share in the same disclosure of being. So again we have to ask how far one can say that this type of exercise is cognitive. An ontological reflection that is deeply colored by feeling and mood, and that expresses itself in a language evocative rather than descriptive is obviously no ordinary kind of knowing. It has affinities with such religious experiences as revelation and mystical vision; or with esthetic experiences of perceiving things in the depth of their inter-relatedness. The only language that in the end seems appropriate to talk about such matters is the language of myth and poetry; or perhaps one can only become silent. And even if something can be said to be known and to receive some indirect expression, it is known only in a situation and from a point of view; even if others can be brought to share the ontological vision, the relativity of an historical situation is not removed.

So we find ourselves in the midst of many difficult questions. Can one still speak of philosophy, of truth and understanding, when one seems to have come into an area where the stringency of thought breaks down and everything begins to shimmer in the haze of poetry and mysticism? Or can one speak of 'knowledge' or use such high-sounding words as 'metaphysics' and 'ontology' for the existentialist vision of being? Assuredly, the existentialist himself is under no illusions about what is possible. He cannot step outside of existence, so to speak, in order to give a universally valid account of being, an account that would be objective and scientific in the broadest sense, an account that would hold true for all times and all places. Perhaps some old-time metaphysicians thought that they could do this. The existentialist renounces anything so ambitious, and, at the best, speaks haltingly and indirectly of being as glimpsed from one unprivileged point of view situated within being itself. Yet he would not agree that his utterance is empty or that it merely evinces a subjective emotion. He wants to claim some knowledge and some participation in truth, though his claim is much more modest and more qualified than the traditional claims of rational metaphysics.

I think we can best assess the nature and claims of an existential metaphysic by considering a concrete example in some detail. I have chosen Jaspers' philosophy—and especially his so-called *periechon-tology*—to serve as our example, but many of the features and contours to be observed in this particular existential metaphysic (if I may be permitted to use the expression) are characteristic of the shape of any existential metaphysic.

The point where the questions of individual existence pass into wider questions of being and reality is, in Jaspers' view, the 'limit-situation' (*Grenzsituation*). This is an idea that appeared in his early work on psychiatry, *Allgemeine Psychopathologie,* published in 1913, and the idea continued to be important for his subsequent philosophical writing. As the name implies, the limit-situation is one in which the existent comes to the boundaries of his existence. It may be death or guilt or suffering that brings him to this situation, but we should notice that although the ideas of finitude and anxiety are present in Jaspers' thought, as they are in most of the existentialists, he does not give just a negative picture. It is true that in the limit-situation existence 'founders' or is 'shattered,' to use a favorite expression of his. The ordinary ways of comporting oneself and of understanding one's world no longer suffice. Yet the limit-situation is also characterized by an awareness that one's existence is the gift of Transcendence—an awareness not altogether unlike the religious experience of grace. In other words, the limit-situation is both a shattering one and a liberating one. It enables man to become fully human. 'Man's freedom is inseparable from his consciousness of his finite nature.'[6] By becoming aware of Transcendence, the infinite which contrasts his own finiteness, man is said to transcend his finiteness and to be directed 'to an origin other than that which science makes intelligible to him in his finite existence.'[7]

Can we say more clearly what is meant by this Transcendence which encounters man on the boundaries of his existence? Is Transcendence, in Jaspers' usage, equivalent to God? Certainly there is a connection, but if one has some definite conception of God, for instance, as a personal God, then this would be no more than a cipher of Transcendence. Thus God and Transcendence are not identical. Transcendence cannot be thought or made the object of thought. This is because it belongs to the realm of the encompassing, that which comes before subject and object. Transcendence is indeed the encompassing of all encompassing. 'The eternal, the indestructible, the immutable, the source, the encompassing of all encompassing —this can be neither visualized nor grasped in thought. . . . When we cover it with categories such as being, cause, origin, eternity, indestructibility or nothingness, when we call it by these categorical ciphers, we have missed it already.'[8]

Yet, having said all this, Jaspers goes on to say that Transcendence

is not an indifferent limit that is thus missed in all thinking. It is not something to which no eye or thought can reach, and which therefore does not concern us. It concerns us so much that no other source of light will make all being, ours included, transparent. Transcendence—which is not a cipher but something we relate to in the cipher language, something unthinkable which we must think all the same—is as much being as nothingness.[9]

Is there cognition here or no cognition? Do we know or do we not know? The answer to these questions depends on how broadly we are prepared to define 'knowing' (see above, p. 100 ff.). There is no conceptual knowledge here, and nothing provable. But Jaspers is not prepared to say that it is all a matter of subjective feeling. However indirectly and indefinitely, the ciphers point to a reality beyond themselves. Jaspers writes frequently of 'philosophical faith.' This is not a series of demonstrable propositions about the universe, but he insists that it is not just a believing state of mind. This faith, moreover, has some content. It implies recognition of Transcendence, of a moral imperative, and of the finite, dependent character of worldly existence.[10]

The road we have traced in Jaspers, or something similar to it, can be seen in other philosophers of existence. It is apparent, for instance, in Heidegger. Admittedly, he began in the hope that one could proceed by a 'scientific' (*wissenschaftlich*) procedure from the analysis of the *Dasein* to the full conceptualizing of the meaning of being (*Sein*). But, as he says himself, he found that the way broke off. He had to find another way, and we can see along it, though in different form and under different names, the landmarks that we have already met in Jaspers' way. It is something like a 'limit-situation' that Heidegger describes in *Was ist Metaphysik?* The self becomes aware of its finitude and nothingness through the ontological experience of anxiety in the face of death; but this is precisely the way that leads to the encounter with being. Although Heidegger speaks of the dissolution of logic in this encounter, he does not try to construct a theory of indirect discourse, comparable to Jaspers' notion of ciphers. His approach is closer to the way of mysticism and negative theology. However, he sees language as the vehicle by which being communicates itself to the *Dasein*, so being is not left entirely without form. It cannot indeed be known or conceptualized in the way that finite beings can be known, for being itself is 'totally other' from beings. Yet it is no mere haze or empty word (as Nietzsche claimed) but the most concrete of realities.

In Sartre too there is an ontology, though in his case existentialism remains much more tied to the phenomena of human existence than it does with Jaspers and Heidegger (if one may still speak of 'existentialism' in their case). It is still true that in Sartre we encounter 'ontological emotion' and something very much like revelation.

But he never comes to that attempted reconciliation of existence and being found in the German philosophers of existence. In fact, Sartre's 'metaphysics' seems to be fundamentally dualistic, because there is an unbridgeable gap between the *pour-soi* and the *en-soi*.

THE SEARCH FOR ULTIMATE REALITY

We have now seen more clearly the shape of an existentialist metaphysic or ontology. It certainly differs from the old-style rationalistic metaphysics and does not claim to be 'scientific' or to have universal and 'objective' validity. But neither is it regarded as merely emotive and subjective. It is true that a parallel is drawn with poetry. But, then, metaphysicians who are not existentialists have also compared metaphysics to poetry. Whitehead is an example. It has not been supposed, however, that poetry is devoid of its own kind of wisdom and insight.

Perhaps the existentialist ambivalence toward metaphysics may point the way toward a new understanding of this recurrent drive toward constructing an account of the ultimately real. On the one hand there is a cutting away of the larger pretensions of traditional metaphysics. Just because of man's finitude, facticity, and historicality, he can never have a final view of the whole. Yet the existentialist refuses to join the positivist. Some glimpse of reality, he claims, is granted to men, however fleeting and fragmentary this glimpse may be. But language too runs out, and only indirectly can anything be said about reality. So vague and elusive does the language sometimes become, and so cautious is the speaker, that one has to ask whether, after all, anything is being said.

However, the philosopher has his own distinctive path, even if at the end that path converges with the paths of mystics and poets. The philosopher's path is the path of rational inquiry and reflection, and is in the broad sense 'scientific.' His aim is to conceptualize, and his thinking is subjected to rational criticism and analysis. Most of the existentialists set out on this path, though they find that it stops short of the goal they had set for themselves. Surely Jaspers voices a truly philosophic spirit when he writes: 'Unless an idea is subjected to the coldly dispassionate test of scientific inquiry, it is rapidly consumed in the fire of emotions and passions, or else it withers into a dry and narrow fanaticism.' This quotation, incidentally, comes from a book which bears in English the significant title, *The Way to Wisdom*.[11] Whatever ways may be taken by the poet or the mystic.

the philosopher's way to wisdom must lead through the rigors of rational thought if he has any claim to be a philosopher.

But in existentialism the critique becomes reciprocal. If science absolutizes itself or if we are dominated by an intellectualism that has grown too narrowly rationalistic and too narrowly empirical, then existence itself makes a protest. The passionate Unamuno cried: 'When mathematics kills, it is a lie.'[12] A saner but essentially similar critique of science is found in Jaspers. A philosophy of existence makes us aware of the limits of science and of what can be attained by the methods of science. Jaspers' view of the matter is admirably summarized by Eugene T. Long:

> Science does not produce knowledge of being itself. It can give only knowledge of particular appearances or objects within the finite order. It cannot provide life with its meaning or goals, its values or directions. Rather, in the midst of scientific thinking we may become aware of its limits and consequently of that which has its source in something other than that available to scientific investigation. We may become aware of striving toward a unity of the particular data of science.[13]

The existentialist is in fact more realistic than the positivist, for he recognizes that, as Kant once said, metaphysics is 'a natural disposition of the reason.' In spite of positivist prohibitions, the human mind will venture out beyond the empirical phenomena. But this is not just an intellectual thirst. It is also an existential drive. The ontological question is already wrapped up in the existential question; and no one can help asking the existential question, for he cannot help deciding about his existence and determining his goals and values. To do this, however, he needs an orientation to his world and some unitary vision. The existentialists, as we have seen, are well aware that no rationally provable metaphysical system can be constructed. Risk and commitment are involved when we decide what we shall take for real and what for unreal. The existentialist philosopher at this point goes beyond the provable, in company with the poets and mystics. Yet what distinguishes him as a philosopher is that his leap can never be an uncritical one, as Kierkegaard seemed to think. Criticism, moreover, will continue to operate after the leap is made.

The desire to know, the drive of the intellect, is subtly intertwined in its roots with the desire to be, the drive of the whole person. There is a personal factor in all knowing, even the kind which seems most matter-of-fact. That personal factor becomes increasingly important as we move toward the kind of knowing that is called 'metaphysical.' For this has to do with the ultimate convictions that also shape our lives. In other words, metaphysics has a religious dimension—using the word *religious* in the widest sense so that it would not be restricted to those who finally come to a theistic metaphysic. F. H. Bradley wrote:

> All of us, I presume, more or less, are led beyond the region of ordinary facts. Some in one way and some in others, we seem to touch and have communion with what is beyond the visible world. In various manners we find something higher, which both supports and humbles, both chastens and transports us. And, with certain persons, the intellectual effort to understand the universe is a principal way of thus experiencing the Deity. No one, probably, who has not felt this, however differently he might describe it, has ever cared much for metaphysics.[14]

But although the personal and even religious dimension becomes very important in the kind of knowing we call *metaphysical*, it does not follow that one can no longer speak of knowing. To be sure, the existentialist acknowledges that one cannot claim for this knowing the universality of science. Metaphysics is conditioned by a stream of history, by a finite point of view, even by the personality of the metaphysician, his sensitivities, and his lack of sensitivities. No ontology is final or adequate. The flash of ontological insight, however, may be reckoned the most precious knowledge that we have. And although its truth cannot be established objectively, it is true to the extent that it yields a fuller interpretation of the existence of the persons who adhere to it. By this I do not mean that it is merely 'life-enhancing' or is to be judged in a purely pragmatic way. I mean rather that it supplies a basis for an ever-widening structure of intelligibility and meaning; and with every widening of this structure, the ontology itself gets confirmation.

Metaphysics is the search for ultimate reality, and in religion ultimate reality has been called God. Sometimes metaphysicians have tried to prove God's existence, and sometimes they have constructed atheistic metaphysics. Of course, it has often been said that the God of the philosophers is not the same as the God of religion, and this is a statement very congenial to the spirit of existentialism. For if the existentialist speaks of God, it is not on the basis of a rational argument establishing God's existence but as a result of reflection on the meaning of human existence, when this is explored to its farthest boundaries.

Some existentialists do speak of God and some do not. We come back once more to the distinction between theistic existentialism (as represented by Kierkegaard, Marcel, Buber, and others) and atheistic existentialism (Sartre and Camus). I have said already that this distinction should not be absolutized, and I think that the discussion in the present chapter has made it clear that it is impossible to make a neat division, ascribing atheism to some existentialists and theism to others. By its very approach to the problem, existentialism lives in a tension between belief and doubt. Kierkegaard's faith involves risk and fragility, while the unfaith of Camus has elements of belief, for if everything were totally absurd and meaningless, it would make no sense to rebel against being treated as an object.

The meaning of 'God' in existentialist metaphysics is to be identified with the sources of grace and judgment that touch on man at the deepest levels of his existence. The distinction between the theistic and atheistic existentialists is to be seen not so much in the question of whether or not they believe in the existence of an exalted suprasensible being (the God of much traditional metaphysics) but on whether they take meaning or lack of meaning, grace or absurdity, to be the more fundamental interpretation of existence. Here we may recall Ricoeur's point that the difference may reflect the contrast between the otherness and the kinship of being, long known in theology as the contrast between the *via negativa* and the *via eminentiae* (see above, p. 134).

Jaspers and Heidegger are especially interesting as showing how the disjunction of theism and atheism in existentialism is by no means clearcut and has quite transformed the traditional debate about God. For these two philosophers stand somewhere between the confessed theists and the confessed atheists. Neither Jaspers' 'Transcendence' nor Heidegger's 'Being' could be identified with God in the traditional sense, yet neither philosopher is atheistic and both Transcendence and Being have godlike characteristics. They remind one of the *Deitas* which Meister Eckhart distinguished from *Deus*, or of the 'God beyond theism' of which Paul Tillich has spoken. It is not surprising that Heidegger is unwilling to be called either a theist or an atheist. Existentialism when developed ontologically does in fact suggest new possibilities for a concept of God, perhaps more viable than the concept of traditional theism. But no more than any other philosophy does existentialism resolve the final ambiguity of the world.

THE DESTINY OF THE INDIVIDUAL

If the quest for ultimate reality, the never-ending debate over the reality and nature of God, is one great problem of metaphysics, another is the desire to know the final destiny of the individual, the hopes and speculations concerning immortality. Usually the two questions are considered to be closely related, and an affirmative answer to one frequently implies an affirmative answer to the other. But this is not always the case, and the existential importance of the two questions seems to vary from one person to another. There have been 'God-intoxicated' men for whom God was everything, and the destiny of the individual mattered nothing—let him lose himself in God, if that will in any way enrich the being of God. There have been others (the British philosopher McTaggart is a notable example) who denied God but believed passionately in the immortality of the individual soul.

One might have expected that the existentialists, stressing as they do the uniqueness and irreplaceability of the individual, would have been much exercised about the problem of his final destiny. But this is not so. No doubt some of them do believe in immortality of some kind. Kierkegaard certainly did, and for him man was still conceived as a synthesis of the temporal and the eternal. Berdyaev denied a natural or metaphysical immortality but believed in the possibility of attaining a quality of existence that would bring 'victory over death.' But it is more typical of the existentialist stance to see death as final. We have already seen the important part played by the concept of death in the thought of such men as Heidegger, Sartre, and Camus (see above, pp. 150–5). For them, it is death above all that constitutes human finitude, and its prominence in their thinking lends a somber tone to their philosophies. Yet even they seek a kind of 'eternal life' in the midst of temporality as they seek to transcend the sheer successiveness of existence.

There are, I think, two considerations arising from existentialist philosophy which have a bearing on the problem of the final destiny of the individual. These considerations are not in any sense like 'proofs' of immortality, in the traditional sense. They are simply pointers, and they do not compel our assent. But I think they are significant and permit a sober hope that the irreplaceable individual is not destined to be utterly lost.

The first consideration has to do with the *intensity* of human existence. In man, life is not merely biological and quantitative. It has undergone a qualitative transformation, and with this goes the desire to break free from the transitory and to perpetuate the intense 'moment.' Some men, at least, have felt deeply that life with this quality cannot perish. Unamuno especially has given classic utterance to this passionate longing for eternity. 'The feeling of the vanity of the passing world kindles love in us, the only thing that triumphs over the vain and transitory, the only thing that fills life again and eternalizes it . . . . And love, above all when it struggles against destiny, overwhelms us with the feeling of the vanity of this world of appearances and gives us a glimpse of another world, in which destiny is overcome and liberty is law.'[15] Whatever 'reasons of the head' may speak against it, this passionate desire of the heart prevails. At least, says Unamuno, let us *deserve* immortality, and if there is only nothing for us, then the universe itself stands condemned: 'If it is nothingness that awaits us, let us so act that it shall be an unjust fate.'[16]

The second consideration is less emotional and more analytic. It consists in the claim that existential analysis reveals in man an emerging essence which cannot be fulfilled within the limit of his earthly life and which therefore points to the possibility of a fulfillment beyond death. Although the German theologian W. Pannenberg would not be considered an existentialist, he has nevertheless used phenomenological analysis of the meaning of hope in human existence to support belief in what he calls *resurrection* rather than immortality. 'The phenomenology of hope indicates that it belongs to the essence of conscious human existence to hope beyond death.' Pannenberg's argument turns partly on man's awareness of death, for to be aware of the limit of death is also to be able to conceive something beyond the limit; and partly on man's openness and self-transcendence, which drive him beyond every given state of himself. It will be seen therefore that his reasoning is guided by two themes that are basic in the reflection of existentialist philosophers.[17]

Of course, to Unamuno one may say that the universe is unjust; and to Pannenberg one may say that the essence of man cannot be fulfilled and is self-frustrating. This is possible, and it may be that the intensity of life and the phenomenon of hope are alike illusory guides to man's final destiny. It seems clear, however, that this question of the destiny of the individual is inseparable from the question about ultimate reality. If the universe is absurd and godless, then there is no final destiny for the individual. But if the universe is a meaningful process in which God, Transcendence, or Being is realizing creative possibilities in finite beings, then it is reasonable to hope that whatever of value is so realized will not be finally lost.

CHAPTER FOURTEEN

Existentialist Influence in the Arts and Sciences

PHILOSOPHY AND CULTURE

What is the relation of a philosophy to the culture in which it has grown up? The question is not easy to answer, and today there is renewed discussion about the social responsibility of the philosopher. As far as existentialism is concerned, the relation to the prevailing culture would seem to be a reciprocal one. On the one hand existentialism brings to explicit intellectual form currents that run deep in contemporary culture, and the historical survey carried out near the beginning of this book gave us evidence of this (see above pp. 18–40). Existentialism has on the other hand something of a prophetic function; it criticizes much in the contemporary world, and above all it criticizes everything that seems to threaten the possibility of authentic humanity.

To say this, of course, is to acknowledge the ambivalence of our present culture. There are in it many conflicting trends, and it certainly does not constitute a unity.

The importance of existentialism (or of any other philosophy) may be judged to some extent by considering how far it has succeeded in bursting out beyond the rather narrow circles of professional philosophers to exercise a wider cultural influence, either by helping to bring to expression the spirit of the culture or by criticizing it. Judged by this criterion, existentialism must be considered very important indeed. In many branches of inquiry and in several of the arts the influence of existentialism is very apparent. Of course, this

203

does not always imply that a psychologist or a novelist, let us say, has consciously studied existentialist philosophy and then proceeded to apply it in his own work (though this has often been true). In some cases the 'existentialism' of a novelist or an educator has arisen independently of the formal philosophical inquiry and is a parallel expression of the same attitudes as these have emerged in recent times.

In this chapter we shall take cognizance of some of the more important areas where existentialist influence has shown itself—psychology (including psychiatry); education; literature; the visual arts; ethics; theology. No doubt one could extend the survey to other areas, but perhaps those that I have named are the most obvious. Among them, psychology, literature, and theology have been especially infiltrated by existentialist ideas. There is indeed already an extensive literature on this influence. Here I can merely open up the various areas, but I shall refer to several writers in whose works the interested reader will find fuller discussion. The bibliography at the end of this volume lists other writings relevant to the themes of this chapter.

EXISTENTIALISM, PSYCHOLOGY, AND PSYCHIATRY

One of the major impacts of existentialism upon another discipline has been upon psychology and its application in psychiatry. A whole new school of existential psychiatry has grown up.

It has been pointed out above (see p. 13) that existential analysis, following the phenomenological method, is different from psychology. Of course, we had in mind empirical psychology, which has tried as far as possible to make psychology a natural science. But some psychologists now believe that the attempt to make psychology conform to the methods of the natural sciences has been mistaken, or at least has only a limited usefulness. Still more, some psychiatrists have come to believe that existentialism offers a better way of understanding the nature of selfhood and personality, both in health and in disorder, than certain of the older models, including the Freudian. It is with these existential psychiatrists that we shall be chiefly concerned in the rest of this section.

We may begin by recalling that some of the existentialist philosophers themselves have been keenly interested in psychology and psychiatry. It has been mentioned (see above, p. 36) that Karl Jaspers began life as a psychiatrist and that his first major work was his *General Psychopathology*. In that book he claimed that human existence cannot be objectified and turned into a scientific datum. What we have to do with is 'a form of inward behavior, a grasp of self, a self-election, a self-appropriation.'[1] Jean-Paul Sartre has also been keenly interested in psychology and has written a good deal on the subject. Toward the end of *Being and Nothingness* he sketches an 'existential psychoanalysis' in which he argues that more fundamental than the *libido* of Freudian analysis is the *desire to be*, arising from the lack of being of the *pour-soi*.[2]

But as well as these philosophers, there is an important group of men whose primary interest is in psychology and psychiatry and whose understanding of these subjects has been shaped by ideas drawn from the philosophy of existence. Important representatives of this school of thought are the Swiss psychiatrists Ludwig Binswanger (1881–) and Medard Boss (1903–). In the United States a similar approach is advocated by Rollo May (1909–) and in Great Britain by R. D. Laing (1927–).

Although both Binswanger and Boss had close relations with Freud, and although all the members of this school speak of Freud with respect, they are nevertheless critical of the kind of model of the self or person with which Freud worked. It is their belief that Freudian psychoanalysis shared with traditional empirical psychology the fault of trying to conceive the person in subpersonal mechanical terms. Boss, for instance, claims that 'Freud thought of the human being as a telescope-like psychic apparatus,' and he asks the question: 'How should a telescope-like psychic apparatus or a self-regulating libidinal system be able to perceive or understand the meaning of anything, or to love or to hate somebody?'[3] Binswanger reports a conversation he had with Freud in which he had suggested that the psychoanalyst must take cognizance of spirit as well as instinct. Freud's reply surprised him: 'Mankind has always known that it possesses spirit; I had to show that there are also instincts. . . . One has to begin somewhere and only very slowly move forward.'[4] Binswanger demands whether we must not move forward by 'enlarging' the Freudian framework so as to give spirit its place as well as the instincts. He goes on to criticize the most 'baleful influence' that has arisen from the Freudian model—the depersonalization of man. 'This depersonalization has by now gone so far that the psychiatrist (even more than the psychoanalyst) can no longer simply say "I," "you," or "he" wants, wishes, etc.—the only phrases that would correspond to the phenomenal *facts*. Theoretical constructs dispose him rather to speak instead of *my*, *your* or *his* Ego wishing something.'[5]

R. D. Laing, whose work has been chiefly among schizophrenics, found two major defects in the traditional vocabulary (and therefore conceptuality) used to describe psychiatric patients. In the first place, the technical vocabulary itself split the patients into parts, so as to make more difficult the restoration of that wholeness of the self at which the psychiatrist aims. 'Instead of the original bond of "I" and "you," we take a single man in isolation and conceptualize his various aspects into the "ego," the "superego" and the "id." '⁶ In the second place, this language goes on the tacit presupposition that the patient is to be described as some kind of mechanism. Many of Laing's schizophrenic patients do in fact think of themselves as automata, robots, machines, and the like, and the psychiatrist's problem is to get them to feel themselves as *real persons*. People who think of themselves as bits of machinery are, says Laing, 'rightly regarded as crazy.' But he asks: 'Yet why do we not regard a theory that seeks to transmute persons into automata or animals as equally crazy?'⁷

The quest then among these existential psychiatrists is to construct an 'authentic science of persons' (Laing) or a 'genuine psychology' (Binswanger). Binswanger and Boss, albeit with some differences, find in the existential analytic of Heidegger the firmest basis on which to erect a science of persons. 'The eminent importance of the "Daseins-analysis" in the sense of Martin Heidegger's fundamental ontology,' writes Boss, 'lies in the fact that it helps overcome just these short-comings of the basic anthropological concepts of our psychological thinking, shortcomings which until now actually kept us in the dark.'⁸ Rollo May has owed much to the work of the philosophical theo-logian Paul Tillich, whose book *The Courage to Be* moves on the boundaries of psychoanalysis, existentialism, and theology. Laing draws on many philosophers, including Heidegger, Kierkegaard, Merleau-Ponty, Sartre, and Macmurray. His notion of 'ontological insecurity' synthesizes insights from several philosophers and provides a link between the kind of analyses of everyday existing found in our earlier chapters through the eccentricities of such men as Hamann, Kierkegaard, and Kafka to the pathological disorders of the 'divided self.'

Even these brief paragraphs have made it clear that existentialism is having a fruitful influence on psychology and psychiatry, and one may expect further developments in this area. Of course, there are dangers, and Rollo May has rightly pointed to some of them, especially 'the anti-scientific tendency in some existential psychiatry.'⁹ There is no single road to knowledge and every new theory is in peril of distortion and exaggeration. But every science must take cognizance of the peculiarities of its subject-matter, and the existential psychologists are wrestling with one of the most difficult problems of all, a science of people.

From the existentialist impact on psychology, it is a short step to education. That existentialism should have consequences for the educational enterprise is not surprising. To educate (Latin, *e-ducare*) is to bring out or to draw out. In the widest sense, 'e-ducation' is the work of bringing a person out into his possibilities. 'Ex-sistence' is a standing out or stepping out into one's possibilities. To educate means no less than to let someone exist, to stand out or transcend into existential space as the unique person that he is.

To be sure, the concern to let the individual exist in his individuality is nothing new. We have noted earlier how Socrates' maieutic approach to education had existentialist traits (see above, p. 24). In modern times too there have been educational philosophies that have eschewed authoritarianism and adopted more or less 'permissive' approaches designed to let the student become himself; but the conception of man underlying these approaches has scarcely been existential—it has in fact varied from the occultism of Rudolph Steiner to the naturalism of John Dewey.

Existentialism offers a new model and a new terminology for the further development of a humanistic type of educational philosophy. It seems too that such a philosophy is demanded by the circumstances of our time. In the vast universities and comprehensive schools of a mass society, the student easily finds himself lost and alienated, or is subjected to conformist pressures that seem determined that he shall not be himself—and surely there is visible here one of the roots of student discontent. An educational philosophy that has more regard to the individual (as a philosophy influenced by existentialism presumably would) seems to be demanded. Such an approach would also help to correct the excessive egalitarianism of recent educational planning and the resulting mediocrity of achievement, for it would give more scope to the full development of excellence in talented individuals who will be increasingly needed in a technological society.

So far as I am aware, the full shape of an existentialist theory of education has still to emerge, but some significant thinking is going on. As an example, I may mention the work of Dwayne Huebner, professor at Teachers' College, New York. In a paper with the title 'Curriculum as Concern for Man's Temporality,' he considers the student as the existent who has 'the capacity to transcend what he is to become something he is not.' Curriculum is to be designed with this temporal self-transcendence in view, while the teacher is visualized as the enabler of the process of self-transcendence. In a further paper entitled 'Language and Teaching: Reflections on Teaching in the Light of Heidegger's Writing about Language,' Huebner spells out his ideas in more detail. Teaching is seen as a mode of being-with, a positive mode of solicitude in which one leaps *ahead* of the other so as to open his possibilities for him, but never leaps in *for* the other, for this would be really to deprive him of his possibilities. This being-with requires, in turn, an authentic use of language. (For the Heideggerian terminology here, see above, p. 82.) These remarks afford a hint of some of the possibilities that lie in the application of existential analysis to education.[10]

EXISTENTIALISM AND LITERATURE

The title of this section announces a vast area, at which we can do no more than take a glimpse. Because of its emphasis on the concrete, existentialism can come to expression perhaps more tellingly in plays and novels than in philosophical treatises. Some of the leaders of the school have been well aware of this and have distinguished themselves as much in the capacity of creative writers as in that of philosophers. Camus, Sartre, and Marcel are perhaps the most illustrious examples. Such literary productions as *La Peste*, *La Nausée*, and *Huis Clos* must have carried the existentialist teaching to scores of thousands of people who would never read a formal philosophical treatise.

It is in the area of literature, however, that we become especially aware of the reciprocity mentioned in the introductory paragraphs of this chapter. There has been much literary production independent of any direct or even indirect philosophical influence from the existentialists, yet itself 'existentialist' in its affinities and sometimes coming to exert an influence on the philosophers. One thinks, for instance, of the impact that Hölderlin's poetry has made upon Heidegger.

But we have to be careful not to lump together as 'existentialist' any literature that happens to show penetration into the problems of human existence, or we shall be in danger of voiding the term of any significant content. If we are going to venture to talk of existentialist influences in literature, then we have to point to something more definite than just vague and possibly accidental resemblances between the understanding of man found in literary writers and that found in the existentialist philosophers. We must restrict ourselves to those literary productions where prominence is given to what we have called the 'recurring themes' of existentialism (see above, p. 12f.). I mean such themes as freedom, decision, and responsibility; and, even more, finitude, alienation, guilt, death; and perhaps not least, that peculiar and indefinable intensity of feeling that is apparent in most of the existentialists from Kierkegaard on. I think we find a useful pointer in the following sentences of Lionel Trilling:

> If we compare Shakespeare and Kafka, leaving aside the degree of genius that each has, and considering both only as expositors of man's suffering and cosmic alienation, it is Kafka who makes the more intense and complete exposition. And, indeed, the judgment may be correct, exactly because for Kafka the sense of evil is not contradicted by the sense of personal identity. Shakespeare's world, quite as much as Kafka's, is that prison cell which Pascal says the world is, from which daily the inmates are led forth to die; Shakespeare no less than Kafka forces upon us the cruel irrationality of the conditions of human life, the tale told by an idiot, the puerile gods who torture us not for punishment but for sport; and no less than Kafka Shakespeare is revolted by the fetor of the prison of this world, nothing is more characteristic of him than his imagery of disgust. But in Shakespeare's cell, the company is so much better than in Kafka's, the captains and kings and lovers and clowns of Shakespeare are alive and complete before they die. In Kafka, long before the sentence is executed, even long before the malign legal process is instituted, something terrible has been done to the accused.[11]

To some extent, I think these sentences explain why one would call Kafka an existentialist writer, but not Shakespeare. The existentialist of the 19th and 20th centuries seems to be aware of a crisis, a threat, a fragmentation and alienation that are new in their chilling intensity. Writing of this sense of crisis, William Barrett has remarked: 'The image of modern man lies in T. S. Eliot's line: "Men are bits of paper, whirled by the cold wind." '[12]

Let us go back for a few moments to Johann Christian Friedrich Hölderlin (1770–1843), as he may be regarded as the literary pioneer of the modern existentialist mood in literature. Already at the beginning of the 19th century he was giving expression to that changing mood that eventually came to philosophical expression in Nietzsche

—the increasing sense of alienation and lostness in the cosmos. His own sense of 'ontological insecurity,' to use Laing's expression, eventually brought him, like Nietzsche, to madness. In a poem *Brot und Wein* ('Bread and Wine') he expresses the nascent, almost Gnostic, mood thus:

> But, friend, we have come too late. To be sure, the gods are
> living,
> But in another world far above our heads.
> They are endlessly active, but seem to give little heed
> As to whether we live—that's how much the heavenly ones care.
>
> You see, some time ago—to us it seems a long time—
> All those who were favorable to our life withdrew themselves
> above.
> When the Father averted his face from man
> And, very properly, mourning began over the whole earth.[13]

These words do not indeed say that God is dead. But he is absent and silent—the Father has averted his face. Man feels his intense loneliness, as the latecomer on a scene once joyful but now made mournful by the departure of those who bestowed the joy. These and similar themes are treated in many other poems of Hölderlin, but we have no space to extend the discussion here.

I have already alluded to two great Russian novels that in the 19th century introduced some of the themes of existentialism— Tolstoy's study of death in *The Death of Ivan Ilyitch* and Turgenev's study of nihilism in *Fathers and Sons*. But surely the greatest literary exponent of existentialism in their time was their fellow countryman Fyodor Dostoevsky (1821–81), especially in such works as *The Brothers Karamazov* and *Notes from the Underground*. About the latter, Walter Kaufmann has declared that it contains 'the best overture for existentialism ever written.' He continues: 'With inimitable vigor and finesse the major themes are stated here that we can recognize when reading all the other so-called existentialists from Kierkegaard to Camus.'[14]

The trickle of such writers in the 'century of progress' has swollen to a flood amid the disillusionments of the 20th century. Perhaps Franz Kafka (1883–1924) must be reckoned the greatest existentialist writer of all. Where else, for instance, is the idea of thrownness set forth with such vividness as in *The Trial*, where a man finds himself suddenly hailed before the court and cannot even discover the nature of the charge against him? Or where is the modern sense of ontological lostness and bewilderment set forth so well as in

The Castle, as we read of the surveyor's unavailing attempts to get into touch with the real forces that determine his life? Alongside Kafka may be ranged many of the most brilliant writers of this century—T. S. Eliot, Samuel Beckett, James Joyce, and a host of others.

The advocates of technology and affluence tend to become impatient with the literature of alienation, absurdity, and despair. These writers, we are told, are pessimists who cannot see the good in the contemporary world. Admittedly, the existentialist writers have been one-sided. Yet surely contemporary society has needed their critique, for it is in danger of becoming one-sided in the opposite direction, of lapsing into a brash complacent optimism dominated by a materialistic scheme of values. They are reminding us that techniques alone cannot solve the human problem, for this is finally an existential problem. They are not so much pessimists as realists who know that there are no utopian solutions to the pathos of existence. 'People will be cleverer and more penetrating,' wrote Goethe, 'but not better, not happier, not more energetic.' His prophecy has been fulfilled by the course of events, and it is naive to suppose that mankind's problems are going away or that they can be grappled with effectively if we shut our eyes to the questions opened up to us in existentialist literature.

EXISTENTIALISM AND THE VISUAL ARTS

To discuss existentialism and the visual arts is again to introduce a subject so vast that it could easily provide the theme for a whole book. Furthermore, this is again an area where the relation is reciprocal. It is not so much the case that modern art has been directly influenced by existentialism as that in the various forms of modern art—cubism, surrealism, and the rest—we can see parallels to existentialism, as these forms of art bring to expression in their own medium ideas that are given their philosophical formulation by the existentialists.

Paul Cézanne (1839–1906) is customarily regarded as the most influential figure in modern art, and perhaps his work does indicate some kind of parallel to the existentialist movement. For in him we see the break up of traditional forms and the eventual creation of new ones, allowing us to see things in a new way and in new relationships. One critic says of Cézanne:

Eighteenth-century art had been rational and orderly; official nineteenth-century art had vainly tried to maintain this rational orderliness (which became more and more insipid as it receded from contemporary needs) against the assaults of brilliant and original artists who in various ways used art to express their personal emotions, or to capture the fugitive aspects of nature; and last of all a queer and laborious old man . . . . was seen to have worked his way back, by solitary and prolonged experiment, to the starting-point from which art is viewed as a definite reordering of the natural world.[15]

Two points in Barton's comments are, I think, important for perceiving the existentialist aspects of modern art. First, Cézanne is distinguished from artists who used their art 'to express personal emotions.' This is not to say that Cézanne did not express personal emotion—obviously he did, and this would be true even more of a painter like Vincent van Gogh. The point is that they are not expressing emotion for emotion's sake but that (and here we strike the parallel with the existentialists) emotion itself is a way of lighting up the world. Second, the abandonment of one conception of form and order does not mean the abandonment of all form. Modern art has become aware of the sharp discontinuities that were concealed in traditional forms, and perhaps it is the shock of encountering such discontinuities that produces the impression in some people that form has been abandoned. On the contrary, we may well be shown things in a new configuration of which we have hitherto been unaware. A good illustration is Picasso's picture 'Guernica.' It consists of persons, things, objects from the Spanish town of Guernica, destroyed in the Spanish Civil War, set down by the artist in apparently quite 'unreal' relationships. But, as Paul Tillich has remarked, this picture 'shows the human situation without any cover.'[16] This picture is also instructive for the parallel with existentialist philosophy, for in this philosophy too the starting-point was Kierkegaard's relentless revealing of the discontinuities that had been covered up in the 'system,' but this was at the same time the beginning of a search for a new form and of the quest for new relationships. It is the quest for a new and more dynamic ontology, just as in the arts. Samuel Terrien has writen: 'For the past seventy years there has been a new enterprise by which the artist labors to gain access to the beingness of the world. His painting looks unfinished because it beats, it pulsates and even throbs with the universe. The ontology which is now in process of emerging cannot yet be set in propositional discourse, because it is still related to a mode of implicit questioning.'[17]

It is clear too that in terms of this dynamic ontology beauty is not considered to be an eternal value laid up in the heavens. Rather—

like the existential concept of truth—it has to be realized in a historical situation. We can agree with Albert Hofstadter's claim that 'beauty is not a mode of value but a unique mode of validity.'[18]

The foregoing paragraphs receive confirmation when we turn to some leading existentialist philosophers and inquire about their views on art. Heidegger is insistent that the work of art is not to be understood as expressing the feelings of the artist. Rather, it brings being itself into the light of truth. The artist and his work are equally primordial. 'The artist is the origin of the work. The work is the origin of the artist. Neither *is* without the other.'[19] This reciprocity is exhibited in a well-known passage in which he discusses a Greek temple. The temple does not represent anything, but it is not therefore something quite indefinite. It embodies both a world and the earth. The world is a cultural historical entity in which the fate of human beings is worked out; the earth is the primordial material which has emerged and been disclosed in the temple. The truth of the work of art takes place in the revelation occasioned by this conjuncture. In a somewhat similar fashion, Karl Jaspers considers that 'the basic meaning of art is its revealing function.' It reveals being by giving form to what we perceive.[20] We have already noted Jaspers' comments on the great architectural wonder of the Boro Buddor which, as a kind of non-verbal language, takes us beyond even the ciphers in disclosing being in its transcendence and its all-encompassing character (see above, p. 116).

However, it was Nietzsche who pointed out the impossibility of tracing all art to a single principle and the consequent danger of generalizing. Let us content ourselves by saying that in the art of our time a spirit akin to that of existentialism is widely active.

EXISTENTIALISM AND ETHICS

We have touched on the subject of ethics at several points in the course of this book (see above, pp. 14, 53, 161). We need not repeat here what has already been said. However, it has seemed desirable to bring together the gist of these scattered remarks on ethics, since the evaluation of any philosophy will depend in no small measure on the kind of ethic it generates.

In sum, existentialist ethics turns away from any kind of legalism. Laws and rules are considered to be external impositions, forcing the existent into a predetermined pattern and so preventing him from realizing his unique authentic selfhood. Thus existentialism tends to encourage what is usually called a 'situation' ethic. In such an ethic the course of action is determined by the unique situation in which the agent finds himself. How, in this situation, is he true to himself?—and since we have seen that authentic selfhood has its communal dimension, one could not consistently interpret this situational criterion of action in a purely self-regarding fashion.

In point of fact, all ethics have combined a rule-element and a situation-element. Even legalistic ethics have had some built-in mechanisms to allow for the exceptional case, and in many cases such systems of laws and rules have been in practice remarkably flexible. However, existentialist ethics exalts the situational element over the rule element. The latter may be reduced almost to vanishing point, so that one comes close to a kind of antinomianism—just as I suggested that probably the existentialist ideal in politics would be anarchy, strictly understood.

It is easy to criticize an extreme situation in ethics, and certainly such a position has many weaknesses. It suffers from individualism and subjectivism and prizes the intensity of choice above the building up of moral wisdom and virtue. Furthermore, it fails to understand how law itself can become internalized and appropriated. The existentialist has a hard time understanding the words of the psalmist:

> I will keep thy law continually,
>   for ever and ever;
> And I shall walk at liberty,
>   for I have sought thy precepts.
> I will also speak of thy testimonies before kings,
>   and shall not be put to shame;
> For I find my delight in thy commandments,
>   which I love.
> I revere thy commandments, which I love,
>   and I will meditate on thy statutes.
>   [Psalm 119: 44-8; RSV translation]

Yet, in spite of its weaknesses and its proneness to extravagant hostility toward laws and rules, an existentialist ethic has its own merits, and these are not without relevance today. On the whole, an ethic that stresses law is an ethic that looks to the past—to tradition, custom, the way things have always been done. Such an ethic brings stability, but also the danger of stagnation. An ethic that stresses the situation is, on the contrary, future-oriented; it looks to the new, and action is determined with regard to the new. Every ethic, I have said, experiences something of this tension. The existentialist ethic takes the risk of stressing the situation rather than law, the futural and the new rather than the traditional. I deliberately use the word *risk*, and indeed all action involves risk. Yet today when the conditions of life are changing so fast we have to meet situations that are new and for which no rules or precedents seem available. Hence, within limits, the existentialist stress in the situation and the future can be helpful and constructive on the contemporary world.

I have suggested elsewhere that the risks may be reduced by rethinking the meaning of natural law in dynamic and existential terms—that is to say, a law that is truly internal to man and that is nothing other than the thrust of existence itself toward fuller humanity. Such a view does not, I think, imply some fixed pattern of existence, though it is hardly compatible with the idea that man creates himself out of nothing. In other words, it is compatible with moderate forms of existentialism, but hardly with the more extreme type associated with Sartre.[21]

EXISTENTIALISM AND THEOLOGY

Throughout the course of history, theology has lived in a kind of love-hate relationship with philosophy. To be sure, the theologian bases himself on faith and revelation, as he has learned these in a community of faith, but if he is to articulate his ideas and express them in a language that communicates with the contemporary culture, he finds that he cannot do without the philosopher. Sometimes we do come across theologians who, in reaction against a supposed philosophical domination, try to break away from any connection with philosophy. But they drift back, or perhaps the next generation drifts back, or the truth may even be that they have never got away from some involvement with the philosopher.

In recent decades existentialism has in fact been the type of philosophy most influential with theologians. The early Barth, Bultmann, Tillich, Buri, Ott, Ebeling, Rahner—these are only some of the theologians of recent and contemporary times who have been significantly and, in some cases, deeply influenced by existentialist philosophy. The influence has taken many forms. In Barth it came from Kierkegaard; in Bultmann, from Heidegger; in Buri, from Jaspers; in Barth, it led to kerygmatic theology; in Bultmann, to demythologizing; in Tillich, to ontology. But whatever the variety of forms has been, it may be claimed that much of the most creative theological thinking in this century has sprung from the encounter with existentialism.

The first obvious point of contact between existentialism and theology is that both offer a doctrine of man. If most contemporary philosophy has turned away from speculative questions, such as the existence of God, this fact can be a useful reminder to the theologian that theology is also anthropology, or that perhaps we should even speak of 'theanthropology.' Christian theology is not speculation about God 'in himself' but of God in relation to man, and the Christian faith is therefore as much an understanding of man as it is of God. There is much to be said for the view that a contemporary theology should take as its methodological starting-point the doctrine of man rather than the traditional starting-point of the doctrine of God. Existentialist theologians do in fact follow this procedure and try to unfold the meaning of Christian faith in terms of a phenomenology of Christian existence. Obviously this does help to get theology off the ground in a secular age. The question about man is still asked when the question about God seems to have faded into the background. Of course, it may turn out that the two questions are inseparable and that the one implies the other. But at the present day, when many theories of man are circulating, Christian theology finds a point of entry into the debate by probing the nature of the human existent, his hopes and loves, his finitude and sin, in the conviction that the study of man in depth opens up the dimension of transcendence.

In carrying out this study, the theologian finds in existentialism both models of existence and the resource of a language in which the structures of existence can be expressed. Just as psychiatrists have been attracted by existential analysis and have taken over some of its concepts and terminology, so have theologians. In the Bible and in traditional Christian theology, the doctrine of man is obscured by an antiquated and quasi-mythological terminology. In the Old Testament, we hear of man compounded of the dust of the ground and the breath of life; while St. Paul, in spite of his penetrating insights into Christian existence, has to express himself in such imprecise and obscure terms as *flesh*, *spirit*, *heart*, and the like. Existentialism offers a new and better model, and an updated terminology for expressing the Biblical understanding of man. For instance, the 'dust of the ground' may be understood as facticity and the 'breath of life' as possibility, and the ancient story receives a new intelligibility.

Existentialism provides not only isolated terms but also wider principles of interpretation and articulation. The Biblical terms themselves have their home so to speak, in contexts of myth, of history, of cultic and legal institutions, or whatever it may be. Bultmann's 'demythologizing' is the best known example of the systematic application of existential interpretation to wide areas of New Testament material, and the translation of the 1st-century images and myths into a contemporary language of existence. The so-called 'new hermeneutic' developed by Ebeling and others seeks to probe further into the problems of interpretation, and the philosophy of existence continues to play an important role in the discussion.

But is an existential interpretation of the Bible and of theological doctrines valid? Or are we seeing a modern philosophy replacing traditional religious material that has become outmoded? Presumably this style of interpretation and this way of doing theology may, like any other, become distorting through exaggeration. Yet there seems to be sufficient affinity between the Biblical understanding of man and the philosophy of existence to ensure that existential interpretation does not force the Biblical material into an alien mold. We must remember too that all interpretation implies reciprocity.

But what about God in these existentialist theologies? Is not existentialism a humanism, as Sartre says, and does not its employment in theology lead to reducing Christianity from a faith in God to a humanistic ethic?

It is true that this style of theology dwells on the human side of the faith relationship, and describes Christian existence in the world. However, I have already pointed out that the existentialist theologian believes that when one analyzes human existence in depth, one uncovers experiences where God-language becomes appropriate. By its very nature, existentialism offers no 'proofs' of the existence of God, but it does push the analysis of human existenc. to those very limits of existence where faith arises.

As far as God-language is concerned, I think that existentialist theologians can be divided into two fairly distinct groups. Neither abolishes God, but their ways of speaking of him differ very considerably.

The first group is represented by Bultmann and Buri. They tell us that one can speak of God only in the moment of faith. He cannot become the object of thought but is known as the unconditioned demand (or the unconditioned grace) that touches human life in certain concrete moments.

The second group is most typically represented by Tillich. Following those existentialist philosophers who go on to construct some kind of ontology or metaphysic, Tillich too seeks an ontological as well as an existential basis for God-language. I believe myself that the ontological question cannot finally be evaded. In particular, I would see in Heidegger's notion of being a very helpful model for an ontology of God. Of course, it need hardly be said that in this context we are thinking of an existential ontology of a vastly different kind from the speculative ontologies of the older styles of metaphysics. There is the possibility of developing an existential ontology which might be a modern counterpart to the old-fashioned and largely discredited natural theology.

One could mention many other links between existentialism and theology. For instance, the theology of revelation has found several helpful models in existentialism, from the notion of encounter, developed by Buber and others and employed widely by such theologians as Brunner, to the primordial thinking of Heidegger, which Ott has seen more recently as illuminative for the phenomenon of revelation. It is clear that in theology, as well as in the other areas surveyed in this chapter, the influence of existentialist thought has been far-reaching.

CHAPTER FIFTEEN

An Evaluation of Existentialism

SOME CRITICISMS CONSIDERED

At the very beginning of our study we noted that although existentialism has its recurring themes there are very great differences among those who in a general way are labeled 'existentialists' or 'philosophers of existence.' Because of these wide differences, existentialism is too protean a phenomenon to lend itself to general criticism. The very fact that each of its practitioners consciously struggles against conformity and is unwilling to be accounted a member of a 'school' means that generalizations about existentialism are bound to be unfair to some of its manifestations. Criticisms that may be very much to the point as regards some forms of existentialism miss the mark when extended to others. Individualism is a charge that may with some plausibility be leveled against Kierkegaard, but it does not apply to Buber. Irrationalism may be laid at the door of the quixotic Unamuno, but Jaspers has specifically championed the cause of reason against the demonic unreason that has several times broken loose in the 20th century. A deep pessimism runs through Nietzsche, Sartre, and Camus, but Marcel talks of hope. In some of these cases we are witnessing deliberate attempts to correct exaggerations in existentialism. Yet in the three cases that I have mentioned, Buber, Jaspers, and Marcel must be counted exceptions to the prevailing existentialist tendencies. A philosophy that was predominantly social, rational, and optimistic could hardly qualify as existentialism, any more than a religion that had abolished the papacy, the hierarchy, and the Mass could still be called Roman Catholicism.

Certain tendencies do keep recurring in existentialism, and even if they are not to be found in all forms of existentialism, they are, as it were, representative of the prevailing drift of existentialist thought. Correspondingly, certain criticisms and questions have arisen at various points in this book. We shall now gather these together and ask how damaging they are to the existentialist enterprise.

1. Let us begin with the complaint that existentialism is irrationalist in its tendency. If this charge could be established, then I think it would disqualify existentialism as a philosophy, for the philosopher must surely be the man who hearkens to reason and allows himself to be guided by it. He is the 'lover of wisdom,' almost by definition. Our respect for the philosopher depends on his supposed capacity to see things for what they really are, with a vision that is unclouded by passion and prejudice. This does not mean, let me say, that the philosopher must be neutral and disengaged. Perhaps no one can attain to such neutrality, and perhaps no one should even attempt it. The rationalism of the philosopher is not to be equated with a non-involvement in human affairs or with the attempt to become a godlike spectator of the human scene rather than a participant. But even so, we do expect the philosopher to be critical, analytical, free from partisan bias, devoted to truth for truth's sake—and these qualities do seem to demand a measure of detachment.

I think it must be conceded that the call of the existentialist for passionate participation does set in motion a tendency that, unless carefully kept under control, can indeed lead to a state of mind which conflicts with the philosopher's obligation to reason. Unamuno's Don Quixote and Kierkegaard's knight of faith may be admired for various reasons, but scarcely as philosophers. And philosophers may not find much to admire in them at all. H. J. Paton may have gone too far when he wrote the following words, but I do think that we have to heed the warning: 'The rejection of reason finds its most elaborate modern expression in the voluminous writings of Kierkegaard, and his popularity today is a sign of the dangerous pass to which we have come—a mark of desperation and despair.'[1] The warning is that when men do begin to let reason slip, to claim that intensity and passion are above rational criticism, and to prize the absurd and paradoxical, a terrible danger looms on the horizon. It is the danger not just of the irrational but of the anti-rational, and the anti-rational can as easily assume the forms of inhuman cruelty as of quixotic generosity. What, for instance, are we to say about what Ulrich Simon has called the 'pagan madness' and the 'dark ecstatic nihilism' of Auschwitz?[2] That there is some affinity between that monstrous madness and some features of existentialism is not to be denied.

Men are only too ready to be swayed by senseless passion, and it cannot be the philosopher's business to encourage this. However, existentialism at its best is neither irrational nor anti-rational but is concerned rather with affirming that the fullness of human experience breaks out of the confines of conceptual thought and that our lives can be diminished by a too narrow rationalism. In fairness to H. J. Paton, it should be said that to his harsh criticism of Kierkegaard he adds these words: 'It is reasonable enough to recognize the limits of human knowledge and to insist that in the religious life there must be a decision or commitment which is not the result of discursive reasoning.'[3]

What is healthy and valid in the existentialist collision with rationalism is not the attack on logic or the exaltation of the absurd—these are in fact dangerous and negative characteristics that must be resisted in the name of reason. Rather what is valid is the insistence that there are many rich strands in human existence that ought not to be ignored or downgraded just because they cannot be fitted into the logic of mathematics or of the empirical sciences. This is not to condemn logic or to embark on intellectual anarchy. At its best, it is an attempt to develop a logic of persons in addition to our logic of things.

2. Closely related to the charge of irrationalism is that of amoralism (if not indeed of immoralism). Because of the gravity of this charge, I have already spent some time in a discussion of it and need not repeat here what has been said above (see pp. 161–8). We have seen that the answer to this problem cannot be a return or attempted return to some rigid legalism. But if man is to claim for himself the moral freedom which the existentialists urge, then this can only be acceptable if there go along with it a heightened sense of responsibility and a more penetrating ethical analysis that will elucidate some norms and directions drawn from the structure of existence itself. Just as we have acknowledged that men are only too ready to embrace the irrational, so we have to say also that they are only too ready to set aside the moral demand, and some unguarded ways of expressing the existentialist approach to ethics do encourage conduct that turns out to be finally destructive of our humanity. The mere summons to authenticity is not enough, until there is an adequate ethical analysis of what authenticity implies. The terms in which Hans Jonas has criticized one existentialist philosopher have obviously

a wider application. Talking of the call of being as a summons to authentic existence in Heidegger, he says: 'So was the Führer and the call of German destiny under him; an unveiling of something indeed, a call of being all right, fate-laden in every sense; neither then nor now did Heidegger's thought provide a norm by which to decide how to answer such calls.'[4] Heidegger's own association with the Nazis may be put down to political naiveté, in which he was certainly not alone in the early 1930s. But was there more to it? Can we find the roots of it in the existentialist reluctance to acknowledge the place of norms in the moral life, in the stress on being true to oneself no matter where this leads?

I am aware, of course, of the many ambiguities in these matters. I believe that Heidegger's own record is more defensible than some of his critics would have us believe. Furthermore, one cannot simply blame Nietzsche for the Nazi phenomenon. (Why not Hegel as well?—Camus suggests that they both have some share in the matter.) But it must be said that Kierkegaard introduced a very dangerous idea when he first talked of the 'teleological suspension of ethics.' I have acknowledged above that sometimes we have to take the risk of being exposed to this danger, otherwise we could never break out of the *status quo*. But here I want to register the seriousness of the matter and to say that the ambiguities of existentialist ethics constitute a weakness in existentialism. This weakness will not be overcome until there emerges a clearer and more affirmative account of the place of norms and guidelines in conduct—an account that might take the form of a dynamically conceived 'natural law' or 'law of existence.'[5]

3. I turn next to the criticism that existentialism is infected with an undesirable degree of individualism; and at the same time we shall consider the closely allied complaint that existentialism is a subjectivism.

To be sure, there are elements of both individualism and subjectivism in existentialism, and up to a point I suppose that these are defensible. Wherever individual judgment and responsibility are in danger of being submerged in some impersonal kind of collectivism, it is necessary to champion the rights of the individual; and, furthermore, since complete objectivity and detachment in philosophy would seem to be a myth and a delusion, it is as well for the philosopher to recognize that he does have his own point of view and his own historical stance and to acknowledge that there is therefore a personal factor in his philosophizing.

When the factors of individualism and subjectivism are represented in the moderate way I have just suggested, they could not be regarded as specially objectionable. But the question must be faced whether in fact these two characteristics go far beyond the moderate extent that might be considered permissible—whether indeed they do not run riot in most existentialist philosophies. I have myself sometimes argued that the individualism of the existentialists is an accidental and transient phase of their philosophizing, called forth as a protest against distorted forms of being-with-others; and that their subjectivizing tendencies are likewise not to be considered endemic to their basic philosophical approach but as due to particular historical factors. However, I am not sure that this defense stands up.

Let us recall for a moment Kierkegaard, the so-called father of modern existentialism. His individualism is explicit. He does not hesitate to say bluntly, in one of his most mature works, that ' "fellowship" is a lower category than the "single individual," which everyone can be and should be.'[6] The remark is made in connection with an analysis of the Christian life, which was of course for Kierkegaard the highest and most authentic form of human existence. The same writer also exemplifies the subjectivism of the existentialist in a signal manner, for again and again his argument alludes to matters in his own personal experience, especially his relations to his father and his fiancée. Even if we agree that a personal factor is inevitably present in philosophy, we do not expect philosophy to be in any major degree autobiographical. Surely the philosopher has an obligation to transcend as far as he can a narrowly personal point of view. Again, H. J. Paton is unduly harsh in his judgment, yet not entirely wide of the mark when he writes: 'We should be particularly on our guard when the guide makes no pretence at objective thinking, which stands or falls by the argument independently of the personality of the thinker, but rests his case on the inwardness of his own personal experience. If ever a person was self-centered, it was Kierkegaard: he hardly ever thinks of anyone but himself.'[7]

What can be said about Kierkegaard can be said also about many of his successors in the existentialist tradition. Obviously, for instance, Sartre is in similar case.

Of course, Buber and Marcel break out of a narrow individualism into a theory of intersubjectivity. But it may well be asked whether even they have gone far enough. The interpersonal and intersubjective relations of which they speak still tend to be on the intimate and domestic level. They are relations between individuals. But so many of the most pressing problems of the contemporary world concern the relations between groups or corporate entities—national and international bodies, corporations, races, trade unions and the like. As far as these problems are concerned, existentialism and 'situation ethics' are apparently of little help. Here we again strike upon the political critique of existentialism. I have pointed out that the political role of existentialism may be simply that of criticizing all dehumanizing forms of collectivism (see above, p. 189). But we need some positive guidance in these areas, and it is doubtful if existentialism has much to offer. In spite of their genuine insistence that all existence is inescapably a being-with-others, most existentialist philosophies take the existence of the individual as the starting-point, and when this first step has been taken, perhaps the bias toward the existence of the single individual makes itself felt in all the subsequent analyses.

4. Sometimes one meets the criticism that existentialism is too narrowly humanistic in its outlook. This is not to be understood as a complaint that existentialists are interested in the well-being of man—there is no objection to humanism in that broad sense. The complaint is rather that man is made the measure of all things, with the result that everything is seen in anthropomorphic terms. There is no philosophy of nature, for instance, and no interest in the kind of entities investigated by the natural sciences.

Although this criticism might seem to apply most forcibly to the Sartrean type of existentialism, which is explicitly identified with a humanism, it applies in some measure also to existentialist ontology and metaphysics. Thus, although Heidegger in his *Brief über den Humanismus* sharply differentiates his own position from Sartre's and claims that the interest of his philosophy is centered in Being rather than in human existence, it would surely be just to say that he too has little to say about nature and non-human reality in general, and that he shows little appreciation for the natural sciences.

The danger of an exclusively man-centered philosophy is not just that it gives us an unduly anthropomorphic understanding of reality, but that finally it may react unfavorably on man himself. For when man is isolated as the center of interest and the cosmos is understood as simply the setting for human life and the field for human conquest and exploitation, a powerful impetus is given to those unfortunate tendencies that today have become a major problem—air and water pollution, unexpected side-effects of technology, and the like. The new importance of ecology and the rediscovery of the significance of the 'balance of nature' call for a broadly based philosophy. Such a philosophy would encourage a respect for non-human realities and an interest in them for their own sakes. Existentialism has not provided this motivation.

5. Existentialism is said to be pessimistic and even morbid. Its adherents are accused of looking on the nightside of life. In particular, they are said to be blind to the promise of the contemporary world. They are anti-technological and anti-democratic and out of sympathy with the aims and achievements of modern society.

To be sure, there is some truth in these charges. Although the man-centeredness of existentialism has provided a thrust toward technological exploitation, as we have seen in the existentialist understanding of the world (see above, p. 62), the personalism of the existentialist clashes with the growing impersonalism of technology, and sometimes gives rise to an escapist, nostalgic longing for a simpler mode of life, and occasionally to a cult of the primitive. Again, while the existentialist penetration through all externals to the very springs of authentic existence consorts very well with some aspects of the democratic ideal, the very thrust toward authenticity and excellence encourages the ideal of the superman and depreciates the mass.

I do not know however how far these criticisms can be accepted as a negative evaluation of existentialism. Often the criticisms come from shallow optimists who are in turn criticized by existentialists for their failure to appreciate the pathos of life. The contemporary world and its institutions are certainly ambiguous. Let us agree that existentialists may have been excessively negative in their evaluation of what is going on in the world today, yet we would still have to acknowledge that they have pointed to real evils and dangers, and we would have been much poorer without their critique.

CONCLUDING REMARKS

What are we to say finally about this philosophy that has captivated so many of the best minds of the 20th century and has exercised so widespread an influence?

Like any other philosophy, existentialism has its weaknesses, its blind spots, its exaggerations. I have tried to present it fairly, not glossing over its defects, but rather pushing the objections as far as I could. Yet it seems to me that the merits of this type of philosophy outweigh the objections. Existentialism has yielded many fresh and penetrating insights into the mystery of our own human existence, and it has thereby contributed to the protection and enhancement of our humanity in the face of all that threatens it today. As a philosophy, it offers us a frame of reference against which we can interpret and evaluate the perplexing events of the contemporary world.

For my own part, I certainly could not identify myself with any one form of existentialism. Indeed, as has been evident from our discussion, I would want to modify or broaden or alter the existentialist way of philosophizing at so many points that the result may not be recognizably 'existentialist' any more. Yet I would still have to say that from existentialism we can learn truths that are indispensable to our condition and that will be essential to any sane, human philosophy of the future.

Notes

NOTES TO CHAPTER ONE

1. Jean-Paul Sartre, 'Existentialism Is a Humanism,' *Existentialism from Dostoevsky to Sartre*, ed. Walter Kaufmann (Cleveland, 1956), p. 289.
2. H. Diem, *Kierkegaard: An Introduction*, trans. D. Green (Richmond, Va., 1966), p. 81.
3. Paul Sponheim, *Kierkegaard on Christ and Christian Coherence* (New York, 1968), p. 14.
4. Martin Heidegger, *Being and Time*, trans. J. Macquarrie and E. S. Robinson (New York and London, 1962), p. 49 ff.
5. Thomas Langan, *The Meaning of Heidegger: A Critical Study of an Existentialist Phenomenology* (New York, 1959), p. 41, n. 46.
6. Miguel de Unamuno, *The Tragic Sense of Life*, trans. J. E. C. Flitch (New York, 1954), p. 28.
7. Sartre, 'Existentialism Is a Humanism,' *loc. cit.*, p. 290.
8. John Macmurray, *The Self as Agent* (New York and London, 1957), p. 84 ff.
9. Roger L. Shinn, ed., *Restless Adventure: Essays on Contemporary Expressions of Existentialism* (New York, 1968), p. 13.
10. Søren Kierkegaard, *Concluding Unscientific Postscript*, trans. D. F. Swenson (Princeton, 1941), pp. 96–97.
11. Karl Jaspers, *Nietzsche and Christianity*, trans. E. B. Ashton (Chicago, 1961), p. 6.
12. Cf. Richard Kroner, 'Heidegger's Private Religion,' *Union Seminary Quarterly Review* 11 (1956): 23–37.
13. Cf. Hans Jonas, 'Heidegger and Theology,' *Review of Metaphysics* 18 (1964): 207–233.

14. This paragraph and the preceding summarize Heidegger, *Being and Time*, pp. 49–63.
15. Cf. Jean-Paul Sartre, *Being and Nothingness: An Essay on Phenomenological Ontology*, trans. Hazel Barnes (New York, 1956), pp. xlv–1.
16. Nikolai Berdyaev, *The Beginning and the End*, trans. M. French (New York, 1957), p. 62.
17. *Ibid.*
18. Roger L. Shinn, *Man: The New Humanism* (Philadelphia, 1968), p. 170 ff.
19. Heidegger, *Über den Humanismus* (Frankfurt, 1949), p. 10.
20. Heidegger, *Was ist Metaphysik?*, 7th ed. (Frankfurt, 1949), pp. 15–16.
21. Sartre, *Being and Nothingness*, p. li.
22. Berdyaev, *The Beginning and the End*, pp. 47–48.
23. José Ortega y Gasset, *Man in Crisis*, trans. M. Adams (New York, 1959), p. 112.
24. Jaspers, *Nietzsche and Christianity*, p. 91.

NOTES TO CHAPTER TWO

1. Karl Jaspers, *The Origin and Goal of History*, trans. Michael Bullock (New Haven and London, 1953), p. 2.
2. Henri Frankfort, *Kingship and the Gods: A Study of Ancient Near Eastern Religion as the Integration of Society and Nature* (Chicago, 1948), p. 4.
3. Cf. Mircea Eliade, *Cosmos and History: The Myth of the Eternal Return* (New York, 1959).
4. Martin Buber, *The Prophetic Faith*, trans. C. Witton-Davies, 2d ed. (New York, 1960), p. 96 ff.
5. Rudolf Bultmann, *Primitive Christianity in Its Contemporary Setting*, trans. R. H. Fuller (Cleveland and New York, 1956), p. 42.
6. E. R. Dodds, *The Greeks and the Irrational* (Berkeley, Calif., 1951), pp. 17 and 254.
7. Cf. George J. Seidel, *Martin Heidegger and the Pre-Socratics* (Lincoln, Neb., 1964).
8. Søren Kierkegaard, *Philosophical Fragments, or A Fragment of Philosophy*, trans. David F. Swenson (Princeton, 1936), p. 6.
9. D. T. Suzuki, *An Introduction to Zen Buddhism* (New York, 1964).
10. Yoshenori Takeuchi, 'Buddhism and Existentialism: The Dialogue Between Oriental and Occidental Thought,' *Religion and Culture*, ed. W. Leibrecht (New York, 1959), pp. 291–318.
11. Cf. Rudolf Bultmann, *Theology of the New Testament*, trans. Kendrick Grobel (New York, 1951), vol. 1, pp. 3–22.
12. *Ibid.*, p. 187 ff.
13. *Ibid.*, p. 164.
14. Hans Jonas, *The Gnostic Religion*, 2d ed. (Boston, 1963), p. 324.

15. Adolf Harnack, *History of Dogma*, ed. B. Bruce, trans. N. Buchanan et al. (London, 1897), vol. 1, p. 17.
16. *Ibid.*, p. 22.
17. Quotations are from *An Augustine Synthesis*, ed. E. Przywara (New York, 1958), p. 421.
18. *Ibid.*, p. 33.
19. *Ibid.*, p. 23.
20. *Ibid.*, p. 75.
21. *Ibid.*, p. 75.
22. *Meister Eckhart: A Modern Translation*, trans. Raymond B. Blakney (New York, 1941), p. 243.
23. *Ibid.*, p. 246.
24. Giovanni Pico della Mirandola, *Oration on the Dignity of Man*, trans. A. Robert Caponigri (Chicago, 1956), pp. 4–5.
25. Ronald Gregor Smith, *Johann Georg Hamann: A Study in Christian Existence with Selections from His Writings* (London, 1960), p. 22.
26. *Ibid.*, p. 253.
27. *Ibid.*, p. 40.
28. *Ibid.*, p. 42.
29. Søren Kierkegaard, *Journals*, ed. and trans. Alexander Dru (New York, 1959), p. 40.
30. Kierkegaard, *Either/Or: A Fragment of Life*, trans. Walter Lowrie (Princeton, 1944), vol. 2, p. 141.
31. Kierkegaard, *The Concept of Dread*, trans. Walter Lowrie (Princeton 1944), p. 55.
32. Kierkegaard, *The Last Years: Journals 1853–55*, ed. R. Gregor Smith (New York, 1965), p. 266.
33. Friedrich Nietzsche, *Beyond Good and Evil*, trans. Francis Golffing (Chicago, 1959), p. 46.
34. Friedrich Nietzsche, *The Joyful Wisdom*, trans. Thomas Common (Edinburgh, London, and New York, 1910), p. 125.
35. M. M. Bozmann, 'Introduction,' *Thus Spake Zarathustra*, trans. A. Tille (London, 1933), p. xii.
36. Martin Heidegger, *Was ist Metaphysik?*, 7th ed. (Frankfurt, 1949), p. 45.
37. F. Temple Kingston, *French Existentialism: A Christian Critique* (Toronto, 1961), pp. 26–27.
38. Jean-Paul Sartre, *Being and Nothingness: An Essay on Phenomenological Ontology*, trans. Hazel Barnes (New York, 1956), p. 677.
39. James Somerville, *Total Commitment: Blondel's L'Action* (Washington and Cleveland, 1968), p. 26.

NOTES TO CHAPTER THREE

1. (New York, 1965), p. 72 ff.
2. Martin Heidegger, *Über den Humanismus* (Frankfurt, 1949), p. 17.

I

3. Søren Kierkegaard, *Concluding Unscientific Postscript*, trans. D. F. Swenson (Princeton, 1941), p. 267.
4. Heidegger, *Being and Time*, trans. J. Macquarrie and E. S. Robinson (New York and London, 1962), p. 67.
5. Heidegger, *Über den Humanismus*, p. 15.
6. Jean-Paul Sartre, 'Existentialism Is a Humanism,' *Existentialism from Dostoevsky to Sartre*, ed. Walter Kaufmann (Cleveland and New York, 1956), p. 290.
7. Sartre, *Being and Nothingness: An Essay on Phenomenological Ontology*, trans. Hazel Barnes (New York, 1956), p. 630.
8. Karl Jaspers, *Philosophical Faith and Revelation*, trans. E. B. Ashton (New York, 1967), pp. 63–66. A similar analysis can be found in other of his writings.
9. Theodosius Dobzhansky, *The Biology of Ultimate Concern* (New York, 1967), p. 52.
10. Sartre, 'Existentialism Is a Humanism,' *loc. cit.*, p. 292.

NOTES TO CHAPTER FOUR

1. Jean-Paul Sartre, *Being and Nothingness: An Essay on Phenomenological Ontology*, trans. Hazel Barnes (New York: 1956), p. 104.
2. Martin Heidegger, *Being and Time*, trans. J. Macquarrie and E. S. Robinson (New York and London, 1962), pp. 91–148.
3. Sartre, *Being and Nothingness*, p. 200.
4. Cf. Heidegger, *Being and Time*, p. 102 ff.
5. A. S. Eddington, *The Nature of the Physical World* (New York, 1928), Introduction.
6. Maurice Merleau-Ponty, *Signs*, trans. Richard C. McCleary (Evanston, Ill., 1964), p. 166.
7. Sartre, *Being and Nothingness*, p. 305.
8. On this Pauline idea of the body see John Macquarrie, *An Existentialist Theology: A Comparison of Heidegger and Bultmann*, 2d ed. (New York and London, 1960), pp. 40–46.
9. Heidegger, *Being and Time*, p. 146.
10. *Ibid.*
11. Henri Bergson, *Time and Free Will*, trans. F. L. Pogson (New York, 1910).
12. Nikolai Berdyaev, *The Meaning of the Creative Act*, trans. D. Lowrie (New York, 1955), p. 15.
13. Heidegger, *Being and Time*, p. 75.
14. John Macmurray, *The Self as Agent* (New York and London, 1957), p. 33 ff.
15. John Habgood, *Truths in Tension* (New York, 1965), p. 62.

NOTES TO CHAPTER FIVE

1. Martin Buber, *I and Thou*, trans. R. G. Smith, 2d ed. (Edinburgh and New York, 1958), p. 4.
2. Nikolai Berdyaev, *The Meaning of the Creative Act*, trans. D. Lowrie (New York, 1955), pp. 180–184.
3. Martin Heidegger, *Introduction to Metaphysics*, trans. R. Manheim (New Haven, 1959), p. 156.
4. On these points see Buber, *I and Thou*, pp. 3–4.
5. *Ibid.*, p. 6.
6. *Ibid.*
7. See Harvey Cox, *The Secular City* (New York, 1965), pp. 44–45.
8. Heidegger, *Being and Time*, trans. J. Macquarrie and E. S. Robinson (New York and London, 1962), pp. 158–159.
9. Gabriel Marcel, 'The Ego and Its Relation to Others,' *Homo Viator: An Introduction to a Metaphysic of Hope*, trans. E. Craufurd (New York and London, 1951), p. 15.
10. See especially *Being and Nothingness: An Essay on Phenomenological Ontology*, trans. Hazel Barnes (New York, 1956), pp. 339–430.
11. *Ibid.*, p. 345.
12. *Ibid.*, p. 352.
13. Arthur Gibson, *The Faith of the Atheist* (New York, 1968), p, 71.
14. Søren Kierkegaard, *The Point of View for My Work as an Author*, trans. Walter Lowrie (New York, 1939), p. 193.
15. Kierkegaard, *The Sickness unto Death*, published together with *Fear and Trembling* as *Fear and Trembling and The Sickness unto Death*, trans. Walter Lowrie (Garden City, N.Y., 1954), p. 193.
16. *Ibid.*, p. 165.
17. Friedrich Nietzsche, *The Will to Power*, trans. A. M. Ludovici (Edinburgh, London, and New York, 1909), vol. 1, p. 228.
18. See Heidegger, *Being and Time*, p. 163 ff.
19. *Ibid.*, p. 167.
20. Nietzsche, *The Will to Power*, vol. 2, p. 236.
21. See G. W. F. Hegel, *The Phenomenology of Mind*, trans. J. B. Baillie, 2d ed. (New York and London, 1931), pp. 234–240,

NOTES TO CHAPTER SIX

1. Martin Heidegger, *Being and Time*, trans. J. Macquarrie and E.S. Robinson (New York and London, 1962), p. 88.
2. John Macmurray, *The Self as Agent* (New York and London, 1957), p. 87.
3. See *ibid.*, pp. 100–103, for the discussion of these propositions.
4. Nikolai Berdyaev, *The Meaning of the Creative Act*, trans. D. Lowrie (New York, 1955), p. 123.

5. See the analytic index to *Being and Time* for a list of usages and references.
6. Heidegger, *Kant and the Problem of Metaphysics*, trans. J. S. Churchill (Bloomington, Ind., 1962), p. 94.
7. Karl Jaspers, *The Perennial Scope of Philosophy*, trans. R. Manheim (New Haven and London, 1950), pp. 14–20.
8. Nikolai Berdyaev, *The Beginning and the End*, trans. M. French (New York, 1957), pp. 60–61.
9. See Marshall McLuhan, *Understanding Media: The Extensions of Man* (New York, 1964).
10. Søren Kierkegaard, *Concluding Unscientific Postscript*, trans. D. F. Swenson (Princeton, 1941), p. 319.
11. Martin Heidegger, *Existence and Being*, ed. Werner Brock, trans. R. F. C. Hull and Alan Crick (Chicago and London, 1949), p. 292 ff.

NOTES TO CHAPTER SEVEN

1. Søren Kierkegaard, *Concluding Unscientific Postscript*, trans. D. F. Swenson (Princeton, 1941), p. 267; see above, p. 104.
2. Kierkegaard, *Philosophical Fragments, or a Fragment of Philosophy*, trans. D. F. Swenson (Princeton, 1936), p. 47.
3. Ronald Grimsley, *Existentialist Thought* (Cardiff, 1955), p. 169.
4. Martin Heidegger, *What Is Called Thinking?*, trans. F. D. Wieck and J. G. Gray (New York, 1968), p. 3.
5. Heidegger, *Was ist Metaphysik?*, 7th ed. (Frankfurt, 1949), p. 37.
6. Karl Jaspers, *Philosophical Faith and Revelation*, trans. E. B. Ashton (New York, 1967), p. 125.
7. Martin Buber, *I and Thou*, trans. R. G. Smith, 2d ed. (New York and Edinburgh, 1958), p. 4.
8. See Heidegger, *Being and Time*, trans. J. Macquarrie and E. S. Robinson (New York and London, 1962), pp. 203–210.
9. Jean-Paul Sartre, *Being and Nothingness: An Essay on Phenomenological Ontology*, trans. Hazel Barnes (New York, 1956), p. 372.
10. *Ibid.*, p. 373.
11. Kierkegaard, *The Last Years: Journals 1853–55*, ed. R. Gregor Smith (New York, 1965), p. 262.
12. Heidegger, *Being and Time*, p. 212.
13. David E. Jenkins, *The Glory of Man* (New York, 1967), pp. 14–15.
14. Heidegger, *An Introduction to Metaphysics*, trans. R. Manheim (New Haven, 1959), p. 156.
15. Heidegger, *Über den Humanismus* (Frankfurt, 1949), pp. 10, 21, 43.
16. Heidegger, *An Introduction to Metaphysics*, p. 57.
17. Jaspers, *Philosophical Faith and Revelation*, p. 95.
18. *Ibid.*, p. 140.
19. *Ibid.*, p. 265.
20. *Ibid.*

NOTES TO CHAPTER EIGHT

1. Richard Wollheim, *F. H. Bradley* (London, 1959), p. 226.
2. Paul Ricoeur, *Fallible Man*, trans. C. Kelbley (Chicago, 1965), p. 118.
3. *Ibid.*, p. 156.
4. See *The Random House Dictionary of the English Language* (New York, 1965), p. 519, for a discussion of these synonyms and near-synonyms.
5. Martin Heidegger, *Being and Time*, trans. J. Macquarrie and E. S. Robinson (New York and London, 1962), p. 227, n. 1.
6. *Ibid.*, p. 492.
7. Jean-Paul Sartre, *Being and Nothingness: An Essay on Phenomenological Ontology*, trans. Hazel Barnes (New York, 1956), p. 29.
8. Sartre, *The Emotions: Outline of a Theory*, trans. Bernard Frechtman (New York, 1948), p. 16.
9. *Ibid.*
10. Søren Kierkegaard, *The Concept of Dread*, trans. Walter Lowrie (Princeton, 1944), p. 38.
11. George Price, *The Narrow Pass: A Study of Kierkegaard's Concept of Man* (New York, 1963), p. 46.
12. Heidegger, *Being and Time*, p. 226.
13. *Ibid.*, p. 230.
14. *Ibid.*, p. 231.
15. *Ibid.*, p. 232.
16. Sartre, *Being and Nothingness*, p. 29.
17. *Ibid.*
18. *Ibid.*, p. 32.
19. *Ibid.*
20. Heidegger, *Introduction to Metaphysics*, trans. R. Manheim (New Haven, 1959), p. 1.
21. Heidegger, *Being and Time*, p. 234.
22. Ricoeur, *Fallible Man*, p. 161.
23. *Ibid.*

NOTES TO CHAPTER NINE

1. Søren Kierkegaard, *Journals*, ed. and trans. Alexander Dru (New York, 1959), p. 44.
2. *Ibid.*, p. 46.
3. Gabriel Marcel, *Man Against Mass Society*, trans. G. S. Fraser (Chicago, 1952), p. 1.
4. Donald A. Lowrie, *Christian Existentialism* (New York, 1956), pp. 136–147.

NOTES TO CHAPTER TEN

1. Austin Farrer, *The Freedom of the Will* (New York, 1960), p. 173.

2. *Ibid.*, p. 209.
3. Paul Ricoeur, *Fallible Man*, trans. C. Kelbley (Chicago, 1965), p. 37.
4. José Ortega y Gasset, *The Modern Theme*, trans. James Gleuch (New York, 1933), p. 95.
5. Theodosius Dobzhansky, *The Biology of Ultimate Concern* (New York, 1967), p. 72.
6. Martin Heidegger, *Being and Time*, trans. J. Macquarrie and E. S. Robinson (New York and London, 1962), pp. 279–311.
7. *Ibid.*, p. 307.
8. Albert Camus, *The Rebel: An Essay on Man in Revolt*, trans. Anthony Bower (New York, 1956), p. 100.
9. Arthur Gibson, *The Faith of the Atheist* (New York, 1968), pp. 96–97.
10. See Ricoeur, *Fallible Man*, p. xiii, where his translator, C. Kelbley, notes that he uses the words *faille* ('breach'), *écart* ('gap'), *fêlure* ('rift'), *déchirement* ('tearing') to express what he has in mind.
11. See Heidegger, *Being and Time*, pp. 325–335.
12. F. W. Dilistone, *The Christian Understanding of Atonement* (Philadelphia, 1968), p. 3.

NOTES TO CHAPTER ELEVEN

1. Jean-Paul Sartre, 'Existentialism Is a Humanism,' *Existentialism from Dostoevsky to Sartre*, ed. Walter Kaufmann (Cleveland and New York, 1956), p. 298.
2. *Ibid.*, p. 292.
3. *Ibid.*, p. 293.
4. Albert Camus, *The Rebel: An Essay on Man in Revolt*, trans. Anthony Bower (New York, 1956), p. 10.
5. *Ibid.*, p. 250.
6. Søren Kierkegaard, *Fear and Trembling*, trans. Walter Lowrie (Garden City, N.Y., 1954), p. 75.
7. *Ibid.*
8. George Price, *The Narrow Pass: A Study of Kierkegaard's Concept of Man* (New York, 1963), p. 192.
9. Friedrich Nietzsche, *Thus Spake Zarathustra*, trans. A. Tille, rev. ed. (London, 1933), p. 176.
10. *Ibid.*, pp. 253–254.
11. Martin Heidegger, *Being and Time*, trans. J. Macquarrie and E. S. Robinson (New York and London, 1962), p. 323.
12. *Ibid.*, p. 319.
13. *Ibid.*, p. 322.
14. Karl Jaspers, *Philosophical Faith and Revelation*, trans. E. B. Ashton (New York, 1967), p. 310.
15. Søren Kierkegaard, *The Last Years: Journals 1853–55*, ed. R. Gregor Smith (New York, 1965), p. 226.
16. Heidegger, *Being and Time*, pp. 227 and 238–239.

17. Martin J. Heinecken, *The Moment Before God* (Philadelphia, 1956), p. 361.
18. Kierkegaard, *Training in Christianity*, trans. W. Lowrie (Princeton, 1944), p. 117.
19. Kierkegaard, *The Last Years*, p. 156; see also Heidegger's comments on Kierkegaard's understanding of temporality and eternity in *Being and Time*, p. 497.

NOTES TO CHAPTER TWELVE

1. H. A. Hodges, 'Selected Passages from Dilthey,' *Wilhelm Dilthey: An Introduction* (New York, 1968), p. 142.
2. Martin Heidegger, *Being and Time*, trans. J. Macquarrie and E. S. Robinson (New York and London, 1962), pp. 449–455.
3. Søren Kierkegaard, *The Last Years: Journals 1953–55*, ed. R. Gregor Smith (New York, 1965), p. 151.
4. Kierkegaard, *Philosophical Fragments, or a Fragment of Philosophy*, trans. David F. Swenson (Princeton, 1936), p. 42.
5. Kierkegaard, *The Last Years*, p. 143.
6. Kierkegaard, *Repetition: An Essay in Existential Psychology*, trans. W. Lowrie (Princeton, 1941), p. 4.
7. Friedrich Nietzsche, 'The Use and Abuse of History,' *Thoughts out of Season*, trans. A. M. Ludovici and A. Collins (Edinburgh, London, and New York, 1909), vol. 2, pp. 1–100.
8. *Ibid.*, p. 19.
9. *Ibid.*, p. 27.
10. *Ibid.*, p. 28.
11. *Ibid.*, p. 55.
12. Friedrich Nietzsche, *Thus Spake Zarathustra*, trans. A. Tille, rev. ed. (London, 1933), p. 194.
13. *Ibid.*
14. Heidegger, *Being and Time*, p. 433.
15. *Ibid.*, p. 440.
16. *Ibid.*, p. 443.
17. *Ibid.*, p. 436.
18. *Ibid.*, pp. 448–449.
19. Heidegger, *Introduction to Metaphysics*, trans. R. Manheim (New Haven, 1959), p. 155.
20. W. J. Richardson, *Heidegger: Through Phenomenology to Thought* (The Hague, 1963), pp. 20–21.
21. Heidegger, 'Der Spruch des Anaximander,' *Holzwege* (Frankfurt, 1957), p. 311.
22. Karl Jaspers, *Philosophical Faith and Revelation*, trans. E. B. Ashton (New York, 1967), p. 186.
23. Johannes Metz, *Theology of the World*, trans. William Glen-Doepel (New York, 1969), p. 107 ff.

24. Nikolai Berdyaev, *The Meaning of the Creative Act*, trans. D. Lowrie (New York, 1955), p. 287.
25. Albert Camus, *The Rebel: An Essay on Man in Revolt*, trans Anthony Bower (New York, 1956) p. 241.

NOTES TO CHAPTER THIRTEEN

1. Nikolai Berdyaev, *The Beginning and the End*, trans. M. French (New York, 1957), p. 9.
2. *Ibid.*, p. 39.
3. Karl Jaspers, *Philosophical Faith and Revelation*, trans. E. B. Ashton (New York, 1967), p. 75.
4. See Paul A. Schilpp, ed., *The Philosophy of Karl Jaspers* (New York, 1957), p. 77.
5. R. Grimsley, *Existentialist Thought* (Cardiff, 1955), p. 212.
6. Karl Jaspers, *The Perennial Scope of Philosophy*, trans. R. Manheim (New Haven and London, 1950), p. 64.
7. *Ibid.*, p. 65.
8. Jaspers, *Philosophical Faith and Revelation*, p. 255.
9. *Ibid.*
10. See Jaspers, *The Perennial Scope of Philosophy*, p. 34 ff.
11. Jaspers, *The Way to Wisdom*, trans. Eden and Cedar Paul (New York, and London, 1951), p. 159.
12. Miguel de Unamuno, *Don Quixote Expounded with Comment*, trans. A. Kerrigan (Princeton, 1968), p. 114.
13. E. T. Long, *Jaspers and Bultmann* (Durham, N.C., 1968), p. 121.
14. F. H. Bradley, *Appearance and Reality* (Oxford, 1930), p. 5.
15. Miguel de Unamuno, *The Tragic Sense of Life*, trans. J. E. C. Flitch (New York, 1954), p. 39.
16. *Ibid.*, p. 263.
17. See W. Pannenberg, *Was ist der Mensch?* (Göttingen, 1962); see also his *Jesus—God and Man*, trans. Duane Priebe and Lewis L. Wilkins (Philadelphia, 1968), pp. 83–88.

NOTES TO CHAPTER FOURTEEN

1. Karl Jaspers, *General Psychopathology*, trans. J. Hoenig and M. W. Hamilton (Chicago, 1963), p. 350.
2. Jean-Paul Sartre, *Being and Nothingness: An Essay on Phenomenological Ontology*, trans. Hazel Barnes (New York, 1956), p. 557 ff.
3. Medard Boss, 'Daseinsanalysis and Psychotherapy,' *Psychoanalysis and Existential Philosophy*, ed. H. M. Ruitenbeek (New York, 1965), pp. 81–82.
4. L. Binswanger, *Being-in-the-World*, trans. J. Needleman (New York 1963), pp. 182–183.
5. *Ibid.*, p. 189.

6. R. D. Laing, *The Divided Self* (London and New York, 1960), p. 19.
7. *Ibid.*, p. 23.
8. Boss, 'Daseinsanalysis and Psychotherapy,' *loc. cit.*, p. 82.
9. Rollo May, 'Danger in the Relation of Existentialism to Psychotherapy,' *Psychoanalysis and Existential Philosophy*, p. 180.
10. The references to Dr. Huebner's unpublished writings are made with the kind permission of the author.
11. Lionel Trilling, *The Opposing Self* (New York, 1958), pp. 38–39.
12. William Barrett, 'Existentialism as a Symptom of Man's Contemporary Crisis,' *Spiritual Problems in Contemporary Literature*, ed. S. R. Hopper (New York, 1958), p. 144.
13. The German text of the lines quoted may be found in Michael Hamburger, ed., *Hölderlin: Selected Verse* (Baltimore, 1961), pp. 111–112. The translation is my own.
14. Walter Kaufmann, ed., *Existentialism from Dostoevsky to Sartre* (Cleveland and New York, 1956), p. 14.
15. J. E. Barton, *Purpose and Admiration* (London, 1932), p. 133.
16. Paul Tillich, 'Existentialist Aspects of Modern Art,' *Christianity and the Existentialists,* ed. Carl Michalson (New York, 1956), p. 138.
17. Samuel Terrien, 'Modern Painting and Theology,' *Religion and Life* (1969): 172.
18. Albert Hofstadter, 'Art and Spiritual Validity,' *Journal of Aesthetics and Art Criticism* 22 (1963): 10.
19. Martin Heidegger, 'Der Ursprung des Kunstwerkes,' *Holzwege* (Frankfurt, 1957), p. 7.
20. Karl Jaspers, *Philosophie* (Berlin, 1931), p. 716.
21. See John Macquarrie, *Three Issues in Ethics* (New York, 1970), Chapter 4.

NOTES TO CHAPTER FIFTEEN

1. H. J. Paton, *The Modern Predicament* (New York, 1962), p. 120.
2. Ulrich Simon, *A Theology of Auschwitz* (London, 1967), p. 88.
3. Paton, *The Modern Predicament*, pp. 120–121.
4. Hans Jonas, 'Heidegger and Theology,' *Review of Metaphysics* 28 (1964): 207–233.
5. See John Macquarrie, *Three Issues in Ethics* (New York, 1970), Chapter 4.
6. Søren Kierkegaard, *Training in Christianity*, trans. W. Lowrie (Princeton, 1944), p. 218.
7. Paton, *The Modern Predicament*, p. 120.

Bibliography

The literature of existentialism is vast. The selection of books and articles listed here includes a good representation of the most important primary works, together with some of the most useful books and articles that discuss existentialism in its various aspects. The items are arranged alphabetically by author, and by title under each author.

Adams, J. L. *Paul Tillich's Philosophy of Culture, Science and Religion.* New York: Harper & Row, 1965.

Allen, E. L. *Existentialism from Within.* London: Routledge & Kegan Paul, 1953.

Barnes, H. E. *An Existentialist Ethics.* New York: Knopf, 1967.

Barrett, W. *Irrational Man.* Garden City, N.Y.: Doubleday, 1958.

Berdyaev, N. *The Beginning and the End,* translated by M. French. New York: Charles Scribner's Sons, 1957. Russian original, 1952.

———. *The Destiny of Man,* translated by N. Duddington. 3d ed., New York: Harper & Row, 1960. Russian original, 1931; English translation first appeared in 1937.

———. *The Meaning of the Creative Act,* translated by D. Lowrie. New York: Macmillan-Collier, 1955.

Bertocci, P. A. 'Existential Phenomenology and Psychoanalysis,' *The Review of Metaphysics* 18 (1965): 690–710.

Binswanger, L. *Being-in-the-World,* translated by J. Needleman. New York: Basic Books, 1963.
Selected papers, translated from the German.

Blackham, H. J. *Humanism.* Baltimore: Pelican, 1968, and Harmondsworth: Pelican, 1968.

———. *Six Existentialist Thinkers.* 2d. ed. New York: Harper & Row, 1959, 1st ed. New York: Macmillan, 1952. Lucid studies of Kierkegaard, Nietzsche, Heidegger, Jaspers, Marcel, and Sartre.

239

Blakney, R. B. *Meister Eckhart: A Modern Translation.* New York: Harper & Brothers, 1941.

Boss, M. *Psychoanalysis and Daseinsanalysis,* translated by L. B. Lefebre. New York: Basic Books, 1963. German original, *Psychoanalyse und Daseinsanalyse,* 1957.

Brinton, C. *Nietzsche.* Cambridge, Mass.: Harvard University Press, 1941.

Buber, M. *Between Man and Man,* translated by R. G. Smith. 2d ed. Boston: Beacon, 1955. A collection of essays, first published in German in 1936.

──────. *I and Thou,* translated by R. G. Smith. 2d ed. New York: Charles Scribner's Sons, 1958. German original, *Ich and Du,* 1923.

──────. *The Knowledge of Man,* translated by M. Friedman and R. G. Smith. New York: Humanities, 1965, and London, 1965. A collection of essays.

──────. *Pointing the Way,* translated by M. Friedman. New York: Harper & Brothers, 1957, and London, 1957. A selection of essays written between 1909 and 1954.

──────. *The Prophetic Faith,* translated by C. Witton-Davies. 2d ed. New York: Harper & Row, 1960.

Bultmann, R. *Jesus Christ and Mythology,* translated by R. H. Fuller. New York: Charles Scribner's Sons, 1958.

──────. 'New Testament and Mythology.' In *Kerygma and Myth,* edited by H. W. Bartsch; translated by R. H. Fuller. New York: Harper & Brothers, 1957, vol. 1, pp. 1–44.

Buri, F. *Theology of Existence,* translated by H. H. Oliver and G. Onder. Greenwood, S. C.: Attic Press, 1966; German original, *Theologie der Existenz,* 1954.

Camus, A. *The Plague,* translated by S. Gilbert. New York: Knopf, 1948. French original, *La peste,* 1947.

──────. *The Rebel: An Essay on Man in Revolt,* translated by A. Bower. New York: Knopf, 1956. French original, *L'homme révolté,* 1951.

Collingwood, R. G. *The Idea of History.* Oxford: Oxford University Press, 1946.

Collins, J. *The Existentialists: A Critical Study.* Chicago: Regnery, 1952.

──────. *The Mind of Kierkegaard.* Chicago: Regnery, 1953.

Danto, A. C. *Nietzsche as Philosopher.* New York: Macmillan, 1965.

Desan, W. *The Tragic Finale: An Essay on the Philosophy of Jean-Paul Sartre.* 2d ed. New York: Harper & Row, 1960. 1st ed. Cambridge, Mass.: Harvard University Press, 1954.

de Unamuno, M. *The Tragic Sense of Life,* translated by J. E. C. Flitch. New York: Dover, 1957. Spanish original, *El sentimiento trágico de la vida,* 1913.

Diamond, M. *Martin Buber: Jewish Existentialist.* 2d ed. New York: Harper & Row, 1968.

Diem, H. *Kierkegaard: An Introduction,* translated by David Green. Richmond, Va.: John Knox, 1966.

Dobzhansky, T. *The Biology of Ultimate Concern.* New York: New American Library-World, 1967.

Dodds, E. R. *The Greeks and the Irrational.* Berkeley, Calif.: University of California Press, 1951.

Fallico, A. B. *Art and Existentialism.* Englewood Cliffs, N. J.: Prentice-Hall, 1962.

Friedman, M. S. *Martin Buber: The Life of Dialogue.* 2d ed. New York: Harper & Row, 1965.

Gibson, A. *The Faith of the Atheist.* New York: Harper & Row, 1968.

Grene, M. *Martin Heidegger.* New York: Hilary, 1957.

Grimsley, R. *Existentialist Thought.* Cardiff: University of Wales Press, 1955.

Hart, R. L. *Unfinished Man and the Imagination.* New York: Herder and Herder, 1968.

Hegel, G. W. F. *The Phenomenology of Mind,* translated by J. B. Baillie. 2d ed. New York: Macmillan, 1931, and London: G. Allen & Unwin, 1931; German original, *Phänomenologie des Geistes,* 1807.

Heidegger, M. *Being and Time,* translated by J. Macquarrie and E. S. Robinson. New York: Harper & Row, 1962, and London, SCM Press, 1962. German original, *Sein und Zeit,* 1927.

———. *Discourse on Thinking,* translated by J. M. Anderson and E. H. Freund. New York: Harper & Row, 1966. German original, *Gelassenheit,* 1959.

———. *Holzwege.* Frankfurt: Vittorio Klostermann, 1957.

———. *Introduction to Metaphysics,* translated by R. Manheim. New Haven: Yale University Press, 1959. German original, *Einführung in die Metaphysik,* 1953.

———. *Kant and the Problem of Metaphysics,* translated by J. S. Churchill. Bloomington, Ind.: Indiana University Press, 1962. German original, *Kant und das Problem der Metaphysik,* 1929.

———. *The Question of Being,* translated by W. Kluback and J. T. Wilde. New York: Twayne, 1958.
The German original, *Über die Seinsfrage,* published at Frankfurt by Klostermann in 1956, is printed on the left-hand pages, facing the English translation.

———. *Über den Humanismus.* Frankfurt: Vittorio Klostermann, 1949. This was originally published as 'Brief über den Humanismus' in *Platons Lehre von der Wahrheit.* Bern: Franke, 1947, pp. 53–119.

———. *Unterwegs zur Sprache.* Pfullingen: Günther Neske, 1959.

———. *Was ist Metaphysik?* 7th ed. Frankfurt: Vittorio Klostermann, 1949. The original lecture was given in 1929. A Postscript was added in 1943, an Introduction in 1949. The English translation by R. F. C. Hull and Alan Crick in *Existence and Being* (Chicago: Regnery, 1949, and London: Vision Press, 1949) contains the lecture (pp. 353–380) and the Postscript (pp. 380–392). In the Gateway edition of this same title (Chicago: Regnery, 1960) the lecture appears on pp. 325–349 and the Postscript on pp. 349–361. The Introduction is translated by Walter Kaufmann, 'The Way Back into the Ground of Metaphysics,' in *Existentialism from Dostoevsky to Sartre* (Cleveland and New York: Meridian, 1956), pp. 206–221.

————. *What Is Called Thinking?*, translated by F. D. Wieck and J. G. Gray. New York: Harper & Row, 1968. German original, *Was heisst Denken?*, 1954.

Heinemann, F. H. *Existentialism and the Modern Predicament.* New York: Harper & Brothers, 1958.

Heschel, A. J. *Who Is Man?* Stanford, Calif.: Stanford University Press, 1965.

Husserl, E. *Ideas: General Introduction to Pure Phenomenology*, translated by W. R. Boyce Gibson. New York: Macmillan, 1931, and London: G. Allen & Unwin, 1931. German original, *Ideen zu einer reiner Phänomenologie und phänomenologischen Philosophie*, 1913.

Jaspers, K. *General Psychopathology*, translated by J. Hoenig and M. W. Hamilton. Chicago: Regnery, 1963. German original, *Allgemeine Psychopathologie*, 1st ed., 1913, 4th ed., rev., 1942.

————. *Man in the Modern Age*, translated by Eden and Cedar Paul. New York: Humanities, 1933, and London: Routledge & Kegan Paul, 1933; reprinted Garden City, N. Y.: Doubleday, 1956. German original, *Der geistige Situation der Zeit*, 1931.

————. *Nietzsche and Christianity*, translated by E. B. Ashton. Chicago: Regnery, 1961. German original, *Nietzsche und das Christentum*, 1938.

————. *The Origin and Goal of History*, translated by Michael Bullock. New Haven: Yale University Press, 1953. German original, *Vom Ursprung und Ziel der Geschichte*, 1949.

————. *The Perennial Scope of Philosophy*, translated by R. Manheim. New Haven: Yale University Press, 1950. German original, *Der philosophische Glaube*, 1948.

————. *Philosophical Faith and Revelation*, translated by E. B. Ashton. New York: Harper & Row, 1967. German original, *Der philosophische Glaube angesichts der Offenbarung*, 1962.

————. *Philosophie.* 3 vols. Berlin, 1931.

————. *The Way to Wisdom*, translated by Eden and Cedar Paul. New Haven: Yale University Press, 1951, and London: Routledge and Kegan Paul, 1951. German original, *Einführung in die Philosophie*, 1950.

Jonas, H. *The Gnostic Religion: The Message of the Alien God and the Beginning of Christianity.* 2d ed. Boston: Beacon, 1963.

————. 'Heidegger and Theology,' *Review of Metaphysics* 18 (1964): 207–233.

Kaelin, E. F. *An Existentialist Aesthetics.* Madison, Wis.: University of Wisconsin Press, 1962.

Kafka, F. *The Castle*, translated by W. and E. Muir, et al. Definitive edition. New York: Knopf, 1954. German original, *Das Schloss*, 1926; 1st English trans. 1930.

Kaufmann. Walter, ed. *Existentialism from Dostoevsky to Sartre*. Cleveland and New York: Meridian, 1956.

Keen, S. *Gabriel Marcel*. Richmond, Va.: John Knox, 1966.

Kierkegaard, S. *The Concept of Dread*, translated by Walter Lowrie. Princeton: Princeton University Press, 1944. Danish original, 1844.

———. *Concluding Unscientific Postscript*, translated by D. F. Swenson. Princeton: Princeton University Press, 1941. Danish original, 1846.

———. *Either/Or: A Fragment of Life*, translated by D. F. and L. M. Swenson (vol. 1) and W. Lowrie (vol. 2). Princeton University Press, 1944. Danish original, 1843.

———. *Fear and Trembling and The Sickness Unto Death*, translated by W. Lowrie. Garden City, N. Y.: Doubleday, 1954. Danish original, 1843.

———. *Journals*, edited and translated by Alexander Dru. New York: Peter Smith, 1959; first English ed. Oxford University Press, 1939.

———. *The Last Years: Journals 1853–55*, translated and edited by R. Gregor Smith. New York: Harper & Row, 1965.

———. *Philosophical Fragments, or a Fragment of Philosophy*, translated by David F. Swenson. Princeton University Press, 1936. Danish original, 1844.

———. *Stages on Life's Way*, translated by W. Lowrie. Princeton: Princeton University Press, 1940. Danish original, 1845.

———. *Training in Christianity*, translated by W. Lowrie. Princeton: Princeton University Press, 1944. Danish original, 1850.

———. *The Works of Love*, translated by H. and E. Hong. New York: Harper & Row, 1962. Danish original, 1847.

Kingston, F. *French Existentialism: A Christian Critique*. Toronto: University of Toronto Press, 1961.

Kroner, R. 'Heidegger's Private Religion.' In *Union Seminary Quarterly Review* 11 (1956): 23–37.

Laing, R. D. *The Divided Self: An Existential Study in Sanity and Madness*. New York: Tavistock, 1960, and London, 1960.

Langan, T. *The Meaning of Heidegger: A Critical Study of an Existentialist Phenomenology*. New York: Columbia University Press, 1959.

Lauer, Q. *Phenomenology: Its Genesis and Prospects*. New York: Harper & Row, 1965.

Löwith, K. *Heidegger: Denker in dürftiger Zeit*. 2d ed. Göttingen: Vandenhoeck und Ruprecht, 1960.

Macmurray, J. *Persons in Relation*. New York: Humanities, 1961, and London: Faber & Faber, 1961.

———. *The Self as Agent*. New York: Humanities, 1957, and London: Faber & Faber, 1957.

Macquarrie, J. 'Existentialism and Christian Thought.' In *Philosophical Resources for Christian Thought*, edited by Perry LeFevre, pp. 123–140. Nashville: Abingdon, 1968.

————. *An Existentialist Theology: A Comparison of Heidegger and Bultmann.* 2d ed. New York: Harper & Row, 1960, and London: SCM, 1960.

————. *Martin Heidegger.* Richmond, Va.: John Knox, 1968.

————. *Studies in Christian Existentialism.* Philadelphia; Westminster, 1966, and London: SCM, 1966.

————. 'Will and Existence.' In *The Concept of Willing,* edited by J. N. Lapsley, pp. 73–87. Nashville: Abingdon, 1967.

Marcel, G. *Being and Having: An Existentialist Diary,* translated by K. Farrer. New York: Harper & Brothers, 1949. French original, *Être et avoir,* 1935.

————. *Homo Viator: Introduction to a Metaphysic of Hope,* translated by E. Craufurd. New York: Harper & Brothers, 1951. Collection of essays, written 1942–44.

————. *The Mystery of Being,* translated by G. S. Fraser and R. Hague. 2 vols. Chicago: Regnery, 1950–51. French original, *Le Mystère de l'Être,* 1950.

Marx, W. *Heidegger und die Tradition.* Tübingen, 1962.

May, R. *Love and Will.* New York: Norton, 1967.

Merleau-Ponty, M. *Phenomenology of Perception,* translated by C. Smith. New York: Humanities, 1962, and London: Routledge & Kegan Paul, 1962. French original, *Phénoménologie de la perception,* 1945.

Munitz, M. K. *The Mystery of Existence.* New York: Delta, 1965.

Nietzsche, F. *Thoughts out of Season,* translated by A. M. Ludovici and A. Collins. 2 vols. Edinburgh and London, T. N. Forbis, 1909, and New York: Macmillan, 1909. German original, *Unzeitgemässe Betrachtungen,* 1874.

————. *Thus Spake Zarathustra,* translated by A. Tille, revised by M. M. Bozmann. New York: Dutton, 1933. German original, *Also sprach Zarathustra,* 1883.

————. *The Will to Power,* translated by A. M. Ludovici. 2 vols. Edinburgh and London: T. N. Forbis, 1909, and New York: Macmillan, 1909. German original, *Der Wille zur Macht: Versuch einer Umwertung aller Werte,* 1906.

Oden, T. C. *Radical Obedience: The Ethics of Rudolf Bultmann.* Philadelphia: Westminster, 1964.

Ortega y Gasset, J. *Man in Crisis,* translated by M. Adams. New York: Norton, Norton, 1959. Spanish original, *En torno a Galileo,* 1945.

Ott, H. *Denken und sein: der Weg Martin Heideggers und der Weg der Theologie.* Zollikon, 1959.

Pannenberg, W. *Was ist der Mensch?* Göttingen, 1962.

Pascal, B. *Thoughts,* translated by W. F. Trotter. London, 1904. French original, *Les Pensées,* 1670; there are numerous editions, arrangements, and translations.

Polanyi, M. *Personal Knowledge: Towards a Post-critical Philosophy.* Chicago: University of Chicago Press, 1958.

Price, G. *The Narrow Pass: A Study of Kierkegaard's Concept of Man.* New York: McGraw-Hill, 1963.

Rahner, K. *On the Theology of Death,* translated by C. H. Henkey, revised by W. J. O'Hara. 2d ed. New York: Herder and Herder, 1965. German original, *Zur Theologie des Todes,* 1957.

Richardson, W. J. *Heidegger: Through Phenomenology to Thought.* The Hague: Martinus Nijhoff, 1963.

Ricoeur, P. *Fallible Man,* translated by C. Kelbley. Chicago: Regnery, 1965. French original, *L'homme faillible,* 1960.

―――. *The Symbolism of Evil,* translated by E. Buchanan. New York: Harper and Row, 1967. French original, *La symbolique du mal,* 1960.

Roberts, D. E. *Existentialism and Religious Belief.* New York: Oxford University Press, 1957.

Sadler, W. A. *Existence and Love: A New Approach in Existential Phenomenology.* New York: Charles Scribner's Sons, 1969.

Sartre, J. P. *Being and Nothingness: An Essay on Phenomenological Ontology,* translated by Hazel Barnes. New York: Philosophical Library 1956. French original, *L'être et le néant,* 1943.

―――. *The Emotions: Outline of a Theory,* translated by B. Frechtman. New York: Philosophical Library, 1948. French original. *Esquisse d'une théorie des émotions,* 1939.

―――. 'Existentialism Is a Humanism.' In *Existentialism from Dostoevsky to Sartre,* edited by Walter Kaufmann. Cleveland and New York: Meridian, 1956.

―――. *Nausea,* translated by Lloyd Alexander. Norfolk, Conn.: New Directions, 1959. French original, *La Nausée,* 1938.

Seidel, G. J. *Martin Heidegger and the Pre-Socratics.* Lincoln, Neb.: University of Nebraska Press, 1964.

Shinn, R. L. *Man: The New Humanism.* Philadelphia: Westminster, 1968.

―――, ed. *Restless Adventure: Essays on Contemporary Expressions of Existentialism.* New York: Charles Scribner's Sons, 1968.

Somerville, J. *Total Commitment: Blondel's L'Action.* Washington and Cleveland: Corpus, 1968.

Sponheim, P. *Kierkegaard on Christ and Christian Coherence.* New York: Harper & Row, 1968.

Takeuchi, Y. 'Buddhism and Existentialism: A Dialogue Between Oriental and Occidental Thought.' In *Religion and Culture,* edited by W. Leibrecht, New York: Harper & Brothers, 1959. Essays in honor of Paul Tillich.

Tillich, P. *Biblical Religion and the Search for Ultimate Reality.* Chicago: University of Chicago Press, 1955.

―――. *The Courage to Be.* New Haven: Yale University Press, 1952.

―――. *The Dynamics of Faith.* New York: Harper & Brothers, 1958.

―――. *Love, Power and Justice.* New York: Oxford University Press, 1954.

―――. *Systematic Theology.* 3 vols. Chicago: University of Chicago Press, 1953–64.

————. *Theology of Culture*, edited by R. C. Kimball. New York: Oxford University Press, 1959.

Turgenev, I. *Fathers and Sons*, translated by C. J. Hogarth. London, 1921; Russian original, 1862.

Versenyi, L. *Heidegger, Being and Truth*. New Haven: Yale University Press, 1965.

Von Rintelen, J. *Beyond Existentialism*, translated by H. Graef. New York: Humanities, 1961, and London, 1961. German original, *Philosophie der Endlichkeit*, 1951.

Waelhens, A. de. *La philosophie de Martin Heidegger*. Louvain, 1942.

Wollheim, R. *F. H. Bradley*. London: Pelican, 1959.

Index